JOSEPH CONRAD

D1614996

CRITICAL ISSUES SERIES

General Editors: John Peck and Martin Coyle

Published

Jane Austen	*Darryl Jones*
George Eliot	*Pauline Nestor*
Virginia Woolf	*Linden Peach*
Charlotte Brontë	*Carl Plasa*
Charles Dickens	*Lyn Pykett*
Allan H. Simmons	*Joseph Conrad*
Henry James	*Jeremy Tambling*
John Keats	*John Whale*
William Wordsworth	*John Williams*

In preparation

James Joyce	*Kiernan Ryan*
D. H. Lawrence	*Rick Rylance*
Thomas Hardy	*Julian Wolfreys*

Critical Issues Series
Series Standing Order
ISBN 1–4039–2158–X hardcover
ISBN 1–4039–2159–8 paperback
(*outside North America only*)

You can receive future titles in this series as they are published by placing a standing order. Please contact your bookseller or, in case of difficulty, write to us at the address below with your name and address, the title of the series and the ISBN quoted above.

Customer Services Department, Macmillan Distribution Ltd, Houndmills, Basingstoke, Hampshire RG21 6XS, England

---

Critical Issues

Joseph Conrad

Allan H. Simmons

First published 2006 by
PALGRAVE MACMILLAN
Houndmills, Basingstoke, Hampshire RG21 6XS and
175 Fifth Avenue, New York, N.Y. 10010
Companies and representatives throughout the world

PALGRAVE MACMILLAN is the global academic imprint of the Palgrave
Macmillan division of St. Martin's Press, LLC and of Palgrave Macmillan Ltd.
Macmillan® is a registered trademark in the United States, United Kingdom
and other countries. Palgrave is a registered trademark in the European
Union and other countries.

ISBN-13: 978–1–4039–3709–4 hardback
ISBN-10: 1–4039–3709–5 hardback
ISBN-13: 978–1–4039–3710–0 paperback
ISBN-10: 1–4039–3710–9 paperback

This book is printed on paper suitable for recycling and made from fully
managed and sustained forest sources.

A catalogue record for this book is available from the British Library.

A catalog record for this book is available from the Library of Congress.

10   9   8   7   6   5   4   3   2   1
15   14   13   12   11   10   09   08   07   06

Printed and bound in China

To Cindy

Contents

Preface

Polish by parentage and British by adoption, Conrad stands on the cultural cusp between national and Continental influences. Deeply perceptive of various kinds of imperialism, he is no less a transitional figure in the English novel's development. Writing for a late-Victorian readership in his early career, Conrad produced a body of work that includes such essential Modernist texts as "Heart of Darkness," *Lord Jim*, and *Nostromo*, and in the process helped to forge the scepticism that is the early twentieth century's hallmark.

This book deals with all of Conrad's work. In relocating the theoretical, post-colonial and feminist readings of recent decades in a comprehensive and scholarly historical and biographical frame, it seeks to show how our sense of the complexity of Conrad's fiction is immeasurably enriched by a detailed awareness of the circumstances of its writing, including those of Conrad himself. The introduction traces Conrad's extraordinary life and times, and places his texts within the Modernist tradition that his writing helped to fashion. Thereafter, the chapters broadly follow the chronology of Conrad's career, identifying its various phases and grouping the fiction according to shared concerns. Thus, chapters on the Malay fiction, the sea novels, the Marlow tales, and the political novels allow the themes of nationality, Englishness, and the processes of history to emerge as directing strands in Conrad's writing. These chapters situate Conrad's development as a writer and his post-colonial critique of Empire within a historical and textual context. Throughout, the emphasis is on Conrad's achievement in its address to the issues of his time.

Completing the study are chapters devoted to Conrad's short fiction, his period of popular success, during which he addresses contemporary social and political concerns of feminism and the First World War, and his late novels. The final chapter includes a survey of the evolution of Conrad's reputation, charting the changes in critical focus and attitude to his work from the early twentieth century through to the views of the present day. As will be apparent, the questions Conrad's fiction raises are as relevant to our time as when it was written, and just as provocative in terms of its handling of gender, class, social responsibilities and politics. This book represents a contribution to the ongoing assessment of and critical debate about Conrad's writing.

Acknowledgements

While writing this book, I have incurred a number of debts that I should like to acknowledge here. Special thanks are due to Owen Knowles and J. H. Stape, as much for their friendship as for their generous advice and scholarly interest. My gratitude is due, too, to the support of the wider community of scholars gathered round the Joseph Conrad Society (UK), and to the editors and staff of Palgrave from whose expertise and guidance I have benefited, in particular John Peck, Martin Coyle, Kate Wallis, and Sonya Barker. I am also grateful to Stephen Donovan, who kindly shared the photograph that appears on the front cover. On a more personal note, I owe an immense debt to the ever-sympathetic Cindy and Jethro, who have patiently overseen and encouraged the evolution of this book, and to Angel whose purrs and demands for attention determined its rhythms.

Quotations
and Abbreviations

All references to Conrad's works are to *The Uniform Edition of the Works of Joseph Conrad*, 22 vols. (London: J. M. Dent, 1923–28). The following abbreviations are used:

AF	*Almayer's Folly*
LE	*Last Essays*
LJ	*Lord Jim*
NLL	*Notes on Life and Letters*
NN	*The Nigger of the "Narcissus"*
OI	*An Outcast of the Islands*
PR	*A Personal Record*
SA	*The Secret Agent*
TU	*Tales of Unrest*
Y	*Youth: A Narrative, and Two Other Stories*

References to Conrad's letters are to Laurence Davies et al., eds, *The Collected Letters of Joseph Conrad*, 7 vols. to date (Cambridge: Cambridge University Press, 1983–), or to G. Jean-Aubry, *Joseph Conrad: Life and Letters*, 2 vols. (London: Heinemann, 1927). The following abbreviations are used:

CL	*The Collected Letters of Joseph Conrad*
LL	*Joseph Conrad: Life and Letters*

In quotations, a sequence of spaced points [. . .] indicates an ellipsis in the original text; a sequence of unspaced points [...] an elision that I have made.

1

Introduction: Life and Letters

The contours of Joseph Conrad's life seem designed to shape our response to his art. The legend is well known: he was the Polish émigré who learned to speak English while serving as a sailor and officer in the British Merchant Service before becoming one of the country's most celebrated authors. Exiled and rootless, his national identity problematically dual, Conrad lived out the "Modern condition" of alienation while, temperamentally sceptical and technically experimental, his writings reflected its philosophy and mood. Writing to a fellow countryman in 1903, Conrad asserted: "Both at sea and on land my point of view is English, from which the conclusion should not be drawn that I have become an Englishman. That is not the case. Homo duplex has in my case more than one meaning" (*CL3*: 89). The influences, affinities, and conflicts of Conrad's thoughts and poetics stem from the confluence of family, geography, and history. Such a rich inheritance yielded fictions that combine the authenticity of first-hand experience with the insights of profound meditation, and place Conrad alongside Gustave Flaubert, Henry James, Marcel Proust, and James Joyce in the pantheon of Modernist authors.

Serendipity and historical coincidence combined to link Joseph Conrad to the British Empire. He shares the year of his birth, 1857, with Sir Edward Elgar, whose music captured and contributed towards the popular patriotic mood of the country in such well-known pieces as the "Imperial March" (1897), the "Coronation March" (1901), and the "Empire March" (1924). The year 1857 is

1

also the year of the Indian Mutiny. Sometimes regarded as the first step towards a united Independence Movement in India, the rising is remembered as much for the challenge posed to imperial rule – slight, as it turned out – as for the ruthlessness of British reprisals. Like Conrad's writings, Elgar's music celebrates "Englishness," but does so in an era when the Empire was under threat and Britain's global power and industrial supremacy were in decline. Although not final in their subversive impact, the Indian Mutiny and the Crimean and Boer Wars were certainly part of the gradual disenchantment with Empire, challenging any lingering complacency in the existing order. Perhaps inevitably, it was when Britain's global and industrial supremacy was waning that the expression of Englishness is at its most celebratory.

Polish years

Joseph Conrad was the adopted name of Józef Teodor Konrad Korzeniowski, known familiarly to his relations as "Konradek." He was born on 3 December 1857 at Berdichev in Podolia, a part of the Polish Commonwealth that had been appropriated into the Russian Ukraine in 1793. As the Polish Republic would only be restored in 1918 after the First World War, Conrad's was a homeland of the heart rather than a geographical fact. He was the only child of Apollo and Ewelina (Ewa) Korzeniowski, members of the *szlachta* or landowning nobility, whose Nałęcz coat-of-arms displays a knotted handkerchief to symbolise, as myth has it, the field-dressed wound of a patriotic ancestor. His first two given names were derived from his grandfathers and his third, Konrad, from the patriotic hero of Adam Mickiewicz's poem *Dziady* (1832). Following his financial failure as an estate manager, Apollo Korzeniowski channelled his energies into his twin passions: literature and political agitation. In October 1861, shortly before Conrad's fourth birthday, Apollo's clandestine political activities led to his arrest by the Russian authorities and imprisonment in the Warsaw Citadel. According to Conrad, "in the courtyard of this Citadel – characteristically for our nation – my childhood memories begin" (*CL1*: 358). The following year, the family was exiled to Vologda, three hundred miles northeast of Moscow, where the harsh conditions soon took their toll and, in early 1863, they were allowed to move south to Chernikhov, near Kiev, on account of their failing health. Here Apollo translated works by Shakespeare,

Dickens, and Victor Hugo, which, together with Polish Romantic poetry that he read aloud, provided Conrad's first contact with literature.

After a rapid deterioration of her health, Ewa died in the spring of 1865, leaving the melancholy Apollo, supported by an allowance from her brother, Tadeusz Bobrowski, to oversee the upbringing of their son. Conrad's recollection of his father is of a "man of great sensibilities; of exalted and dreamy temperament; with a terrible gift of irony and of gloomy disposition; withal of strong religious feeling degenerating after the loss of his wife into mysticism and despair" (CL2: 247). His birth, upbringing, and experience left Conrad temperamentally sceptical, and his writings repeatedly turn to chance or accident as the driving force behind human life: "Our captivity within the incomprehensible logic of accident is the only fact in the universe" (CL1: 303). Typically, the tone of Conrad's writings is one of ironic detachment, matched by a penchant for opening up dual perspectives through the use of doubles and alter egos that encourages a multiplicity of interpretations.

In failing health himself, Apollo was finally granted permission to leave Chernikhov in late 1867, determined "to bring up Konradek not as a democrat, aristocrat, demagogue, republican, monarchist, or as a servant and flunkey of those parties – but only as a Pole" (Najder, ed., 1983: 113). His death in Cracow in May 1869, at the age of 49, put paid to these ambitions. Instead, the eleven-year-old Conrad found himself at the head of a funeral procession, several thousand strong, and "a manifestation of the national spirit seizing a worthy occasion." Apollo's gravestone describes him as "the victim of Muscovite tyranny." To Conrad he was "simply a patriot in the sense of a man who believing in the spirituality of a national existence could not bear to see that spirit enslaved" (PR: x). In honour of his father, the Municipal Council of Cracow gave Conrad the freedom of the city in December 1872, and, in an essay of 1915, entitled "Poland Revisited," Conrad recalled: "It was in that old royal and academical city that I ceased to be a child, became a boy, had known the friendships, the admirations, the thoughts and the indignations of that age" (NLL: 145).

Care of Konradek passed to family and friends, with Tadeusz Bobrowski becoming Conrad's guardian, overseeing his education and financial affairs and providing practical support and avuncular advice until his own death in 1894. Conrad described his relation with Bobrowski as "more in the relation of a son than a nephew"

(*CL2*: 246). His first novel, *Almayer's Folly* (1895), is dedicated "To the memory of T. B." Although little is known of Conrad's early education, his reading included sea and travel writers, such as Frederick Marryat, James Fenimore Cooper, and Mungo Park, alongside such novels as Dickens' *Bleak House*, Cervantes' *Don Quixote*, Hugo's *Les Travailleurs*, and Turgenev's *Smoke*. Of his schooling he would later admit "a latent devotion to geography which interfered with my devotion (such as it was) to my other schoolwork" (*LE*: 12). In the same essay, "Geography and Some Explorers," Conrad identifies himself as "a contemporary of the Great Lakes" (14) and records an incident that earned him the derision of his school friends: "One day, putting my finger on a spot in the very middle of the then white heart of Africa, I declared that some day I would go there" (16). This boast would be realised eighteen years later when Conrad stood on the deck of "a wretched little stern-wheel steamboat" near the Stanley Falls on the Congo River. His experiences in Africa yielded source material for his most famous work, "Heart of Darkness."

Sea years: Marseilles

In 1872, Conrad scandalised his relatives by declaring his ambition to go to sea. His uncle viewed this as "a betrayal of patriotic duties" (Najder, ed., 1983: 141) and his private tutor, Adam Pulman, a medical student, was charged with dissuading the "incorrigible, hopeless Don Quixote" (*PR*: 44) from his dreams. Pulman's failure led to Conrad making what he later described as "a, so to speak, standing jump out of his racial surroundings and associations" (*PR*: 121). In September 1874, Conrad left Poland for Marseilles where he joined the shipping firm Delestang et Fils whose trading orbit extended as far as the French Antilles and in whose employ he made three voyages to the Caribbean in the *Mont-Blanc* and the *Saint-Antoine*. Although he could not have known it at the time, these voyages were already adding to the treasury of experiences that Conrad would plunder for material as a writer. His third voyage, for instance, may have provided a glimpse of the South American coast he would draw upon for the setting of *Nostromo* (1904), while the *Saint-Antoine*'s first mate, Dominique Cervoni, was to be recalled in *The Mirror of the Sea* (1906) and provide a prototype for both Nostromo and Peyrol in *The Rover* (1923).

Leaving Poland, Conrad joined the ranks of immigrants in a restless age. It is estimated that, between 1801 and 1921, 8 million people alone left Ireland for abroad, while, in the half century before 1914, 3.6 million people emigrated permanently from Poland. In *Jude the Obscure* (1895) Hardy refers to "the modern vice of unrest" (68) while Conrad, whose first collection of short stories was entitled *Tales of Unrest* (1898), writes in *The Nigger of the "Narcissus"* (1897): "On men reprieved by its disdainful mercy, the immortal sea confers in its justice the full privilege of desired unrest" (90). Alongside mass immigration, lower death rates and rising birth rates saw the population of the United Kingdom climb from 35.3 million in 1880 to 45 million in 1914 (Hobsbawm, 2002: 152, 342). The trend of Irish immigrants to England and Scotland in the nineteenth century would, in time, be reversed as Irish, Scots, and English emigrants turned their eyes westwards: in the twenty years between 1851 and 1871, 3.7 million immigrants left the United Kingdom for America (Thompson, 1991: 137).

To the Marseilles period of Conrad's life belong tales of gun-running along the Spanish coast and of his being wounded in a duel – now thought to be a deliberately botched suicide attempt in order to extract money from his uncle. Tantalisingly, reliable information about these adventures continues to elude biographical researchers, but what is certain is that he ran up debts that were met by the dependable Bobrowski and generally revelled in the bohemian Mediterranean atmosphere. In the summer of 1877 Conrad jumped ship, as it were, from the French to the British Merchant Service, a decision that ostensibly resulted from a disagreement with Delestang but which must also have been influenced by the fact that, still legally a Russian subject, he was liable for service in the Russian army. In *A Personal Record*, Conrad recalls how the moment of transition occurred while he was working as a water-clerk in Marseilles harbour: "I bore against the smooth flank of the first English ship I ever touched in my life, I felt it already throbbing under my open palm" (137). Doubtless embellished by hindsight, the sensuous description conveys Conrad's intimate regard for the service in which he would serve for the next fifteen years, under the Red Ensign, "the symbolic, protecting warm bit of bunting flung wide upon the seas, and destined for so many years to be the only roof over my head" (138). Consistent with his rootless early life and symbolic of his state of exile, there is a satisfying symmetry in Conrad's choice of the ship as "home."

The British Merchant Service

In April 1878, Conrad shipped as an unofficial apprentice in the *Mavis*, a British steamer bound from Marseilles for the Sea of Azov via Constantinople. After this first sustained contact with the English language and the British merchant marine he landed on English soil at Lowestoft on 10 June 1878. Here he served briefly as an ordinary seaman in a coastal schooner, the *Skimmer of the Sea*, sailing between Lowestoft and Newcastle, and earning the nickname "Polish Joe." Conrad later recalled this experience as a "Good school for a seaman," adding: "In that craft I began to learn English from East Coast chaps each built as though to last for ever, and coloured like a Christmas card" (*CL2*: 35). Fittingly, since his fictions would be haunted by their origins, this exile from across the continent first touched English soil near Lowestoft Ness, England's most easterly extremity. But Conrad's eyes were already turning to further horizons and, in October 1878, he joined the full-rigged wool clipper *Duke of Sutherland* in London for his first overseas voyage, to Sydney.

Conrad's period of employment in the British Merchant Service corresponded with the heyday of Empire. By the late-Victorian period, Empire was the great fact of British life, and the British Empire extended to a quarter of the globe. Britain was the world's trader: her economic supremacy, sustained by her dominance on the oceans, was built upon overseas markets and sources of primary products. In one sense, Britain was imperialist because she had to be economically: by the time of the Boer War of 1899–1902, Britain was dependent upon imports for two-thirds of her food, and British shipping accounted for half the world's tonnage. Across the nineteenth century, the pattern of British exports indicates rejection of modern, competitive markets in Europe and America for underdeveloped overseas markets: in 1820, Britain exported 60 per cent of her cotton to Europe and America, and 31 per cent to the underdeveloped world; by 1900, the figures were 7 per cent and 86 per cent (Hobsbawm, 1969: 121). At the peak of Empire, nearly half of British cotton exports went to India, the jewel in her imperial crown and central to her strategic global policy. Integral to the British economy, of course, was the merchant marine in which Conrad served. But Britain's maritime supremacy, built upon iron steamships after 1860, was no bulwark against a world of increasing economic and military competition, and, compounding the decline in British manufactured goods after 1870, by 1900 her maritime dominance was under threat from Germany and America, resurgent after the Civil War. In the face of increasingly professional foreign competition, the sheer scope of the Empire strained Britain's ability to meet her demand for sailors, and foreign sailors were common in the "British" Merchant Service.

Describing himself as "a Polish nobleman, cased in British tar" (*CL*1: 52), Conrad's service in the overseas trade spanned the years from 1878 to 1893, during which time he ascended the ranks, gaining his captain's certificate in November 1886. Officially "a British master mariner beyond a doubt," he had succeeded against the understandable early resistance of his uncle, Tadeusz Bobrowski. He recalled his success in *A Personal Record* as "an answer to certain outspoken scepticism, and even to some not very kind aspersions. I had vindicated myself from what had been cried upon as a stupid obstinacy or a fantastic caprice" (120). After early voyages to Australia in the late 1870s, in September 1881 Conrad shipped as second mate in the *Palestine*, an old barque carrying a cargo of coal to Bangkok, beginning a decade of service in Eastern, especially Malayan, waters that provided such a rich vein of inspiration for his writings. The ill-fated voyage in the *Palestine*, which took a year to leave English waters, ended when her cargo caught fire due to spontaneous combustion and the crew were forced to abandon her off Sumatra. These experiences provide the basis for "Youth" (1898) in which the ship is renamed the *Judea*.

In terms of their impact upon his subsequent career as an author, the most significant of Conrad's eastern voyages was not in an international ocean-going vessel but in the *Vidar*, an Arab-owned steamer he joined as first mate in August 1887 and in which he made four local trading voyages between Singapore and small Dutch East Indies ports on Borneo and Celebes between September and December that year. It was in this service that Conrad gained the knowledge of topography and people – including Willem Carel Olmeijer – that would not only inspire his first two novels, *Almayer's Folly* (1895) and *An Outcast of the Islands* (1896), but inform his Malay fiction generally. In *A Personal Record*, he claims: "If I had not got to know Almayer pretty well it is almost certain there would never have been a line of mine in print" (87). First-hand experience enabled Conrad to endow the exotic in his fiction with a sense of geographical and historical reality. Sambir, the setting for both *Almayer's Folly* and *An Outcast of the Islands*, is based upon the remote coastal region of Berau in north-east

Borneo that Conrad visited on his trading rounds in the *Vidar* and where he met Olmeijer. Furthermore, geographical coincidence is complemented by historical verisimilitude that identifies the temporal setting of *Almayer's Folly* as the mid-1880s and *An Outcast of the Islands* as the early 1870s.

Leaving the *Vidar* in early 1888, Conrad secured his only berth as captain, in the *Otago*, an Australian-owned barque. Becalmed in the Gulf of Siam and with a fever-stricken crew, the *Otago* took three weeks to sail from Bangkok to Singapore, where she took on medical supplies and signed fresh crew before sailing to Sydney. Conrad recalled this ordeal in *The Shadow-Line* (1916), which he described in his "Author's Note" as "personal experience seen in perspective with the eye of the mind and coloured by that affection one can't help feeling for such events of one's life as one has no reason to be ashamed of" (xi). The ship's departure for Australia marks Conrad's last contact with the East, and Conrad's command lasted just over a year, during which time the *Otago* carried cargo between various Australian ports, including Melbourne and Port Adelaide, and completed a round-trip to Mauritius. Shortly afterwards, in the spring of 1890, Conrad returned to the Polish Ukraine for the first time in sixteen years to visit his uncle. *En route* he stopped in Brussels to meet a distant cousin, Aleksander Poradowski, and found him terminally ill. He died two days later. Conrad's introduction to his widow, Marguerite Poradowska, proved timely. She was a published novelist, and Conrad had recently begun to write *Almayer's Folly*, which would occupy him for the next five years. Conrad soon declared a "deep attachment" (*CL*1: 48) for "aunt" Marguerite with whom he shared an important friendship and his early thoughts about creative composition.

1890 was to prove a turning point in Conrad's life for quite another reason: in May, he travelled to the Congo Free State, in the employ of the Société Anonyme Belge pour le Commerce du Haut-Congo [Belgian Limited Trading Company for the Upper Congo], to take up a three-year appointment to command one of the company's steamboats whose previous captain had been killed by native tribesmen. In the event, Conrad's stay lasted six months before the physical and moral shock of conditions in King Leopold II's Congo Free State forced him back to Europe. Twenty years later, he confessed to Lady Ottoline Morrell that he had "never recovered" from his trip to the Congo; and, in the judgement of Edward Garnett, who replaced Poradowska as Conrad's literary mentor and became a lifelong friend: "The sinister voice of the Congo with its murmuring undertone of human fatuity, baseness and greed, had swept away the generous illusions of his youth and left him gazing into the heart of an immense darkness" (Ray, ed., 1990: 28, 78). The rare respite was provided by a meeting with Roger Casement, who was knighted in 1911 for his humanitarian efforts in exposing barbarities being perpetrated in the equatorial forests of Africa and South America by buccaneering European powers lured by the wealth to be gained from rubber trees at the dawn of the motorcar age. An estimated ten million Africans were either worked to death or simply killed during Leopold's reign, from 1885 to 1908. Casement would later seek Conrad's first-hand testimony about conditions in the Congo Free State. By then, Conrad had recorded his first-hand experience of brute colonialism in "An Outpost of Progress" (*TU*: 1898) and "Heart of Darkness" (*Y*: 1902).

Conrad's final berth in a sea career that lasted nearly twenty years was as first mate in the *Torrens*, a passenger clipper and one of the fastest ships of her day, in whom he made two return voyages to Australia between 1891 and 1893. The second voyage in the *Torrens* proved auspicious for Conrad's next career. During the outward voyage the still incomplete manuscript of *Almayer's Folly* had its first reader, W. H. Jacques, a passenger and Cambridge graduate, who pronounced it "Distinctly" worth finishing, leaving Conrad feeling "as if already the story-teller were being born into the body of a seaman" (*PR*: 17). The homeward leg brought two English friendships that would endure. Among the passengers, Conrad met two travelling companions, Edward ("Ted") Sanderson and John Galsworthy (the future writer), to whom he would dedicate *An Outcast of the Islands* and *Nostromo*, respectively. The *Torrens* returned to London on 26 July 1893. Unbeknown to Conrad, signing off would mark the end of his sea-going career.

Conrad's early sense of what it was to be English was fashioned by his service in the British Merchant Service. In his "Author's Note" to *The Mirror of the Sea* he identified "the ultimate shapers of my character, convictions, and, in a sense, destiny" as "the imperishable sea, ... the ships that are no more, and ... the simple men who have had their day" (xii). Writing to a fellow Polish émigré from Singapore in October 1885, he claimed: "When speaking, writing or thinking in English the word Home always means for me the hospitable shores of Great Britain" (*CL1*: 12). The following year, on 19 August 1886 Conrad officially became a naturalised subject of Great Britain, a subject of Queen Victoria rather than Tsar Alexander III (although he would only be released from his status as a Russian subject in 1889). Whether Conrad realised it or not, there was already a public clamour to restrict immigration. In a letter to *The Times* of 31 May 1904, the young Liberal, Winston Churchill, defended "the old tolerant and generous practice of free entry and asylum to which the country has so long adhered and from which it has so often greatly gained" (10), but the Conservative government's "Aliens Act" of 1905 restricted immigration into Britain for the first time.

Paradoxically, Conrad's dislocated life as an itinerant sailor provided him with the sense of stability, community, and duty to which his fictions turn in their implicit appeal to human solidarity and commitment as a counterweight to the central themes of betrayal and threatened identity. In the British Merchant Service, Conrad was a cog in the greatest imperial machine the world had ever seen at a time when Britain dominated the oceans. But the merchant marine in which he served was undergoing a technological transformation that saw the transition from sail to steam. He described himself as "the last seaman of a sailing vessel" (*CL*3: 89). To A. N. Wilson, "Technology is the vital fact in the Imperial story" (2002: 493). If *The Nigger of the "Narcissus"* constitutes an elegy for the vanishing era of sailing ships, then "Typhoon", with its less romantic steamship the *Nan-Shan*, is a tribute to the mechanisation necessary for Britannia to continue to "rule the waves". In the Age of Steel, the *Nan-Shan* had stolen the seas from the *Narcissus* even as Conrad was writing his novella.

Conrad, England, and English letters

The divergent preoccupations in Conrad's work trace a rhythm of successive stages in his life. Set in north-east Borneo and drawing on his experiences in the *Vidar*, Conrad's first two novels quickly aligned him with the popular genre of exotic adventure literature. The boys' adventure stories of G. A. Henty or the colonial fantasies of H. Rider Haggard, for instance, reflected and fed the popular taste for the new imperialism. Although, in Conrad's writing, this genre of exotic fiction was forced to encounter alien ways of thinking that placed in question its logic and coherence. After nursing Conrad through two abandoned works, *The Sisters* and *The*

Rescuer, Edward Garnett, who guided the fledgling author's early writing and business affairs, suggested to Conrad that he write a novel about the sea. Dedicated to Garnett, *The Nigger of the "Narcissus"* (1897) is generally acclaimed the greatest sea-novel in the English language; it is also the first novel in which Conrad's subject – the enduring tradition of British seafaring – strikes an identifiably national chord. Conrad's summary of his subject in *The Nigger of the "Narcissus"* – "the crew of a merchant ship, brought to the test of what I may venture to call the moral problem of conduct" (*LE*: 95) – typifies his attitude to the sea in his writings: it is the great testing ground for human experience.

On 24 March 1896, shortly after the publication of *An Outcast of the Islands*, Conrad married Jessie George, whom he described to a relation as "a small, not at all striking-looking person (to tell the truth alas – rather plain!) who nevertheless is very dear to me" (*CL1*: 265). Jessie, or "Chica" as he called her, admirably combined the roles of wife, mother, homemaker, and typist for the often irascible Conrad. Their first home was in Stanford-le-Hope in Essex, near the Thames estuary, and close to that of Conrad's oldest English friend, G. F. W. Hope. (Like Conrad, Hope had been an officer in the merchant marine, and they shared leisure trips in Hope's yawl, the *Nellie*, immortalised as the setting for Marlow's narration in "Heart of Darkness.") The Conrads moved house frequently, occupying eight rented residences in all, in southern England, mainly in Kent and, as Virginia Woolf observed, "in the depths of the country, out of ear-shot of gossips, beyond reach of hostesses" (1925: 282). Living here, Conrad was part of a coterie of émigré authors that included Henry James, Stephen Crane, and W. H. Hudson, leading a near neighbour, H. G. Wells, to complain humorously of "a ring of foreign conspirators plotting against British letters at no great distance from his residence" (Ford, 1962: 276).

Although a late-starter – he was 37 when his first novel was published – Conrad quickly immersed himself in the world of letters. Despite ubiquitous references in his correspondence to writer's block, and to the poor quality of his output, he was a ferociously industrious author, producing on average a volume per year, over half of which continue to attract serious critical consideration. The first half of Conrad's writing career, however, was beset with financial hardships. Critically acclaimed by his peers, he failed to achieve popular success and was reliant upon helpful friends and subsidies from his agent, J. B. Pinker, to make ends meet.

Having experimented with a new narrative voice in *The Nigger of the "Narcissus,"* Conrad embarked on a series of tales that were to inaugurate his major phase and establish his place in the modern canon. "Youth," "Heart of Darkness," and *Lord Jim,* composed between 1898 and 1900, include the figure of Marlow as character-narrator. In her obituary of Conrad, Virginia Woolf claimed that he was a "compound of two men; together with the sea captain dwelt that subtle, refined, and fastidious analyst whom he called Marlow." This leads to her "rough-and-ready distinction" that "it is Marlow who comments, Conrad who creates" (1925: 285–86, 287). As the "sea stuff" confirms and contributes to a sustaining national myth of the sea, so Marlow's presence as an English narrator weaves Conrad's own life into the life of the nation through the no less potent myth of English literature. Conrad encouraged posterity to bracket the man and the work, claiming:

> "Youth" is a feat of memory. It is a record of experience; but that experience, in its facts, in its inwardness and in its outward colouring, begins and ends in myself. "Heart of Darkness" is experience, too; but it is experience pushed a little (and only very little) beyond the actual facts of the case for the perfectly legitimate, I believe, purpose of bringing it home to the minds and bosoms of the readers. ("Author's Note," *Y*: xi)

Character and narrator, positioned between the tale and the reader, Marlow can be thought of as Janus-faced, seeing and addressing both the international British "world" of the tales and the national British "island" of the reader. Indeed, his attitude towards England (and Empire), now questioning and now reverent, depends upon this perspective: it enables the irony that defines his poetics. Rooted in the marine and colonial worlds, Marlow's tales blend the facts and myths of Empire, yet it is also through Marlow that Great and Greater Britain are brought into critical contiguity and focus. Even as he mediates between his audience and the fictional world he creates, Marlow's narratives dramatise the transformative energy of orality: this is storytelling for an audience prepared to listen to the world's voices. Commentator and character, outsider and insider, Marlow mimics Conrad's own wariness as an immigrant author writing for an English audience. To Knowles and Moore, "Marlow unites within his apparently single identity the position of both welcoming English host *and* disconcerting stranger" (2000: 40). Located between cultures, Conrad wrestles with issues of identity with the result that our sense of the way our culture feels from the inside is enriched by the perspective afforded by one of Britain's greatest outsiders.

All three Marlow-narratives were serialised in *Blackwood's Magazine*, known familiarly as *Maga*, whose ethos was conservative and imperialist. More than a decade later, Conrad remembered this period fondly in a letter to Pinker, saying: "One was in decent company there and had a good sort of public. There isn't a single club and messroom and man-of-war in the British Seas and Dominions which hasn't its copy of Maga – not to speak of all the Scots in all parts of the world" (*CL4*: 506). "Heart of Darkness" was chosen for inclusion in the thousandth number of *Maga*, where it sits awkwardly with the journal's prevailing imperial attitude. British politics of the 1890s were dominated by ideas of "imperialism" and "race." Eric Hobsbawm notes that the word "imperialism" first became part of the political and journalistic vocabulary at this point "in the course of arguments about colonial conquest" (2002: 60).

Viewed by Kipling as "the first battle in the war of [19]14–18 – a little before its time but necessary to clear the ground" (Lycett, 1999: 296–97), the Boer War of 1899–1902, fought against an enemy of European origin, was possibly the least victorious of the colonial wars won by Britain, largely because of the methods used to quell Boer resistance: farm burning, block houses, and concentration camps. The number of Boer women and children who died in the concentration camps (28,000) exceeded the number of combatants killed on both sides (20,000 British and 7,000 Boers) and must have focused the immigrant Conrad's feelings towards his adopted home (Pakenham, 1991: 580–81.) He referred to the war as "idiotic" and his view that the war would "become repugnant to the nation" (*CL2*: 207, 211) was borne out in the national mood: there were no celebrations in Trafalgar Square to mark its end as there had been after Ladysmith was relieved in March 1900. Conrad thus espoused his new national identity at a moment when the sense of Englishness was itself being reformulated. As G. K. Chesterton asked: "What can they know of England who know only the world?" (1905: 42).

Conrad's family history complicates his political allegiance to an Empire composed of territories whose boundaries took no account of tribal origins. He was British, as he assured David Bone, "by choice," adding: "I am more British than you are. You are only British because you could not help it" (Bone, 1955: 160). And the

Britain of Conrad's choice was imperial. The great fact of British life, the Empire, provided Conrad with a living, with security, and with a sense of communal recognition and belonging. As a member of the British Merchant Marine, engaged in the practical reality of Empire, Conrad was part of the great web of communication that assimilated remote areas of the world into the British economy. It would be surprising if his early political allegiances were not those of the enlightened Conservative. But while Conservative imperialism dominates British politics at this period, the age is equally characterised by portents of imperial disintegration, and, related to this, strains between old hierarchies of authority and power and an incipient democracy.

British political life mirrored the changing configurations and realignments of national identity. Its leanings towards socialism were evident in the founding of the Fabian Society in 1884, whose members included Sidney and Beatrice Webb, George Bernard Shaw, and H. G. Wells. In 1886, unemployed East Enders rioted in Trafalgar Square and looted shops in Oxford Street; in the two years that followed, strikes by East End match-girls and dockworkers launched the new and formidably powerful unionism. The need for an increasingly unionised working class to be represented in the House of Commons led to the formation in Bradford in 1893 of the Independent Labour Party, founded by Keir Hardy, an Ayrshire coal miner who had helped to form the Scottish Parliamentary Labour Party in 1888. Membership of the trade union movement increased steadily: it doubled in the Edwardian years, from two million in 1901 to over four million in 1913 (see Matthew and Morgan, eds, 1992: 60). Co-ordinated through such organizations as Mrs Fawcett's National Union of Women's Suffrage Societies in 1897 and the Pankhursts' Women's Social and Political Union in 1903, the campaign for women's votes (which Conrad supported) politicised gender in the pursuit of a revised concept of British "citizenship." The term "feminism" came into use in the 1890s.

* * *

After the publication of *Lord Jim* in 1900, Conrad spent the early months of the new century writing "Typhoon" (published in the United States in 1902 and in England in 1903). A sea novella set aboard a steamship, the *Nan-Shan*, and hence a companion piece to *The Nigger of the "Narcissus,"* "Typhoon" earned the plaudit that "Conrad has no equal on the seas" (Sherry, ed., 1973: 18). Although friends and associates – among them Garnett, Wells, and James – disapproved of the plan, Conrad also entered into a period of collaboration with Ford Madox Ford, his junior by sixteen years and whom he first met in 1894. The collaborative venture produced *The Inheritors* (1901), *Romance* (1903), and *The Nature of a Crime* (1909), but failed to bring either the material rewards or the popular recognition aimed at by both men.

This period also saw a variety of writing ventures as Conrad, beset by illnesses and self-doubt, and now with a young family to support – the Conrads had two sons, Borys, born in 1898, and John, born in 1906 – cast around for new ways of making money with his pen. Alongside the shorter fiction – collected in *Youth, A Narrative and Two Other Stories* (1902), *Typhoon, and Other Stories* (1903), *A Set of Six* (1908), and *Twixt Land and Sea* (1912) – Conrad turned his hand to a series of semi-autobiographical pieces, collected in *The Mirror of the Sea* (1906), and play-writing: his story "To-morrow" was adapted as a one-act play entitled *One Day More* and performed by the Stage Society in June 1905. In addition, he wrote essays, literary reviews, and occasional pieces. Notorious for his inability to live within his means, such writing served to keep the author's name before the public while providing Conrad with the means to pay his weekly household bills and supplement his income from fiction writing whose progress was, equally notoriously, slow. Conrad confessed to writing "pour la marmite" [for the money] (*CL3*: 204).

Collected in two volumes, *Notes on Life and Letters* (1921) and *Last Essays* (published posthumously in 1926), the essays and occasional writings that spanned Conrad's writing career show that he had an active not, simply a legal bond with British public life. He was a professional twice over, a professional seaman and a professional writer, and professionalism, by definition, is exclusive. Citizenship, by contrast, is inclusive. Despite such off-hand comments as "I never look at the papers, so I know nothing of politics and literature" (*CL2*: 138), the subject matter of Conrad's essays suggests that they emerge from his reflections on the pages of the daily press – now responding to the Russo-Japanese War of 1904–05; now attacking theatrical censorship; now bringing his maritime expertise to bear on the *Titanic* disaster of 1912, and charging the Board of Trade and the press with irresponsibility; now discussing Poland's re-emergence as a nation state after the First World War.

And if there is more continuity in their belletristic style than their subject matter, then the divergent preoccupations of such writings, following the rhythm of successive stages of his writing career, not only cast a revealing light on his public engagement with and contribution to the cultural and political life of his adopted home-land, but also allow the principles he lived by as an author to be reworded, whether positioning his own "sea stuff" within the tradition of maritime fiction in "Tales of the Sea" or asserting underlying truths of his craft – "Fiction is history, human history, or it is nothing" – in his essay on "Henry James" (*NLL*: 17).

Conrad's next move as a novelist was audacious. He turned his attention to the subject of politics, and over the next decade composed three of the greatest political novels in the English lan-guage: *Nostromo* (1904), *The Secret Agent* (1907), and *Under Western Eyes* (1911). Set, respectively, in South America, Lon-don, and St Petersburg and Geneva, these works, each initially conceived as a short story, delineate the moral complexities of choice and betrayal in particular historical and political moments, revealing individual entrapment within alienating power systems. Conrad described *Nostromo* as "the most anxiously meditated" of his longer novels ("Author's Note": vii): in it he vividly creates the history and politics of a fictional South American country, Costa-guana. Domesticity and the seedy underworld of politics become enmeshed in *The Secret Agent* and *Under Western Eyes*. Looking for a wider public, Conrad assured Pinker that *The Secret Agent* had "an element of popularity in it" (*CL3*: 439). Based in London, the novel draws upon a real incident: in 1884, an anarchist named Martial Bourdin had accidentally blown himself up in Greenwich Park. The "mad dynamiter" was the great bugaboo of the late-Victorian press and in its subject matter and, particularly, the figure of the Professor, *The Secret Agent* courted the popular market. In the event, Conrad declared it "an honourable failure," continuing: "I suppose there is something in me that is unsympathetic to the general public ... Foreignness I suppose" (*CL4*: 9–10).

References to his "foreignness" had surfaced in reviews of *The Secret Agent* by both the general "ruck" and Garnett: Conrad was an "alien of genius," an "alien spirit," and, most irritatingly, "Slav" [see Sherry, ed., 1973: 25–26]. His protest to Garnett is direct: "I've been so cried up of late as a sort of freak, an amazing bloody foreigner writing in English (every blessed review of S.A. had it so – and even yours) that anything I say will be discounted on that ground by the public" (*CL3*: 488). A review of his next volume, *A Set of Six* (1908), described Conrad as "without either country or language," someone who had "found a new patriotism for himself in the sea. His vision of men, however, is the vision of a cosmopolitan, of a homeless person" (Sherry, ed., 1973: 211). Though a naturalised British subject for more than twenty years by this time, such reminders of his status as both insider and outsider rankled. In April 1899, he had been attacked in the Polish magazine *Kraj* for his "desertion" of his native land in order to write "popular and very lucrative novels in English" (Najder, ed., 1983: 187). However unfounded – Conrad was barely eking out a living of print runs of a couple of thousand copies – the charges echo in readings of Conrad's works that interpret them as coded allegories of national betrayal.

The Garnetts were keen Russophiles (Constance Garnett is remembered for her translations of the major Russian authors) and Conrad's next novel would engage directly with "a reading of the Russian character," a subject that, he confessed, had "long haunted me" (*CL4*: 14). Symptomatic of this "haunting" are the links that critics have detected between *Under Western Eyes* and Dostoevsky's *Crime and Punishment*. Conrad's engagement with the Russian character in *Under Western Eyes* taxed him severely. Added to the problems of composition – composition of this "most deeply meditated novel" (*CL6*: 695) took over two years – he had become estranged from both Ford and, when he submitted the complete manuscript in January 1910, from Pinker. A row between the two men included Pinker's accusation that Conrad "did not speak English" (*CL4*: 334).

Conrad's unremitting pessimism about political institutions was starkly voiced in his essay on Anatole France (1904): "political institutions, whether contrived by the wisdom of the few or the ignorance of the many, are incapable of securing the happiness of mankind" (*NLL*: 38). Always fascinated by how people cope, or rather fail to cope, *in extremis*, Conrad's subject is man's vulnerability and corruptibility. Correspondingly, his philosophy was bleak: in a meaningless universe, civilization and virtue were relative, fragile, and constantly under threat. This vision is borne out in fictions whose conclusions afford bleak, fatalistic visions of darkness and where the positive occupies a restricted domain. Human solidarity provides the only source of value in life, and mutual responsibility the only ethic. In his scepticism, Conrad was acutely of his time.

But it is in his letters to a fellow aristocratic-adventurer-turned-writer, Robert Cunninghame Graham, that Conrad is most self-revealing about his sceptical outlook, particularly when challenging his friend's active and outspoken socialist commitment. Graham, who was sentenced to six weeks in prison for his part in the "Bloody Sunday" riots in Trafalgar Square in 1887, had represented North-West Lanarkshire as a Liberal Member of Parliament from 1886 to 1892. Seeing Graham's "ideals of sincerity, courage and truth" as "strangely out of place in this epoch of material preoccupation," Conrad chided: "What you want to reform are not institutions – it is human nature" (*CL2*: 25). Yet this same human nature is, fundamentally, alienated within a purposeless universe:

> Life knows us not and we do not know life – we don't even know our own thoughts. Half the words we use have no meaning whatever and of the other half each man understands each word after the fashion of his own folly and conceit. Faith is a myth and beliefs shift like mists on the shore; thoughts vanish; words, once pronounced, die; and the memory of yesterday is as shadowy as the hope of to-morrow. (*CL2*: 17)

As Christian certainty faltered in the wake of the Darwinian revolution, so science became the modern mythology, supplying the ideas that shape human knowledge. *Almayer's Folly* shares its year of publication, 1895, with the invention of the telephone and the discovery of X-rays by Röntgen; it was also the year in which Freud published his first work on psychoanalysis and Marconi sent his first message over a mile by wireless. But the technological advances of the age were tempered by despair, too. In April 1912, the "unsinkable" White Star liner *Titanic* struck an iceberg and sank on her maiden voyage, while the battlefields of the First World War saw death and destruction on an industrial scale, previously unimaginable. Advances in Western technology, such as the first automatic machine-gun, invented by Hiram Maxim in 1884, led to ludicrously one-sided battles with colonial enemies: in the decisive defeat of the Mahdists in 1898, ten-thousand Sudanese were killed at the Battle of Omdurman at a cost to General Kitchener of less than 50 men. As the poet, essayist, and historian Hilaire Belloc (1870–1953) put it in "The Modern Traveller" (1898): "Whatever happens, we have got / The Maxim Gun, and they have not."

* * *

After two decades of struggling to make his writing pay, and never able to live within his means, the next phase in Conrad's career was transformative. With the publication of *Chance* in 1914, *Victory* the following year, and *The Shadow-Line* in 1917, he achieved a dramatic popularity and financial success. After novels whose world was predominantly masculine and in which women were relegated to the margins, as Conrad addressed such concerns as flawed heroism, *Chance* turns upon the presence of a central female figure, Flora de Barral, and foregrounds the presence of thwarted desire. The later novels repeatedly return to the theme of emotional repression. Conrad's fictional response to the popular social climate, especially the "woman question," proved well timed: the Women's Social and Political Union was founded in 1903 and the Women's Freedom League, a secessionist group, in 1908. Led by Christabel Pankhurst, the suffragettes became increasingly more militant, resorting to a wave of crime that included arson, bomb-throwing, and slashing paintings in public galleries. *Chance*, which Conrad described as one of his "greater successes" (*CL5*: 664), was able to capitalise on this public interest. The comparative figures speak for themselves: published on 12 September 1907, *The Secret Agent* sold 5,000 copies in England that year; *Chance*, published on 15 January 1914, sold 13,200 copies in two weeks (Sherry, ed., 1973: 30). Even more remarkably, the next two novels followed this trend despite being published during the First World War: *Victory* appeared in America in late March 1915 and its popularity was such – 11,000 copies sold in the first three days – that export orders depleted the domestic stock with the result that the English publication, in May, was accompanied by reprintings; the first English edition of *The Shadow-Line*, 5,000 copies, was published on 19 March 1917 and sold out within a week.

Public tastes are notoriously fickle and, according to Garnett, "it is probable that the figure of the lady on the 'jacket' of *Chance* (1914) did more to bring the novel into popular favour than the long review by Sir Sidney Colvin in *The Observer*" (1928: xx). Now part of the literary establishment, Conrad was lionised and befriended by a new generation of writers, including Edward Thomas, Stephen Reynolds, and Hugh Walpole. His popularity meant, for instance, that in early 1916 he sat for a portrait by William Rothenstein, was photographed by Alvin Langdon Coburn, and sat for a bust by Jo Davidson, which was later presented to the National Portrait Gallery. During the same period, negotiations about a collected edition of his works progressed and he began to compose a series of Author's Notes; André Gide's French translation of his works began; plans for a dramatisation of *Victory*, adapted by Basil Macdonald Hastings, started to take shape; and critical studies of his fiction appeared on both sides of the Atlantic. Indeed, so internationally popular had Conrad become that in 1917 an "Evening with Conrad's People," comprising 21 *tableaux vivants* from his novels, was planned in Cincinnati to raise funds for the American war-effort. Besides the manifest recognition of Conrad's fame, it was also "all good for business" (*CL6*: 103), as Conrad observed to Pinker.

In July 1914, the Conrads undertook a planned six-week visit to Poland. Only a month after the assassination of Archduke Franz Ferdinand in Sarajevo, the timing was rash, and the party quickly found itself witness to the mobilization for war and precariously cut off from England. Britain declared war on Germany on 4 August 1914. From Cracow, a town "in a state of siege" with "teleg^{ph} and 'phones closed and papers censured" (*CL5*: 409), they journeyed to unmilitarised territory in the Zakopane mountains whence, "destitute of means, without warm clothing and indeed in a very deplorable plight" (*CL5*: 412), Conrad was forced to turn to Pinker for means to return to England. The Conrads had journeyed to Poland with Józef Retinger and his wife. Retinger, a Pole Conrad had first met in 1912, sought the author's help in internationalising the political fate of wartime Poland. The war, inevitably, dramatized Conrad's complicated, *duplex* allegiances to "home": while claiming to view the problem "from the English point of view, which is only tinged with the ineradicable sentiment of origin" (*CL5*: 646), he also described the "cause" of Poland as "sacred; for there is sacredness in the sacrificial fires of misfortune" (*CL5*: 670). In a letter, Conrad confessed: "My strongest feelings are deeply rooted in this country [i.e. England]; but besides my grief at seeing it engaged in this ugly and desperate adventure I've had to stand two months the strain of living amongst the Poles who see with dismay the ruin of their hopes" (*CL5*: 468). His ill-advised visit to Poland yielded the essay "Poland Revisited" (1915). Described as "a retracing of footsteps on the road of life," the essay is nonetheless a paean to Great Britain, "dear to me not as an inheritance, but as an acquisition, as a conquest in the sense in which a woman is conquered – by love, which is a sort of surrender" (*NLL*: 148). The ravages of war itself are formulated in terms of their destructive impact upon his "school-room" of the North Sea coastal fleet, now "desecrated by violence, littered with wrecks, with death slaking its waves, hiding under its waters" (*NLL*: 155).

The First World War was *the* defining historical moment of Modernism, the apogee of its social, cultural, and political scepticism. Henry James described it as "The plunge of civilization into this abyss of blood and darkness" (Kaplan, 1992: 553). To Ezra Pound, the myriad died "For an old bitch gone in the teeth, / For a botched civilization" ("Hugh Selwyn Mauberley"); to T. S. Eliot civilization was reduced to "A heap of broken images" ("The Waste Land"). In a letter to Conrad of December 1916, J. M. Dent wrote: "we are witnessing the birth throes of a new world, and you of all men, it seems to me, should be the prophet of its psychology" (*CL5*: 681n5). The response of Conrad, who pronounced himself "like a man in a nightmare" (*CL6*: 55), was more personal: his eldest son Borys, aged seventeen, had enlisted in 1915 and, as a commissioned officer attached to the heavy artillery of the 34th brigade, saw active service in France, where he was gassed and shell-shocked during the Second Army's advance into Flanders in mid-October 1918, a month before Armistice Day. In late August 1915, Conrad wrote to Ford, also gassed during the war: "Our world of 15 years ago is gone to pieces; what will come in its place God knows, but I imagine doesn't care" (*CL5*: 503).

As part of the war effort, Conrad was asked by the Admiralty to join other writers in contributing pieces on the work of the Royal Navy Reserve. Peter Buitenhuis notes: "It is probably significant that those who have best survived the test of time, Hardy, Conrad, and Shaw, were those who subscribed least to the propaganda myth of the Great War" (1989: 180). Conrad's sense of his redundancy at this time of national crisis is reflected in his wartime correspondence, which reveals symptoms of weariness and creative exhaustion. Significantly, his only work of substance to have been produced during these years of "moral sea-sickness" (*CL5*: 522) was *The Shadow-Line*.

Wartime gloom and paternal anxiety over Borys exacerbated Conrad's increasingly fragile and nervous health, which is a persistent theme in his correspondence. He described himself two years after the war as "gouty, seedy, crusty, moody, stupid, perverse, cynical and lame" (*CL7*: 204). Inevitably the anxieties of these years led to self-reflection and self-evaluation, not least about mortality: "I suppose one must end some day, somehow. Mere decency requires it" (*CL6*: 78) he quipped to Garnett. To Macdonald Hastings, whose stage-production of *Victory* was the most successful of the theatrical ventures Conrad undertook in his last phase, he lamented: "I have been for 20 years performing on a tight rope (without net) and I am still at it ... One would like to see some prospect of getting down at last – if only on the brink of the grave, just for a moment" (*CL6*: 38). As Conrad was writing prefaces for the collected edition of his works, reflection and self-appraisal also mark this period. In spring 1917 he claimed:

> after 22 years of work I may say that I have not been very well understood. I have been called a writer of the sea, of the tropics, a descriptive writer, a romantic writer – and also a realist. But as a matter of fact all my concern has been with the 'ideal' values of things, events and people.   (*CL6*: 40)

Increasingly, severe gout prevented Conrad from writing and *The Arrow of Gold* was the first novel to be largely dictated. Perhaps because of this, he was able to maintain a steady rate of fictional output in his last years: *The Arrow of Gold* was published in 1919, *The Rescue* in 1920, and *The Rover* in 1923; in addition, *Notes on Life and Letters* appeared in 1921, while *Suspense* and *Tales of Hearsay* were published posthumously in 1925. This is not to say that composition came any easier: even while dictating *Suspense* he complained to Pinker of "that mistrust of oneself that has been my companion through all these literary years" (*CL7*: 110). But these years saw Conrad, who died of a heart attack on 3 August 1924, able to reap and enjoy the rewards of his literary fame, so often only bestowed by posterity. In 1919, he received $20,000 for the film rights to four of his works; *Victory*, the first film based upon a Conrad novel, appeared in late 1920. His social circle, that had included many of the foremost novelists writing in English, now extended to such figures as Paul Valéry, Maurice Ravel, and C. K. Scott Moncrieff, the translator of Proust. He also turned down honorary degrees from a number of universities, in both Britain and the United States, and, in 1924, declined a knighthood from the Prime Minister, J. Ramsay MacDonald. As testament to his truly international reputation, in May 1923 Conrad visited America on a promotional tour organised by his American publisher Doubleday. During his visit, that began with an enthusiastic welcome in New York as he stepped off the *Tuscania* on 1 May – "a nerve-shattering experience" (*LL2*: 307), he told Jessie – Conrad was fêted, gave readings from his works, sat for a portrait by Oscar Cesare, had his portrait on the cover of *Time* magazine, and generally basked in the plaudits of an appreciative American audience.

While critics have generally tended to see in Conrad's late fiction signs of creative exhaustion, these works nonetheless offer further distillations of life experience as Conrad turns to France and the Napoleonic era for his setting. In *A Personal Record* he claimed that "of all the countries in Europe it is with France that Poland has most connection" (121). His *szlachta* upbringing ensured that French was his second language; his literary mentors included such French writers as Flaubert, Maupassant, Hugo, Daudet, Anatole France, and Proust; and, of course, his early exile had taken him to Marseilles and a spell in French ships. He even considered moving to France in 1922 as a tax dodge. *The Arrow of Gold* is set in Marseilles, *The Rover* in Toulon and the Giens peninsula, and while *Suspense* is based in Genoa, its historical setting of 1815 ensures that the action is overshadowed by the imminent return from Elba of Napoleon for the Hundred Days that ended at Waterloo. If the completion of *The Rescue*, twenty-four years after its inception in 1896, can be seen as Conrad's final settling of creative accounts, and Peyrol's "sailor's 'return'" (*LL2*: 339) in *The Rover* as Conrad's swansong, then this late phase as a whole can be formulated in terms of a belated tribute to his European inheritance.

Works cited

Bone, David. *Landfall at Sunset*. London: Gerald Duckworth, 1955.

Buitenhuis, Peter. *The Great War of Words: Literature as Propaganda 1914–18 and After*. London: B. T. Batsford Ltd., 1989.

Chesterton, G. K. *Heretics*. London: John Lane, 1905.

Conrad, Jessie. *Joseph Conrad as I Knew Him*. London: Heinemann, 1926.

Edel, Leon, ed. *Henry James Letters. Volume 4: 1895–1916*. Cambridge, Mass.: Belknap Press, 1984.

Ford, Ford Madox. *The Bodley Head Ford Madox Ford*. Vol. 1. London: Bodley Head, 1962.

Garnett, Edward, ed. *Letters from Conrad: 1895 to 1924*. Bloomsbury: Nonesuch Press, 1928.

——. ed. *Letters from John Galsworthy: 1900–1932*. London: Jonathan Cape, 1934.

Hardy, Thomas. *Jude the Obscure*. [1895] "The New Wessex Edition." London: Macmillan, 1986.

Hobsbawm, Eric. *Industry and Empire: An Economic History of Britain since 1750*. London: Weidenfeld and Nicolson, 1969.

——. *The Age of Empire: 1875–1914*. London: Abacus, 2002.

Kaplan, Fred. *Henry James: The Imagination of Genius.* London: Hodder & Stoughton, 1992.

Knowles, Owen, and Gene M. Moore. *Oxford Reader's Companion to Conrad.* Oxford: Oxford University Press, 2000.

Lycett, Andrew. *Rudyard Kipling.* London: Widenfeld and Nicolson, 1999.

Matthew, H. C. G., and Kenneth O. Morgan. *The Oxford History of Britain: The Modern Age.* Oxford: Oxford University Press, 1992.

Najder, Zdzisław, ed. *Conrad under familial eyes.* Cambridge: Cambridge University Press, 1983.

Pakenham, Thomas. *The Scramble for Africa: 1876–1912.* London: Weidenfeld and Nicolson, 1991.

Ray, Martin, ed. *Joseph Conrad: Interviews and Recollections.* London: Macmillan, 1990.

Russell, Bertrand. *Portraits from Memory and Other Essays.* London: George Allen & Unwin, 1956.

Sherry, Norman, ed. *Conrad: The Critical Heritage.* London: Routledge & Kegan Paul, 1973.

Thompson, David. *England in the Nineteenth Century: 1815–1914.* London: Penguin, 1991.

Watts, Cedric, ed. *Joseph Conrad's Letters to R. B. Cunninghame Graham.* Cambridge: Cambridge University Press, 1969.

Woolf, Virginia. *The Common Reader.* London: Hogarth Press, 1925.

2

Malay Novels: *Almayer's Folly* and *An Outcast of the Islands*

In his memoir, *A Personal Record* (1912), Conrad stated: "if I had not got to know Almayer pretty well it is almost certain there would never have been a line of mine in print" (87). As biographers and critics have demonstrated, Conrad transmuted the experiences of his life into the details of his fiction, his remarkably retentive memory ensuring that people and incidents from his past, no matter how insignificant, provided grist to his creative mill. *Almayer's Folly* is thus both the novel that launched the writing career of Józef Teodor Konrad Korzeniowski, under the pen-name Joseph Conrad, and the first of several testaments to his time as a sailor in the Eastern Seas in the 1880s.

The fictional setting for *Almayer's Folly* and *An Outcast of the Islands* is based upon the remote coastal region of Berau in north-east Borneo. In both novels, Sambir is the name given to the settlement of Tanjong Redeb that stands at the confluence of two rivers in the Berau estuary. Conrad calls his rivers the "Pantai" – the "Eastern River" that provides the subtitle for *Almayer's Folly* – and "the Sambir reach" (*AF*: 14). About the size of Wales, Berau was divided into two sultanates: Gunung Tabur and Sambaliung. Conrad visited Berau four times, between September and December 1887, while serving as first mate in the SS *Vidar*, a steamer owned by an Arab trader in Singapore, Al Jooffree, that sailed under a British flag and was commanded by a Scot, Captain James Craig.

In *Almayer's Folly*, Abdulla's steamer runs "between Singapore and the Pantai settlement every three months or so" (29) and seems modelled on the *Vidar*, with Captain Ford the fictional counterpart of Captain Craig. Captain William Lingard, one of the models for Conrad's Captain Tom Lingard, established a permanent trading post, Lingard & Co., in Tanjong Redeb in 1886. At Berau, Conrad had the opportunity to meet two of William Lingard's agents: Willem Carel Olmeijer, the prototype for Conrad's Kaspar Almayer, and Lingard's nephew, James (Jim). In his "Author's Note" to *An Outcast of the Islands*, Conrad also claimed to have met the original of Peter Willems in Berau, describing him as "a mistrusted, disliked, worn-out European living on the reluctant toleration of that Settlement" (xlv).

Geographical coincidence is complemented by historical verisimilitude that allows us to identify the temporal setting of *Almayer's Folly* in the mid-1880s and *An Outcast of the Islands* in the early 1870s. The contiguity between fiction and history is everywhere in *Almayer's Folly*: "Other things also woke him up from his apathy. The stir made in the whole of the island by the establishment of the British Borneo Company affected even the sluggish flow of Pantai life. Great changes were expected; annexation was talked of; the Arabs grew civil. Almayer began building his new house for the use of the future engineers, agents, or settlers of the new Company" (33). Established by Royal Charter in 1881, the British North Borneo Company led the Dutch to strengthen their position in north-east Borneo and to the setting up of a joint British–Dutch commission in 1884 to settle boundary disputes. The predicament of the fictional Almayer is thus coextensive with historical and political reality: an agent for the British firm of Lingard & Co., Almayer reasonably expects to prosper under the British but not under the Dutch – the chief of the Dutch Commission tells him that "the Arabs were better subjects than Hollanders who dealt illegally in gunpowder with the Malays" (36). Dain Maroola's arrival in Sambir is similarly grounded in historical fact. His contribution to the fictional plot of *Almayer's Folly* in search of gunpowder can be traced to the Dutch reversals against the Sumatran Achinese in 1881 that fostered unrest throughout the Archipelago.

Of course, a work of fiction need not be in thrall to the real world: while it may be located in geographical and historical reality, its meaning is not finally reducible to these sources. Yet, as Conrad writes in his essay on Henry James: "Fiction is history, human history, or it is nothing" (*NLL*: 17). Conrad's writing career begins with an implicit examination of the correspondences between life and art, demonstrating how, at their intersection, vital affinities are at work that the separation of the two damagingly ignores. Not only do the novel and autobiography flow in and out of each other, offering unusually privileging accounts of how fiction is woven out of the material of life, but through their overlapping codes and discourses, the very process of constructing history is also examined through the process of novel-writing.

Almayer's Folly and An Outcast of the Islands: Sequential Narratives

Almayer's Folly was published in 1895, when Conrad was thirty-eight. Not only Conrad's first novel, it was also the first in a series of three novels set in the Malay Archipelago, charting the declining fortunes of Europeans in the area. The Malay Trilogy (sometimes called the "Lingard Trilogy") is a trilogy-in-reverse, in which *Almayer's Folly*, though written first, is actually the last in chronological sequence and provides the conclusion to the overall narrative. It was quickly followed by *An Outcast of the Islands*, a year later, and *The Rescue*, begun (as *The Rescue*) in March 1896 but which Conrad laid aside (to write *The Nigger of the "Narcissus"*), returning to it intermittently for the next quarter of a century and only completing it in 1919. With their shared cast of characters, repeated settings, and related themes, these narratives are "transtextual" (see Watts, 1984). Thus, *An Outcast of the Islands*, a tale about the ambitious and unscrupulous Peter Willems, introduces the character of another European trader, Kaspar Almayer, whose own demise is recounted in *Almayer's Folly*, while *The Rescue* introduces the figure of Tom Lingard, whose discovery of a navigable entry to the Pantai River has enabled him to establish the trading monopoly at Sambir in north-east Borneo that provides the historical and geographic context for both *Almayer's Folly* and *An Outcast of the Islands*. Read chronologically, the European stranglehold on the island trade is breached in *An Outcast of the Islands*, as the Arab trader Abdulla gains access to the river, and it is, quite literally, destroyed in *Almayer's Folly*, where Almayer himself burns down the trading offices of "Lingard and Co."

While *Almayer's Folly* and *An Outcast of the Islands* must obviously stand or fall as discreet works of art, they share a host of connections and extensions that invite a consideration of them as separate stages in a broader, sequential narrative (that extends to and, chronologically, begins with *The Rescue*). Most obviously, there is a cast of recurring, transtextual characters, depicted at different stages of their lives including Lingard, the Almayers, Lakamba, Babalatchi, Abdulla, and Ali. For instance, in *An Outcast of the Islands* we learn that Ali "had been quartermaster with Lingard before making up his mind to stay in Sambir as Almayer's head man" (279). Ali is indeed Lingard's quartermaster in *The Rescue*, and in *Almayer's Folly* he continues in the role of Almayer's "head man." Similarly, in *An Outcast of the Islands*, Babalatchi reminds Lingard of their first meeting "arms in hand" that leads the old sea captain to recall "the past sweetness and strife of Carimata days" (222, 223). Carimata provides the setting for *The Rescue*.

Sustaining the sense of *Almayer's Folly* and *An Outcast of the Islands* as a single, developmental narrative is the ageing of characters like Nina – a child in *An Outcast of the Islands*, she is a wife and mother by the end of *Almayer's Folly* – and Captain Ford – who is "young Ford" (187) in *An Outcast*. The passing of time is further recorded in such details as Abdulla's ascendancy in Sambir: in *An Outcast* he "has begun to build godowns of plank and stone" (230); in *Almayer's Folly*, Abdulla is already established as "the great trader of Sambir," whose buildings are shown "towering above the Malay structures" (15). In *An Outcast of the Islands*, Willems watches "the up-country canoes discharging guttah or rattans, and loading rice or European goods on the little wharf of Lingard & Co." (64). This trade is a distant memory in *Almayer's Folly*. Read as consecutive stages of the same narrative of European exploitation of the Archipelago, the individual novels gain in historical depth that recasts the backdrop of Malay life from exotic setting to a depiction of prevailing existence, a point of fixity that throws the transient presence of the Europeans into even starker relief.

Almayer's Folly and *An Outcast of the Islands* also share structural, thematic, and ideological parallels. For instance, in terms of basic plot-design, both narratives incorporate flashbacks that undermine the effectiveness of the Europeans and both conclude with epilogues that focus on Almayer's dissolution. There are also similarities in the triangular relationships linking the central characters. Although it seems true to say that the character of Aïssa is not as fully drawn as Nina, the Almayer–Nina–Dain relationship in *Almayer's Folly* is reconfigured in the comparably Oedipal Lingard–Willems–Aïssa relationship in *An Outcast of the Islands*. Incidental echoes abound. The conflagration that destroys "Almayer's Folly" is prefigured in the destruction of Babalatchi's prospective new house, used to accommodate Omar and Aïssa, by Willems in *An Outcast of the Islands*. The subversive force of such echoes is apparent in the very dreams of Europeans: Lingard's unrealised dream – "we shall all go to Europe. The child must be educated. We shall be rich. Rich is no name for it" (*OI*: 196) – is clearly adopted by Almayer in *Almayer's Folly*: "They would live in Europe, he and his daughter. They would be rich and respected" (3). Almayer thus pursues a second-hand, already-failed dream.

Inevitably, it is Almayer himself who unites *An Outcast of the Islands* and *Almayer's Folly*. As his role in *An Outcast* becomes increasingly important, so it anticipates the story of his own demise in *Almayer's Folly*. Most notably, the fifth and concluding part of *An Outcast of the Islands* begins with a vision of Almayer that will be repeated at the opening of *Almayer's Folly*. Almayer is depicted, staring "through and past the illusion of the material world": "propped, alone on the verandah of his house," he watches "a solitary log" being washed down the river top to the sea (291); and while the setting provides "the present sign of a splendid future" (292), his daydream is interrupted by Ali's injunction "Makan Tuan!" (294). The repetition of this moment at the beginning of *Almayer's Folly* confirms the stasis and torpor of Almayer's existence in Sambir while underscoring the ironic intent of Conrad's, slightly misquoted epigraph from Amiel – "*Qui de nous n'a eu sa terre promise, son jour d'extase et sa fin en exil*" [Who amongst us has not had his promised land, his day of ecstasy, and his end in exile?]: Almayer is trapped between *extase* and *exil*.

The connections identified above, together with their shared geopolitical context, make the invitation to read *Almayer's Folly* and *An Outcast of the Islands* as continuous stages of the same story overwhelming. An outline of their respective contents demonstrates shared preoccupations, and, particularly, their sustained focus upon the dissolution of the European self in the face of cross-cultural encounters. (This is less a case of racial degeneration through contact with the Other, as the example of Jim-Eng, who becomes an opium addict, proves; rather, it exposes the flawed European assumption of racial superiority.) *Almayer's Folly* opens with the eponymous Almayer, on the verandah of his "new but already decaying house," dreaming of the wealth that will allow him to leave Sambir after "twenty-five years of heart-breaking struggle" (4) to begin life anew with his daughter, Nina, in Europe. To this end he is awaiting the return of the Balinese prince, Dain Maroola, who is instrumental in his plan to find the fabled "mountain of gold" in the island's interior. A *déclassé* Dutchman, Almayer manages the trading post of the English sailor-adventurer Captain Tom Lingard. Dain Maroola's arrival, under cover of darkness and unattended except for his two boatmen, is inauspicious – a fact that "Almayer, in his elation, failed to notice" (13) – as is his immediate visit to Lakamba, the Rajah of Sambir, across the river. Also unperceived by the racially proud Almayer, but subtly conveyed to the reader by the third-person narrator, is Nina's interested response to news of the young prince's return. Throughout the novel, such privileged insights contribute to the ironic distance from which the reader is invited to view Almayer. From this vantage, he emerges as an ineffectual dreamer, blind to the hopelessness of his predicament and outsmarted by the machinations of his supposedly inferior native rivals.

Compounding the contradiction of Almayer's wish to venture deep into the heart of Borneo in order to escape from it, the structural arrangement of the narrative conspires against Almayer's "dream of splendid future" (1), as Chapters 2 to 5 offer an extended retrospective summary of his failed hopes and past life in Sambir. These chapters chart the failures of Almayer's private and professional life. He has reluctantly married Lingard's "adopted daughter" (10), a woman of Sulu origin, out of "judicious fear of the adopted father-in-law and a just regard for his own material welfare" (23), but plans to abandon her in Sambir. Instead, Lingard's bankruptcy and disappearance to Europe, together with the inter-tribal commercial rivalry in the island, see Almayer outmanoeuvred and bested at every turn. His one consolation in life is his daughter, Nina. But, having spent ten years in Singapore receiving a European education, Nina returns to Sambir disillusioned with colonial society and, increasingly responsive to her Malay heritage, falls in love with Dain Maroola. Mrs Almayer fans the flames of this love, and the young couple plan their elopement to Bali. Thus, by the time that the narrative returns the reader to the present at the end of Chapter 5, any lingering belief in Almayer's hopes has been eradicated.

Following this summary, the narrative concentrates on twenty-four eventful hours during which Almayer is lulled into believing that Dain is dead – a plan orchestrated by Babalatchi to deceive the Dutch authorities – and surrenders to "the utter abandonment of despair" (99) in the collapse of his plans. The scale of his deception is revealed to him when, awakened from a drunken stupor by the slave-girl, Taminah, he learns that his wife and daughter have deserted him and that Nina is preparing to flee with Dain. Confronting the couple, Almayer pleads with, threatens, and finally, with the Dutch authorities in close pursuit, assists Nina in her escape to a new life. In this, his motives are characteristically self-serving and informed by the fear of racial "disgrace": "No, it cannot be ... white men finding my daughter with this Malay. My daughter!" (184). In the wake of the couple's escape, the broken Almayer burns down the offices of Lingard & Co. and retires to "Almayer's Folly" where he seeks oblivion in opium. In a corrosive counterpoint, Almayer's demise coincides with the news that Nina has given birth to a son in Bali, and it is left to his greatest enemy to deliver the epitaph on Almayer's squalid and lonely end: "the beads in Abdulla's hand clicked, while in a solemn whisper he breathed out piteously the name of Allah! The Merciful! The Compassionate!" (208).

In his "Author's Note" to *An Outcast of the Islands*, Conrad recalls Edward Garnett's casual suggestion, following the publication of *Almayer's Folly*, that he "write another" (viii). His decision to do just this, continuing work already in hand, effectively committed Conrad to earning his livelihood by his pen. He published the novel – "certainly the most *tropical* of my eastern tales" (ix) – on 4 March 1896 and married Jessie George later that same month, on 24 March.

The "outcast" of the title is Peter Willems, the erstwhile sailor from Rotterdam who, having jumped ship in Semarang at the age of seventeen, is taken up by Captain Tom Lingard. Finding his protégé "hopelessly at variance with the spirit of the sea" (17), Lingard helps Willems secure employment as the confidential clerk of Hudig and Co. in Macassar. When we first meet him in the opening chapter, on the night of his thirtieth birthday, the ambitious but unscrupulous Willems has "stepped off the path of honesty, as he understood it" (11): to cover his gambling debts he has committed the "idiotic indiscretion" (22) of stealing from his employer. Despite having secretly repaid most of the stolen money, Willems is humiliatingly dismissed by Hudig once the theft is revealed. Willems's arrogance and self-delusion are starkly and ironically presented from the outset. Openly contemptuous of his half-caste wife, Joanna (who, he discovers from Lingard, is Hudig's illegitimate daughter) and her poor relatives, the Da Souzas, all of whom are financially dependant upon him, he yet glories in their apparent awe and respect: "he did not mind them, because, with their humble dependence, they completed his triumphant life" (36). Nothing conveys the scale of Willems's altered fortunes like the ridicule of Joanna and her family in revenge for years of tyrannical abuse. Again Lingard comes to the rescue and takes Willems to his trading post in Sambir, managed by Almayer, intending to leave him there until the scandal blows over.

This scandal, however, is but a prelude to the real threat posed to Willems's exalted self-conception. Banished to Sambir, he falls under the spell of the beautiful Aïssa, daughter of the invalid Omar el Badavi, former leader of the piratical Brunei rovers. Not only does this relationship pose a challenge to Willems's sense of racial superiority – "He seemed to be surrendering to a wild creature the unstained purity of his life, of his race, of his civilization" (80) – but it is also successfully exploited by the wily, one-eyed Malay politician, Babalatchi, in his plot to end Lingard's trading monopoly. With symmetrical irony it is Willems himself who pilots the barque of Syed Abdulla up Lingard's secret river, thus ensuring the Arab trader access to Sambir – and, as an older, rueful Almayer observes in *Almayer's Folly*, "where they [the Arabs] traded they would be masters and suffer no rival" (24). With Abdulla's backing, Lakamba replaces Patalolo as Rajah in Sambir and, as old scores are settled, Willems, much to the natives' delight, takes advantage of the new situation to revenge himself on Almayer. But, his instrumentality having served its purpose, Willems is quickly discarded by the inhabitants of Sambir, and the individualism on which he had insisted becomes his punishment: he finds himself culturally and literally isolated. He and Aïssa, "those two incomprehensible and sombre outcasts" (328), are now shunned by the natives. When, after an absence of some six months, during which his own fortunes have suffered the loss of his brig, Lingard returns to Sambir and discovers Willems's treachery, he condemns his former protégé, already shunned by Sambir society, to permanent exile in the hopeless backwater of Sambir: "You are not a human being that may be destroyed or forgiven. You are a bitter thought, a something without a body and that must be hidden" (275).

In a further act of betrayal, with Lingard preoccupied in navigating Abdulla's schooner down river, Almayer seizes the chance to rid himself of Willems – whom he fears as a potential rival heir to the fortune he mistakenly assumes Lingard to possess. He reunites Willems with his wife and son, who, unbeknown to the "outcast," have accompanied Lingard to Sambir. To the egotistical Willems, their presence offers the prospect of escape: "All at once this thought darted through his brain: How did she come? In a boat. Boat! boat!" (344). The escape plan is foiled when the couple are discovered by Aïssa, herself now a social outcast because of her relationship with Willems, whom she kills with his own revolver. In an epilogue to the tale, "Many years afterwards" (360), a gin-sodden Almayer recounts the tale to "a Roumanian, half naturalist, half orchid-hunter for commercial purposes" (360–61) and of how Aïssa, "tamed" by Nina and now a "doubled-up crone" (366), came to be living among his serving girls. The novel ends with Almayer feeling cheated by Willems's death and questioning the nature of the meaning of existence: "Where's your Providence? Where's the good for anybody in all this? The world's a swindle!" (367).

Both novels chart the disintegration of an egocentric character. In this they capture the sense of doom that colours much *fin-de-siècle* literature. For instance, both Gustave Flaubert's *Madame Bovary* (1857) and Thomas Hardy's *Jude the Obscure* (1895) offer other contemporary studies of the mind's imperviousness to its own failures. In Conrad's fiction, though, this disintegration is played out in a colonial setting that immediately renders its implications both personal and racial. Conrad's subject in *Almayer's Folly* and *An Outcast of the Islands* is nothing less than the European self and thus anticipates the theme of a collapsed civilization that, say, T. S. Eliot responds to in "The Waste Land." One thinks, for example, of the narrator's comment on the confrontation between the half-intoxicated Almayer and the disgruntled, lovesick Willems: "These two specimens of the superior race glared at each other savagely for a minute" (*OI*: 63). Identifying the pair as "specimens" carries the suggestion of a scientific study, whose true focus is to be found in the contrast between the adjective "superior" and adverb "savagely." In what sense are the Europeans "superior"? Related to this, "savagely" connotes European regression to what they think they are above.

Imperialism and commerce

A feature of Conrad's colonial fictions – and one that sets his "romances" apart from those of many of his contemporaries – is that they repeatedly strip the imperial adventure of its claims to anything more than crude commercialism. The history of European involvement in the Malay Archipelago is largely a history of trade. For example, by the early sixteenth century the Portuguese had established strategic bases in the Archipelago in their pursuit of the lucrative spice trade; in 1600, Queen Elizabeth I founded the East India Company; and in 1602 the Dutch formed the United East India Company (*Vereenigde Oostindische Compagnie*, or VOC), which became known as the Dutch East India Company. Such companies enjoyed extraordinary powers: not only were they trading monopolies, but their charters also gave them the right to wage war or make contracts in the name of the Crown or States-General, respectively, to build forts and establish trading posts, to keep soldiers and hire managers.

The seeds of Conrad's concern with material interests as a fictional subject were sown in *Almayer's Folly*, where trade becomes a means to pass ironic comment on Dutch colonialism. The European presence in Sambir is purely economic: Lingard's discovery of a navigable route up the Pantai River has guaranteed him a trade monopoly with the upriver natives, while Almayer has been lured to Sambir to work for Lingard by the prospect of inheriting the old seaman's fortune. Economics provides the basis for aspirations and alliances, political and personal, and conveys the larger forces of history and nationalism within the novel. The Balinese Dain Maroola, so central to the hopes of Almayer, Mrs Almayer, and Nina, is first and foremost a trader (himself an outsider from Bali), and here too commerce is a function of imperialism: Dain comes to Sambir in the first place against a backdrop of colonial conflict, hoping to enlist Almayer's assistance in a plot to obtain gunpowder for his father, the Rajah of Bali, "at a time when the hostilities between Dutch and Malays threatened to spread from Sumatra over the whole archipelago" (81). This threat of war between the islanders in the Archipelago and the Europeans is voiced again near the novel's conclusion, where Babalatchi says to Captain Ford:

> "There will be fighting. There is a breath of war on the islands. Shall I live long enough to see? ... Ah, Tuan!" he went on, more quietly, "the old times were best. Even I have sailed with Lanun

men, and boarded in the night silent ships with white sails. That was
before an English Rajah ruled in Kuching. Then we fought amongst
ourselves and were happy. Now when we fight with you we can
only die!" (206)

The unevenness of the conflict, implied in that final observation,
makes the illegal trade in gunpowder, quite literally, a matter of
national survival. Babalatchi's sentiments here echo those spoken
to Aïssa in *An Outcast of the Islands* after the battle with "white
men" that left her father, Omar el Badavi, blinded and his piratical
band of Brunei rovers destroyed. Following this surprise attack, in
which "The beaten ground between the houses was slippery with
blood, and the dark mangroves of the muddy creeks were full of
the sighs of dying men who were stricken down before they could
see their enemy" (52), Babalatchi says of the enemy: "They are very
strong. When we fight with them we can only die. Yet," he adds
menacingly – "some of us still live! Some of us still live!" (53).

The quest for money – and, through it, power – drives the plots
of these novels. Commercial clichés abound – according to Lingard:
"Every puff of wind is worth money in these seas" (*OI*: 44) –
and human motivation and relationships are financially determined. Almayer admits to Lingard: "I married that girl because you
promised to make my fortune" (*OI*: 162). To Willems, "Happiness
meant money" (*OI*: 142), and his betrayal of Lingard to Abdulla in
An Outcast of the Islands is, essentially, a business deal: in return
for Willems's navigational expertise Abdulla "will have to satisfy
the rapacity of a white man" (119). Nor is avarice confined to
Europeans: "The envy of Lingard's political and commercial successes, and the wish to get the best of him in every way, became
Abdulla's mania, the paramount interest of his life, the salt of his
existence" (111). With Sambir as a contested site, Abdulla, the
Arab, and Lingard, the Englishman, are revealed as comparable
colonists, both being "outsiders."

Conrad's fiction also demonstrates how the relationship between
trade and power extends to the commodification of persons. For
instance, Lingard claims: "I have them all in my pocket. ... My word
is law – and I am the only trader" (*OI*: 43). In *Almayer's Folly*,
in particular, people become commodities to be bought and sold.
Most obviously, there is Taminah, the Siamese slave girl. Owned
by Bulangi, she is sold to Babalatchi at a reduced price by the end
of the narrative. Her death, before Babalatchi can enjoy "the sound
of her laughter" (207), provides a stark comment upon both the

ruthlessness and the vagaries of trade in the novel. The "Malay girl" Almayer marries at Lingard's behest is the "legacy of a boatful of pirates" (10), and Nina is "purchased" by the dowry that Dain pours into the hands of the avaricious Mrs Almayer, a payment that links the twin themes of trade and race. Mrs Almayer's acquisitiveness dramatises Almayer's ineffectuality: while he is dreaming of wealth, she is acquiring it right under his nose by "selling" their daughter.

Far from simply contrasting the European and Oriental races, *Almayer's Folly* demonstrates their essential similarities, in particular their shared rapacity, a theme Conrad inherits from Balzac. Significantly, it is Nina, the Almayers' mixed-race daughter, who observes that whilst both Oriental and Occidental pursue "the uncertain dollar in all its multifarious and vanishing shapes ... the savage and uncompromising sincerity of purpose shown by her Malay kinsmen seemed at least preferable to the sleek hypocrisy, to the polite disguises, to the virtuous pretences of such white people as she had had the misfortune to come in contact with" (43). Nowhere is the connection between commerce and cultural diversity better illustrated than when Abdulla visits Almayer offering to buy Nina as a "favourite wife" (45) for his nephew, Reshid. Of course, Abdulla's proposal deeply offends Almayer's assumed sense of racial and cultural superiority, yet, ironically, the material advantages promised by the match offer the very trappings of civilization for which Almayer yearns:

> "You know, Tuan," he said, in conclusion, "the other women would be her slaves, and Reshid's house is great. From Bombay he has brought great divans, and costly carpets, and European furniture. There is also a great looking-glass in a frame shining like gold. What could a girl want more?" (45)

The reader is invited to laugh at Almayer's unease here both through the narrative tone – "Poor Almayer was nearly having a fit" (45) – and through the blatant hypocrisy of his reaction: unable to accede to Abdulla's offer because of his supremacist attitude, Almayer excuses Nina on the grounds that she is unworthy to join Reshid's harem, being but "an infidel woman" (45). But, even as we ridicule Almayer's reaction, we need to be wary: do *we* really want Nina to be sold to Reshid as one of his wives? As in, say, Dickens's *Great Expectations*, where the reader's desire for Pip to

leave the forge and better himself entails a share in the responsibility for Pip's subsequent snobbery towards Joe, so the reader
of *Almayer's Folly* is uneasily implicated in the racial and cultural
assumptions of the time.

Political machinations among the islanders provide a parallel
with Western influence in the area, centred on the same nexus of
trade and power. Thus, at the beginning of *An Outcast of the
Islands*, Rajah Patalolo presides in Sambir, under Lingard's protection. Realising that Lingard's political influence in the islands is a
function of his trading monopoly, and having in the past sought
unsuccessfully to overthrow the Rajah, Lakamba and Babalatchi
invite the powerful Arab trader, Syed Abdullah, to the settlement.
Willems's desire for Aïssa provides the wily Babalatchi with the
tool he needs to implement this scheme: "His idea was to make
use of Willems for the destruction of Lingard's influence" (60).
Confronted by the successful alliance of Lakamba, Babalatchi, and
Abdullah, Patalolo has no choice but to abdicate, leaving Lakamba
to assume the mantle of Rajah. By the end of the novel, Lakamba
is calling himself a Sultan and Babalatchi "the Shahbandar of the
State" (364).

Superimposed upon these local political intrigues are reminders
of the European colonial presence in the Archipelago. For instance,
the Da Souzas are described as "those degenerate descendents of
Portuguese conquerors" (4), and, as part of Willems's humiliation
of Almayer, he hoists the Dutch flag across the river in emblematic
opposition to the Union Jack flying over Almayer's compound. In
Almayer's Folly, with the arrival of the Dutch man-of-war boats
imminent, the Dutch flag is expediently hoisted in Lakamba's courtyard. To Babalatchi, "this emblem of Lakamba's power" is also
"the mark of his servitude" (132). The juxtaposition of Oriental
and Occidental politics in these novels connects us to times and
places not our own, while the tangled network of political, racial,
and tribal loyalties raise broader questions about the construction
and narration of the history of the Archipelago.

The sheer density of national and cultural groups in these novels,
together with the fact that so many words in these English texts
bear traces of their Malay and Arabic etymologies ("Rajah Laut,"
"godown," "amok," "Sheitan," "Kaffir," and "Houri"), ensure
that no moment is free from cultural ambiguities and conflicts.
For instance, at the end of *Almayer's Folly*, the forces threatening
Dain Maroola's life are Arab, Dutch, and Siamese, while those

facilitating his escape are Sulu, Malay, and Dutch (see Watts, 1984: 51). That Conrad should find equivalences between these cultural groupings – if only because they all confirm his pessimism about human motivation – ensures that his Malay fictions both reflect and transcend the imperial prejudices of their age.

The Far Eastern setting is integral to the narrative in at least three ways. Generically, the exotic backdrop offers a recognisable contemporary artistic trope, supporting and complementing the romance theme. This appropriation of foreign settings also extends to the other arts: one recalls, for instance, that Gauguin left Europe for Polynesia in 1895, the year in which *Almayer's Folly* was published. Autobiographically, the remoteness of the locale, where Europeans are surrounded by an unfamiliar indigenous culture, provides a point of view from which the would-be author from Eastern Europe can codify his own estrangement from and uneasiness with his English readership. In this sense, the Malay islanders become, simultaneously, symbols of Conrad's own strangeness and the means by which he can smuggle in his own view of Western Europeans. The tropical setting has ideological prolongations, too, as Conrad presents humanity as an extension of the natural world, driven by the same impetus for survival, thus contextualising human behaviour in terms of evolutionary theory. For example, it is consistent that Nina's and Dain's vows to each other are spoken amid "the intense work of tropical nature": "plants shooting upward, entwined, interlaced in inextricable confusion, climbing madly and brutally over each other in the terrible silence of a desperate struggle towards the life-giving sunshine above" (71). Similarly, in *An Outcast of the Islands*, where Willems's inimical presence is humorously shown to be sufficient to frighten the local buffaloes (66), the natural world is "indifferent" to him: he fears "the loneliness of his soul in the presence of this lofty indifference and ardent struggle, of this lofty indifference, of this merciless and mysterious purpose" (337). Aïssa, by contrast, "The very spirit of that land of mysterious forests" (70), is described as "the animated and brilliant flower of all that exuberant life which, born in gloom, struggles for ever towards the sunshine" (76). In *An Outcast of the Islands*, Aïssa subdues a representative of the conquering race through the passion she inspires in Willems. But while this passion allows him to forget his previous failures and offers some way of saving his ego from its own humiliations and degradation, it also involves a rejection of one set of cultural codes (European/"us") for another (Malay/"them"). Within the historical framework of the novel, Aïssa might be said to reverse the imperial process: she destructively "colonises" Willems. Like the jungle that defies all attempts to tame it and with which she is symbolically identified, Aïssa remains beyond Willems. The scale of his tragedy can be measured in the claim that "She was too different from him. He was so civilized! ... and he could not live without her" (128). This is Almayer's tragedy, too, in *Almayer's Folly* where he discovers that Nina has dreams of her own and he has, at last, to look beyond "the impenetrable mantle of selfishness he wrapped round both their lives: round himself, and that young life that was also his" (*OI*: 300).

Us and them: the politics of race

When we place the belief of Almayer and Willems in their racial superiority within the context of evolutionary theory, Conrad's sardonic comment upon colonialism in *Almayer's Folly* and *An Outcast of the Islands* becomes clear. Conrad began writing his first novel in the autumn of 1889, less than twenty years after the publication of Charles Darwin's *The Descent of Man* (1871). One of the books to which Conrad turned both to revive his own memories of the East and for source material was *The Malay Archipelago: The Land of the Orang-Utan and the Bird of Paradise* (1869) by the British naturalist, Alfred Russel Wallace (1823–1913). Wallace's travels in the Amazon Basin and the Malay Archipelago led him to develop the idea of natural selection independently of Darwin. For instance, happening to sail the fifteen miles between the islands of Bali (home of Dain Maroola in *Almayer's Folly*) and Lombok (noted for its ponies and mentioned in this context in *An Outcast of the Islands* [8]), Wallace discovered the discontinuity in fauna now known as "Wallace's Line" that defines the boundary between Australian and Asiatic zoogeographical zones: the western island of Bali has predominantly Oriental birds and mammals while the fauna of Lombok, to the east, is mostly Australian. Wallace's own *Contributions to the Theory of Natural Selection* (1870) amplified Darwin's *Origin of Species* (1859).

To the twenty-first-century reader, social theories based on evolutionary ideas can seem to offer a risible alibi for Victorian colonialism. For instance, describing the European settlement of

Tasmania and the consequent eradication of its indigenous population, Darwin concludes: "The grade of civilisation seems to be a
most important element in the success of competing nations" (1871:
45). Such claims gave "scientific" credence to already widespread
racial assumptions, such as those of the Poet Laureate, Tennyson:
"Even the black Australian, dying, dreams he will return a white"
("Locksley Hall Sixty Years After" [1886]). None the less, Darwinism's creed of the "survival of the fittest" chimes with Conrad's
presentation of human behaviour as motivated by egotism rather
than altruism – for example, a jealous concern for her own interests
leads Taminah to betray Dain to the Dutch authorities in *Almayer's
Folly*, and, for this brief moment, she ceases to be a mute slave – but
with a crucial proviso: in Conrad's world, race is no guarantee of
superiority. Instead, as their mutual pursuit of wealth in *Almayer's
Folly* and *An Outcast of the Islands* demonstrates, the races are
bound by common avarice. That the less inhibited non-Europeans
emerge financially victorious mischievously invites the conclusion
that, even at this shabby level of greed, the Europeans are unequal
to their supposed inferiors.

Contemporary magazines, such as *Punch*, lampooned Darwin
and Darwinism in simian caricatures. But the humorous depiction of evolutionary theory concealed real and deep-seated fears
of degeneration and atavism. These fears surface as a recognisable
literary trope in late-Victorian literature. H. G. Wells' *The Time
Machine* (1895) offers a social parable in which of the decadent
Eloi are dependent upon, yet at the mercy of, the subterranean
Morlocks, while, in Stevenson's *The Strange Case of Dr. Jekyll and
Mr. Hyde* (1886), Hyde manifests an "ape-like fury." At the conclusion of *Almayer's Folly*, such fears are explicitly linked to European
supremacist dreams in Conrad's depiction of the eponymous hero
symbolically and ignominiously descending the evolutionary lad-
der: defeated by his rivals, Almayer is literally taken in hand and
led around by his pet monkey, "Jack."

As these novels repeatedly demonstrate, Occidental racist attitudes towards the Oriental imbue the observations and assumptions
of both Willems and Almayer. In *An Outcast of the Islands*, for
example, Willems feels "disappointed with himself. He seemed to
be surrendering to a wild creature the unstained purity of his life, of
his race, of his civilization. He had a notion of being lost amongst
shapeless things that were dangerous and ghastly" (80). And when
Almayer taunts Willems, it is on grounds of race: "Don't shout like

this. Do you think yourself in the forest with your ... your friends? This is a civilized man's house. A white man's. Understand?" (88). To address the subject of racism, it is necessary to introduce the methods Conrad uses in treating it, since the two cannot be isolated from each other. To do this, we need briefly to examine the opening of *Almayer's Folly*, a novel whose protagonist is, if anything, more virulent in his racist attitudes, whether concerning his prospective wife – "Easy enough to dispose of a Malay woman, a slave, after all" (10–11) – who he agrees to marry with "a confused consciousness of shame" (10), or Dain, on whom the success of his dreams depends: "It is bad to have to trust a Malay" (18).

Crucial to understanding *Almayer's Folly* is Conrad's manipulation of point of view, or what we would now term "focalisation." Arguably the most important decision that a writer has to make when planning a novel is that of whose point of view orients the narrative, regulating the flow of information and conditioning the reader's response to it. Here is the narrative's opening:

> "Kaspar! Makan!"
> The well-known shrill voice startled Almayer from his dream of splendid future into the unpleasant realities of the present hour. An unpleasant voice too. He had heard it for many years, and with every year he liked it less. No matter; there would be an end to all this soon. (3)

Challengingly, Conrad's first address to his English readership is in a foreign, even "exotic," language: the injunction to Kaspar Almayer to come and eat – *makan*, in Malay. In the succeeding paragraph, the first sentence appears to be spoken by an objective, omniscient narrator, but the verbless, notational second sentence is Almayer's weary gloss on the "well-known" voice. This alerts the reader to the fluid interrelation between external and internal perspective: the opening sentence both anticipates and is coloured by Almayer's startled response ("shrill"/"unpleasant"). The next two sentences then repeat this shift in point of view, from the narrator's statement to Almayer's desire, structurally re-emphasising the inward movement from narrator to character. The balance between the narrator's description of Almayer's "dream of splendid future" and the character's participation in it ("No matter; there would be ... ") advertises perspective as a continuum, extending from the detached objectivity of the omniscient narrator, at one extreme, to the direct access to the subjective thoughts of the characters, at the other. Shared focalisation is thematically essential in a narrative that explores the imperviousness of Almayer's mind to his own folly: his dream needs to be understood as a function of his character. Thus, while Almayer's imagined future is presented from both perspectives in the quoted passage, there is a subtle but significant difference: in the narrator's version, the unpleasant reality succeeds the "dream of splendid future"; Almayer's version, however, ends with the future after the unpleasant reality.

Interpretively, this blend of the voices/thoughts of the narrator and Almayer in "free indirect style" affords simultaneous versions of the same situation. Tacitly this strategy alerts the implied reader to the importance of perspective; pragmatically it ensures that Almayer's attitudes and dreams can be debunked in his own words, often with unconscious self-irony. Time and again, Almayer is caught in the morass of his own racist contradictions: motivated by his own cheap dream of wealth, he fails to see that Nina has her own dreams, and, even more damningly, driven by his desire to buy a way into Amsterdam society for himself and Nina, he steadfastly refuses to see her for what she is, a half-caste. It is a cruel irony that when Almayer eventually surrenders his daughter to Dain Maroola, he does the right thing for the wrong reasons: Almayer helps the couple escape not because he is reconciled to their love for each other, but to protect himself from the disgrace of "white men finding my daughter with this Malay. My daughter!" (184).

As our first view of Nina in *Almayer's Folly* demonstrates, not even simple description is free of racial assumptions: "She was tall for a half-caste, with the correct profile of the father, modified and strengthened by the squareness of the lower part of the face inherited from her maternal ancestors – the Sulu pirates" (16–17). Here, such qualifications as "for a half-caste" and the racially loaded adjective "correct" call attention to themselves, but whether these judgements are Almayer's or the narrator's is difficult to tell. As the narrative develops, the narrator's attitudes become increasingly distanced from those of Almayer, suggesting that they undergo a transformation. The result is a more nuanced attitude to race. This is not to suggest that the racism is altogether eradicated – it is not; rather, the narrating voice begins to reflect doubts about the supremacy of the European, and, in doing so, threatens the simplistic distinctions between colonizer and colonized endorsed elsewhere. In particular, this tension is played out in the distinction between the terms "savage" and "civilized," a distinction that

Conrad addresses in his "Author's Note" to *Almayer's Folly*. In this note, which is Conrad's first critical essay, he takes issue with Alice Meynell, a popular poet and essayist of the 1890s, who, in an essay entitled "Decivilized" (1891), had dismissed colonial literature on the grounds that its subject matter could but yield a "decivilized" art that runs counter to the civilized English norm. Conrad's answer, that "there is a bond between us and that humanity so far away" (viii), removes at a stroke the easy distinction between "us" and "them," together with its inherent claim to cultural superiority where there is only cultural difference.

Throughout *Almayer's Folly*, the term "savage" is repeatedly used to describe and categorize the Malays. Thus, Mrs Almayer is described as a "savage tigress" with a "savage nature," who treats her husband with "savage contempt" using "savage invective" (25–27). Whilst such an obsession may be attributed to Almayer's own hysterical anger at his entrapment in Sambir, the narrator too shares some responsibility for attributing this epithet freely to the Malays. For example, it is not Almayer who describes Lingard's young captive as having a "savage manner" (21), or Taminah's "savage mind" and "savage nature" (116). Here, the narrator might be said to endorse Almayer's Western view of the Oriental.

Alongside this set of references to the Malays as "savage" is another, equally obsessive, set describing European culture as "civilized." For example, Nina's education and life in Singapore are said to afford her a "civilized morality" and a "glimpse of civilized life" in "civilized surroundings" (42). In opposition, the terms "savage" and "civilized" help to define each other and, if the narrative simply left it at that, one could argue that this novel contrasts them in order to express or endorse the superiority of one culture over the other. Instead the distinction between these two cultural markers becomes increasingly blurred, causing a subtle redefinition of their relationship to each other. On the one hand, the connotations of "savage" are offset by their combination with praiseworthy attributes – as, for instance, when Dain speaks with "the rude *eloquence* of a savage nature" or Babalatchi feels pity for Lakamba in "his savage and *much sophisticated* breast" (69, 86; emphases added) – whilst, on the other, the implicit claims of the "civilized" are undermined: it is but a "narrow mantle of civilized morality" in which Nina is wrapped (42), whilst Dain's love for her is expressed with "all the unrestrained enthusiasm of a man totally untrammelled by any influence of civilized self-discipline" (64), a description that casts serious doubt upon the value of such "self-discipline." Such revisions create an instability in the narrating voice that, in turn, suggests its unease with the savage/civilized opposition. In fact, at one point the narrator goes so far as to question the very notion of "civilized": "There are some situations where the barbarian and the, so-called, civilized man meet on the same ground" (67). That "so-called" is a crucial concession for it reduces the very terms of the distinction on which the colonial attitude rests. In this way, Conrad's first novel is simultaneously an example of the colonial literature of its age and an important critique of the ideas implicit in such literature.

The representation of race in *An Outcast of the Islands* is also characterised by familiar colonial tropes. For instance, the racial other is typically reduced to a "type" that can be "known": Almayer "knew his Malays" (318), while Abdulla is described as "Restless, like all his people" (111). Gesture, too, is assimilated into what might be termed colonial iconography. Once one starts to look for it, it is remarkable how often the natives are described as squatting. Babalatchi squats at various firesides and at Lakamba's feet; Abdulla's waiting boatmen are depicted "squatting by the gun-wales" (136), and Lingard's as "squatting over the fire" (239); as Lingard departs, Aïssa "squatted" at Willems's feet (281); and so on. At times this attitude reflects dejection; more usually it conveys the reality of tending or being near a fire – it is the characteristic pose of Omar's old woman-servant, for example. That this pose conveys culturally iconographic status in the novel's depiction of race is demonstrated when Lingard breaks one of the few pieces of furniture Almayer possesses. His response is: "By and by I will have to eat squatting on the floor like a native" (173). When Ali addresses the crew of Lingard's canoe in Malay – "Dayong!" – he does so in "the squatting attitude of a monkey" (280).

Inevitably, though, the novel's racial attitudes find their clearest expression in the relationship between Willems and Aïssa. Willems repeatedly defers to his European descent to claim his superiority: "He was carried away by the flood of hate, disgust, and contempt of a white man for that blood which is not his blood, for that race which is not his race; for the brown skins; for the hearts false like the sea, blacker than night" (152). The European's thoughts enact the mechanics of racism: assumed superiority of his own cultural group allows him to disregard the culture of others. Thus it is with satirical appropriateness that Lingard's judgement strips Willems of colour-allegiances during their confrontation: "You are alone ... Nothing can help you. Nobody will. You are neither white not brown. You have no colour as you have no heart" (276). European attitudes towards the natives are reconfigured in terms of a post-colonial, revisionist gaze, from which perspective, as Aïssa points out, "All whites are alike" (333). From here, the Europeans can be reduced to a simple set of principles and generalisations: "I know white men, Tuan ... always the slaves of their desires ... They know how to keep faith with their enemies, but towards each other they know only deception" (60), says Babalatchi; when Lingard and Willems fight on the quay-side it is "like wild beasts, after the manner of white men" (37); and Aïssa chides Willems: "Your tongue is false. You are white indeed" (144). In a word, racialist stereotypes cut both ways in Conrad's fiction, being neither the unique possession of the Europeans nor of the Malays.

In Part IV, the omniscient, narrating voice enters into this debate, as it were, when generalising and, in the process, elevating to the status of truth Lingard's attitude to the hapless Aïssa:

> The fragments of her supplicating sentences were as if tossed on the crest of her sobs. Lingard, outwardly impassive, with his eyes fixed on the house, experienced that feeling of condemnation, deep-seated, persuasive, and masterful; that illogical impulse of disapproval which is half disgust, half vague fear, and that wakes up in our hearts in the presence of anything new or unusual, of anything that is not run into the mould of our own conscience; the accursed feeling made up of disdain, of anger, and of the sense of superior virtue that leaves us deaf, blind, contemptuous and stupid before anything which is not like ourselves (253–54).

Reader-sympathy is steered somewhat heavy-handedly: presented as interior monologue, Lingard's thoughts that support these conclusions would have condemned him. But this is not the real issue. For this we need only consider the possessive pronouns. Who is included in "our"? This is an English novel for an English audience, and Conrad's interest in translations of his work, signalled in his letters, suggests that he had his sights trained on a larger, European audience. But as has been shown, the claim must surely extend more widely to mankind generally. This pervasive scepticism of the human condition is integral to the Conradian narrative. It colours narratorial judgement in his fiction that repeatedly returns to the subject of individuals, stripped of the mantle of civilization, forced to confront their own self-defining values, often exposing the fragility of their "civilization" in the process.

The collapse of the European "self"

Conrad's presentation of Almayer and Willems in these novels is severely critical, and both characters seem to merit their shabby end. By contrast, Lingard, the romantic European trader-adventurer might seem to offer an idealised counterpoint. But he is implicated in – indeed, makes himself "responsible" (*OI*: 38) for – the lives of Almayer and Willems (just as he is bound up with the fates of Mrs Almayer, Nina, and the inhabitants of Sambir generally). The "ideal" European is thus inextricably linked to the outcast European. Furthermore, since Lingard offers Almayer and, more obviously, Willems chances to establish themselves in the Archipelago, *Almayer's Folly* and *An Outcast of the Islands* are tales of potentially parallel destinies. For example, the seventeen-year-old Willems is taken up by Lingard aboard his ship only to prove himself "hopelessly at variance with the spirit of the sea" (17); in consequence, Lingard secures him employment with Hudig, whom he defrauds and by whom he is dismissed; and again Lingard comes to his rescue and takes him to Sambir. That this "clever young fellow" (17) should come to nought suggests that *An Outcast* is simultaneously concerned with Willems's failure and the failures of Lingard's judgement. When condemning Willems to exile in Sambir, Lingard confesses: "You are my mistake. I shall hide you here.... You are my shame" (275). This regret ensures Lingard's continued responsibility for Willems's fate and implicates him in what the narrator terms "divine folly" (273). Perhaps, by involving himself in Willems's fate, Lingard lends the outcast a dignity that he does not deserve.

Apart from the brute realities of trade, Lingard justifies his involvement in the life of Sambir paternally: it is his "deep-seated and immovable conviction that only he – he, Lingard – knew what was good for them" (200). In this estimation, according to the narrator, Lingard was "not so very far wrong." The use of litotes in this backhanded compliment anticipates the qualifications in the overview that follows: "His trade brought prosperity to the young state, and the fear of his heavy hand secured its internal peace for many years" (200). On its own, such a judgement chimes with contemporary imperial clichés about the "white man's burden"; that such claims are only half of the equation is demonstrated by Babalatchi's rhetorical questions: "What was he, that man of fierce aspect, to keep all the world away from them? Was he a government? Who made him ruler?" (115).

The coexistence of such competing views ensures that the narrative of nation coexists with, and responds to, the narrative of empire and allows us to see Abdulla's ascendancy over Lingard in Sambir as one outsider displacing another outsider within the island's broader history of colonisation. Provocative parallels reformulate cultural and ethnic difference as essential similarity, often with corrosive effect. For example, descriptions of the one-eyed Babalatchi as the "statesman" of Sambir that seem initially ironic ultimately serve to identify him with his stereotypical frock-coated European counterparts. The consequences of such comparisons are profound: to place European supremacy within the broader context of historical change is to relativize it. Similarly and sardonically, through Babalatchi, the myopia of political processes is exposed. That said, while the societies presented in these novels exhibit many shared or similar forms, such parallels do not amount to a process of homogenisation in which all differences are erased. On the contrary, as the Europeans discover, the indigenous peoples of the Malay Archipelago remain irrepressibly independent, without sacrificing their distinctive identities.

Nowhere is the collapse of European power better reflected in *Almayer's Folly* and *An Outcast of the Islands* than in the corrosive depiction of the collapse of European identity. Indicators of this are everywhere, from the exchange of cultural markers – whereby Willems exchanges his Western dress for a sarong (*OI*: 87) – to Almayer's opium trance in the closing stages of *Almayer's Folly*. But it is the dramatisation of the disintegrating self in both novels that is most arresting. For instance, lying in Aïssa's arms Willems envisions

> a man going away from him and diminishing in a long perspective of fantastic trees, whose every leaf was an eye looking after that man, who walked away growing smaller, but never getting out of sight for all his progress. ... There was something familiar about that figure. Why! Himself! (145)

While this example clearly reflects Willems's lover's swoon, it is consistent with the image of the European psyche in exile, detached from meaningful existence and condemned to a torpid existence:

> The very savages around him strove, struggled, fought, worked – if only to prolong a miserable existence; but they lived, they lived! And it was only himself that seemed to be left outside the scheme of

creation in a hopeless immobility filled with tormenting anger and with ever-stinging regret.   (65)

The disintegration of the European self receives more sustained treatment in *Almayer's Folly* when, with the Dutch man-of-war's boats pursuing him to Sambir, Babalatchi and Mrs Almayer contrive Dain's "death" to fool the authorities. To make this deception plausible, Almayer himself needs to be deceived and, at the moment when Almayer is convinced that the dead man before him is Dain, and so represents the end of his hopes of ever escaping from Sambir, he experiences a breakdown in his sense of self. (Again, the reactions of characters such as Nina to the "death" quickly assure the reader that the body is not Dain's, placing us in a superior position to Almayer.) Almayer starts by recognising the folly of his erstwhile hopes: "It seemed to him that for many years he had been falling into a deep precipice. Day after day, month after month, year after year, he had been falling, falling, falling" (99). The reality of his predicament has finally been brought home to him, stripped of the dream that had obscured it. But this separation of reality and dream, which had been indistinguishable to him, triggers a further dissolution in Almayer's sense of himself as an individual:

> He seemed somehow to himself to be standing on one side, a little way off, looking at a certain Almayer who was in great trouble. Poor, poor fellow! Why doesn't he cut this throat? He wished he could encourage him; he was very anxious to see him lying dead over that other corpse. Why does he not die and end this suffering? He groaned aloud unconsciously and started with affright at the sound of his own voice. Was he going mad?   (99–100)

In *Almayer's Folly* Conrad reveals that human action is motivated by egoism. But, as Almayer demonstrates, extreme egoism is blinding and dangerous. Dain's "death" brings home to Almayer once and for all that he is trapped in a real world, shaped by forces other than his subjective desires. Reality and dream have been indistinguishable for Almayer but, confronted by the fact that his dream is over, they become detached. Up to this point, his inability to admit the truth of his position has led to Almayer's wholly subjective view of reality, but now two competing visions of himself, subjective and objective, emerge. Denied the illusion of success, Almayer is no longer certain of his sense of self and, anticipating the opium-oblivion into which he lapses at the novel's conclusion, he is reduced to a form of madness. In this sense, the novel's French title, *La Folie-Almayer* (it was translated by Geneviève Séligmann-Lui in 1919), is more directive than the English title in preserving connotations of madness.

In a novel where the colonial enterprise is equated with the dynamics of trade, and where the colonizer is outmanoeuvred by the colonized, the disintegration of Almayer's personality powerfully underscores Conrad's presentation of the vulnerability and relativism of European culture. As we have already seen, *Almayer's Folly* and *An Outcast of the Islands* show that the civilized/savage distinction between the Europeans and the Malays is untenable and, instead, suggests a substratum of identification between them, based upon their shared impulses.

* * *

So how well does European culture fare in this novel? Its claims to exclusivity are humorously undermined, for instance, at the end of Chapter 6 in *Almayer's Folly* where, much to Babalatchi's chagrin, Lakamba insists upon listening to the "Misere" from Verdi's opera *Il trovatore*, with the suggestion that the very trappings of European cultural heritage have been appropriated by Almayer's enemies. Comparably, in *An Outcast of the Islands*, Omar is identified as "that piratical and son-less Æneas" (54) and Aïssa with Medusa (150). The universality of myth thus serves to connect characters at a fundamental level, beneath apparent differences of skin-colour or cultural gesture. Nor is this appropriation only one-way: were it so, it would imply the supremacy of European over Malay culture. Not only does Babalatchi call Lingard: "A man of the sea – even as we are" (222) and Jim-Eng identify himself as European when he refers to Almayer and himself as "We white men" (182), but the very dream of wealth that motivates Almayer – and, before him, Lingard – has itself also been appropriated from the islanders. When we learn that "The coast population of Borneo believes implicitly in diamonds of fabulous value, in gold mines of enormous richness in the interior" (*AF*: 25), the adjective "fabulous" warns us against accepting this belief as truth, yet both Europeans adopt this dream, so much so that Almayer's quest in this novel is nothing less than "Gunong Mas – the mountain of gold" (57).

Caught between two cultures, Nina in *Almayer's Folly* passes the most damning comment upon racial conflict in her decision to identify with "the ideal Malay chief of her mother's tradition" (43) rather than "the white side of her descent represented by a feeble and traditionless father" (28): Dain may well be an "ideal" chief, but he offers a sense of cultural belonging that the chameleon Almayer, who expediently changes his allegiances to suit his ends, does not. Indeed, Almayer ultimately lacks a sense of belonging to the very European culture that, he feels, elevates him above the Malays. His illegal involvement in Dain's gunpowder smuggling leads to the death of two Dutch sailors, and he has never even been to Amsterdam, towards which his dreams of a glorious future with his daughter are constantly directed. In other words, Dain offers Nina a cultural "home" for which Almayer lacks an equivalent. In his culturally orphaned status, Almayer reflects the plight of the Modernist hero.

Written at the end of the nineteenth century, *Almayer's Folly* reflects an important thematic shift between the Victorian novel and the Modernist one. In general terms, the nineteenth-century novel of, say, Dickens and Trollope, is obsessed with the idea of homecoming, the idea that one can regain and reclaim the family (and, generally, the fortune) that one has lost; by contrast, its twentieth-century counterpart repeatedly stresses alienation and exile without reprieve, the impossibility of any return to lost beginnings. For Almayer and Willems there is no homecoming, there is only homesickness.

Works cited

Darwin, Charles. *The Descent of Man*. [1871] (Second Edition) New York and London: Merrill & Baker, 1874.

Knowles, Owen. "Introduction." *Almayer's Folly*. Edited by Owen Knowles. xvii–xliii. London: Everyman, 1995.

Sherry, Norman. *Conrad's Eastern World*. Cambridge: Cambridge University Press, 1971.

——, ed. *Conrad: The Critical Heritage*. London: Routledge & Kegan Paul, 1973.

Wallace, Alfred Russel. *The Malay Archipelago: The Land of the Orang-Utan, and The Bird of Paradise*. [1869] Kuala Lumpur: Oxford University Press, 1998.

Watts, Cedric. *The Deceptive Text: An Introduction to Covert Plots*. Brighton: Harvester, 1984.

3

Conrad and the Sea: *The Nigger of the "Narcissus"* and "Typhoon"

Conrad's maritime experiences shaped his philosophy of life: "A wrestle with wind and weather has a moral value like the primitive acts of faith on which may be built a doctrine of salvation and a rule of life. At any rate men engaged in such contests have been my spiritual fathers too long for me to change my convictions" (*CL2*: 354). And five years later he described *The Mirror of the Sea* (1906), his collection of essays on sea life, as "the best tribute my piety can offer to the ultimate shapers of my character, convictions, and, in a sense, destiny – to the imperishable sea, to the ships that are no more, and to the simple men who have had their day" (xii). Among these "Memories and Impressions" that illustrate Conrad's relationship with the British maritime tradition is that of "poor Captain B—." Conrad's anecdote begins with a roll-call of sea ports: Captain B—is a "Plymouth man" in command of a "big London ship, fairly well known in her day" (9), now docked in Dundee after an eighteen-month voyage, having brought "a full cargo of jute from Calcutta" (9). Such are the points of "Landfall and Departure" that "mark the rhythmical swing of a seaman's life and of a ship's career" (3). At their parting Captain B—learns of his second mate's plans to take his master's certificate:

> He commended me for not wasting my time, with such an evident interest in my case that I was quite surprised; then, rising from his chair, he said:

"Have you a ship in view after you have passed?"

I answered that I had nothing whatever in view.

He shook hands with me, and pronounced the memorable words:

"If you happen to be in want of employment, remember that as long as I have a ship you have a ship, too."

In the way of compliment there is nothing to beat this from a ship's captain to his second mate at the end of a voyage, when the work is over and the subordinate is done with. And there is a pathos in that memory, for the poor fellow never went to sea again after all. He was already ailing when we passed St. Helena; was laid up for a time when we were off the Western Islands, but got out of bed to make his Landfall. (9–10)

This blend of service and tradition, on the one hand, and "pathos" and exoticism, on the other, captures the balance between realism and romanticism that typifies Conrad's sea fiction. Success in the examination and the abrupt end of Captain B—'s sea career are summarily reported; instead, the emphasis falls on the final meeting of the two men and the sense that the torch of marine service is passing from one generation to another. The implication is clear: Conrad is "one of us." Listening to his old commander's sea history, Conrad's thoughts are tempered by reminders of the price of a sea career. Captain B—'s wife "had not, perhaps, lived with him more than five full years out of the thirty or so of their married life" (10–11). The arrival of the captain's youngest son, who "chattered enthusiastically of the exploits of W. G. Grace" (11), ensures that the tradition of seamanship is juxtaposed with another reflection of the English national character: cricket. The anecdote concludes with Conrad's speculations on what his, obviously dying, host saw when looking round the room at his wife and possessions:

Was he looking out for a strange Landfall, or taking with an untroubled mind the bearings for his last Departure?

It is hard to say; for in that voyage from which no man returns Landfall and Departure are instantaneous, merging together into one moment of supreme and final attention. Certainly I do not remember observing any signs of faltering in the set expression of his wasted face, no hint of the nervous anxiety of a young commander about to make land on an uncharted shore. He had too much experience of Departures and Landfalls! And had he not "served his time" in the famous copper-ore trade out of the Bristol Channel, the work of the staunchest ships afloat, and the school of staunch seamen? (12–13)

No longer merely "the rhythmical swing of a seaman's life," here "Landfall and Departure" serve as metaphors for life itself. The maritime and literary traditions of Conrad's adopted homeland are discreetly connected as Captain B—'s "voyage from which no man returns" echoes Hamlet's account of "death": "The undiscover'd country, from whose bourn / No traveller returns" (*Hamlet*, III.i.78–79). It is, of course, pre-eminently Conrad himself who stands at the intersection of these traditions. The final rhetorical flourish, authenticated by the familiarity of quoted cliché, celebrates in legendary terms "the famous copper-ore trade out of the Bristol Channel" in its paean to the work ethic that produced "the staunchest ships" and schooled "staunch seamen." The anecdote is thus far more than Conrad's memory of a former captain. It is simultaneously an assertion of identity with various traditions of Englishness.

The Nigger of the *"Narcissus"*

Conrad sailed in the actual *Narcissus* as second mate for the voyage from Bombay to Dunkirk in 1884. Shortly before his death, he claimed: "Most of the personages I have portrayed actually belonged to the crew of the real *Narcissus*, including the admirable Singleton (whose real name was Sullivan), Archie, Belfast, and Donkin" (*LL*1: 77). Despite its international cast, *The Nigger of the "Narcissus"* can safely be called Conrad's first "English" novel: not only is the *Narcissus* sailing home to England but the novel's celebration of life at sea is also a celebration of the maritime tradition on which the glory of his adopted homeland rested. He described the novella as "a respectable shrine for the memory of men with whom I have, through many hard years lived and worked" (*CL*1: 308–09).

Conrad's account of his first contact with an English ship, in Marseilles harbour, is recorded with sensuous – indeed, even sexual – vividness at the end of *A Personal Record*: "when I bore against the smooth flank of the first English ship I ever touched in my life, I felt it already throbbing under my open palm" (137). This communion leads to his memory of the Red Ensign hanging from the ship's flagstaff: "The Red Ensign – the symbolic, protecting warm bit of bunting flung wide upon the seas, and destined for so many years to be the only roof over my head" (138). Admittedly written with the benefit of hindsight – *A Personal Record* was first published serially in the *English Review* from December 1908 to June 1909 – Conrad's recollections do more than idealise the Red Ensign, the flag of the merchant service, they simultaneously illustrate how he mythologizes things English, and testify to his enthrallment by the English language:

> for the very first time in my life, I heard myself addressed in English – the speech of my secret choice, of my future, of long friendships, of the deepest affections, of hours of toil and hours of ease, and of solitary hours too, of books read, of thoughts pursued, of remembered emotions – of my very dreams! (136)

The fact that this first address is no more than the pragmatic "Look out there!" to warn of a rope being flung down serves, fittingly, to associate the romance of the English language with the craft of seamanship. Fittingly, too, the manuscript of *Almayer's Folly*, begun during a period of shore leave in 1889, acquired its first reader during a voyage to Australia in the *Torrens* (in which Conrad served as first mate). Their ensuing discussion left the budding author feeling "as if already the story-teller were being born into the body of a seaman" (*PR*: 17).

In this respect, it seems apt that Conrad should have expressed what many have seen as his artistic credo in his "Preface" to *The Nigger of the "Narcissus."* Conrad's statement of intent is clear: "My task which I am trying to achieve is, by the power of the written word, to make you hear, to make you feel – it is, before all, to make you *see*" (x). He refined this emphasis upon the visual quality of the novel in a letter to the influential critic Arthur Quiller-Couch of 23 December 1897, saying: "it has been my desire to do for seamen what Millet ... has done for peasants" (*CL*1: 430–31). The enduring appeal of Millet's paintings lies in their iconography of labour. Following Millet, Conrad dignifies and romanticises the manual work of the sailors in the *Narcissus* through his recourse to pictorialism and the formal demands of symmetry and balance. *The Nigger of the "Narcissus"* begins with the mustering of the crew in Bombay harbour and ends with their paying-off in London. By thus framing his tale of the voyage, Conrad signals the degree to which his narrative borrows from the techniques of painting.

Conrad's choice of subject is felicitous: as his storm scene confirms, the sea lends itself to pictorial representation, whether evoking maritime life in all its dangerous splendour or serving as a mirror for comparable "storms" in the lives of the sailors. The portrait of the *Narcissus*'s voyage is compositionally elegant, balancing the two "storms": the actual storm off the Cape of Good Hope and the near-mutiny at the Equator. Their juxtaposition ensures that the dangers they pose are critically equated, as is the restitution of order in the face of dangers both elemental and emotional. Surviving the first storm depends upon selfless acts of heroism: the rescue of James Wait; Podmore making coffee for the men; and, of course, Singleton's thirty hours at the wheel. The threatened mutiny founders when the crew re-enter the matrix of duty and collective responsibility. Surmounting both storms involves subordinating individuality to a greater design.

The broader structural balance provided by the two storm scenes is ingrained in the fabric of Conrad's prose to evoke an idealised sense of symmetrical rhythm. For instance, the description of the *Narcissus* leaving Bombay harbour is characterised by paired adjectives: "The loose upper canvas blew out in the breeze with soft round contours resembling small white clouds ... the ship became a high and lonely pyramid gliding, all shining and white, through the sunlit mist" (27). This sense of order is threatened when the balanced descriptions are no longer compatible. Confronted by James Wait, for instance, the crew "oscillated between the desire of virtue and the fear of ridicule; we wished to save ourselves from the pain of remorse, but did not want to be made the contemptible dupes of our sentiment" (41). Belfast voices the confusion of the crew more succinctly when he yells: "Knock! Jimmy darlint! ... Knock! You bloody black beast!" (69). Such formal patterning constitutes a tacit appeal to proportion and order in a narrative composed of stark binary opposites – storm and calm, white and black, appearance and reality, and land and sea, to name but a few. Conrad's approach is emphatically Modernist in its appeal to art as a locus of coherence for what he elsewhere called the "irreconcilable antagonisms" of life (*CL2*: 348).

Appropriately, since this is a portrait of a sailing ship, Conrad draws, too, upon the techniques of nineteenth-century narrative painting. These include the use of framed images, such as that of Singleton, standing, caryatid-like, in the forecastle doorway, "with his face to the light and his back to the darkness" (24), symbolically on the threshold between two worlds, and iconographic portraits, whereby James Wait is transformed into a "black idol" in "a silver shrine" (105). To Henry James, *The Nigger of the "Narcissus"* represented "the very finest and strongest picture of the sea and sea-life that our language possesses – the masterpiece in a whole great class" (Edel, ed., 1984: 232).

* * *

Conrad's first fictional engagement with Englishness and his developing sense of himself as an English writer are reflected in the style of *The Nigger of the "Narcissus."* First, the novel represents Conrad's earliest attempt to render phonetically British vocal inflections and dialects. Thus the authorial ventriloquism that produces Belfast's "Jimmy, darlin,' are ye aloive?" (66), or Donkin's "You 'aven't the bloomin' nerve – so you inventyd this 'ere dodge" (111), individuates characters on the basis of their speech. Second, as few critics have failed to notice, the narrating voice (and, hence, the narrative authority) varies across the novel, describing the action now from without and now from within. The narrating is shared between a detached, third-person, omniscient narrator and a first-person narrator who is one of the crew. (For instance, the use of the inclusive "we" during the rescue of James Wait in Chapter 3 identifies the narrator as one of the rescue party.) Not only this, but the first-person "community soul" narrator ("we") gives way to the first-person singular "I" narrator in the novel's final pages – stylistically reinforcing the claim that "The men scattered by the dissolving contact of the land" (167). The shift from plural to singular pronoun here enacts a central theme: individual worth and identity stem from the very collective endeavour they challenge. Simultaneously, this expression of identity asserts the narrator's authority: we have been reading *his* tale. As Michael Levenson (1984) argues, these inflections in narrative voice ensure that *The Nigger of the "Narcissus"* occupies a pivotal point in the development of the English novel, charting the replacement of nineteenth-century omniscience by the fragility of first-person narration that is one of the hallmarks of the Modernism.

To today's reader, *The Nigger of the "Narcissus"* poses a problem. The description of James Wait as "nigger" is offensive. The novel was indeed re-christened *The Children of the Sea* by its first American publishers, but the reasons for altering the title were risible: "The argument was that the American public would not read a book about a 'nigger'" (Smith, n.d.: 8). That the term was in common parlance in 1897 there is no doubt. In the novel, though, it is clearly understood to be a term of abuse as Wait demonstrates in his, similarly racist, retort to Belfast: "You wouldn't call me nigger if I wasn't half dead, you Irish beggar!" (80). Hawthorn notes perceptively that Wait provides a focus for the ideological contradictions and uncertainties of both the author and the age in which he was writing: "Conrad's artistic instinct led him to choose the figure of the Negro as the central character in this work with good grounds, for if anything symbolized contradiction and unclarity in the late Victorian popular mind it was the figure of the Negro" (1990: 102). Expressing the psychology of the crew, the narrator's references to Wait as "our nigger" preserve this ambiguity in their antipathetic combination of fellowship and casual abuse. Thus, their jarring racial abuse is symptomatic of the crew's general confusion about Wait. Is he shamming illness or genuinely dying?

But the depiction of race is only one of the interpretive problems caused by Wait's presence in the *Narcissus*. Another concerns the place of the supernatural that, by seeming to show that the contours of fact can be altered to fit the contours of the imagination, threatens the tale's realism. With the *Narcissus* frustratingly becalmed in the tropics and Wait's imminent death now obvious to everyone except himself, the normally taciturn Singleton voices a sailor superstition: "He said that Jimmy was the cause of head winds. Mortally sick men – he maintained – linger till the first sight of land, and then die; and Jimmy knew that the very first land would draw his life from him. It is so in every ship. Didn't we know it?" (142). It is tempting to dismiss this belief as belonging to a less rational age. Singleton himself is, after all, described as "a lonely relic of a devoured and forgotten generation" (24) – and recourse to the homophone Wait/weight to explain why the ship's progress is retarded seems equally spurious. And yet, with the island of Flores on the eastern horizon, Wait *does* finally die, and no sooner is he buried at sea than the wind freshens to drive the ship home. Nor is superstition the only threat to rational interpretation. When interviewed by Captain Allistoun, Wait coughs "all over the old man's meteorological journals" (45). In the light of the storm that follows, should we read this as Wait "infecting" the ship's progress? Clearly intended as inclusive, Conrad's "tribute" to sea-life in The Nigger of the *"Narcissus"* offers a range of perspectives, old and new, and each with its own claims to truth. As he wrote to Edward Garnett, to whom this novel is dedicated: "There are so many touches necessary for such a picture" (*CL1*: 310).

* * *

The novel's initial subtitle, "A Tale of the Forecastle," immediately establishes Conrad's focus. His "shrine" is erected to the able-bodied and ordinary seamen who make up the crew of the *Narcissus*. The opening of the narrative reinforces this focus: between Mr Baker's order for the crew to be mustered and the boatswain's carrying it out, the narrative pauses to dramatise the gathering of the crew in the forecastle earlier that evening. The order and the response thus serve to frame this retrospective portrait of the crew. Whilst it is tempting to read the novel as a romantic evocation of a bygone age, it is, rather, a testament to individual worth that which results from collective endeavour. Repeatedly the voyage homeward, from Bombay to London, is presented in terms of the psychology of group dynamics. While such references to her as "a small planet" (29) identify the *Narcissus* as a microcosmic world, they equally emphasise the crew's fluctuating interdependence and isolation. When the crew disperse at the end of the novel, the first-person narrator, and participant in their shared experience, says: "I never saw them again" (172). Unthinking collective endeavour is thus seen as the means by which the crew protects itself from threatening individuality. Like Narcissus in Greek mythology, the crew become enamoured of their own reflections at times, as the journey provides experiences that test and mirror their inner worth. By never identifying the ship's cargo, Conrad implies that the *Narcissus* is freighted with the sum of these recognitions.

In his essay "Stephen Crane" (1923), Conrad describes *The Nigger of the "Narcissus"* as "my effort to present a group of men held together by a common loyalty and a common perplexity in a struggle not with human enemies, but with the hostile conditions testing their faithfulness to the conditions of their calling." His subject, he says, is "the psychology of the mass ... the crew of a merchant ship, brought to the test of what I may venture to call the moral problem of conduct" (*LE*: 94, 95). The opening portrait of the crew in the forecastle strikes the novel's keynote: the group and what threatens its unity. From the outset, this is suggested by the crew's need to define their place within the hierarchical structure aboard ship. The issue of hierarchy is introduced in the novel that Singleton is reading – Bulwer Lytton's *Pelham*, a story about an aristocratic dandy – and quickly followed by Belfast's tale (whose veracity is questioned) about how he poured tar over a second mate. Then, as if conjured up by Belfast's tale of insubordination, Donkin introduces himself with the warning: "I can look after my rights! I will show 'em!" (9). Thus what is presented as a potential threat to stability acquires real force even before the homeward voyage has begun.

Hawthorn (1990) sees in the command-structure aboard the *Narcissus* a reflection of the hierarchy within society at large. In this light, the novel is "conservative," as the revolutionary tendencies of the crew are ultimately "tamed" and the prevailing order reaffirmed. For much of the work, however, this hierarchy is tested and questioned by the crew – for instance, in their conversations about what constitutes a gentleman. Nor is this theme restricted to the crew: performing his final duties aboard, Mr Baker muses on how he has no chance of promotion while Mr Creighton, the second mate, is "quite a gentleman . . . swell friends . . . will get on" (167). For Mr Baker the twice-used epithet "a model chief mate" (166, 167) clearly has an ironic ring to it. That said, the threat of instability is repeatedly offset by the crew's unquestioning responses to calls to duty. In Chapter 4, both the talk of mutiny and the mutiny itself are forgotten when duty calls: the group attending Jimmy "vanish" at the order to "Haul the spanker out" (109), while the call "Helm up!" (124) immediately stifles any thoughts of uprising. As these examples show, beneath thoughts of insubordination and enlightened self-interest there exists a substratum of duty, of allegiance to the very hierarchy they question. In "Well Done!" (1918), his essay praising the efforts of the British Merchant Service during the First World War, Conrad writes: "seamen and duty are all the time inseparable companions" (*NLL*: 191).

The use of nautical expressions throughout the text extends this sense of professionalism. At a superficial level, these maritime terms simply serve to embed the action within a professional context. But their precision and technical nature – identifying and distinguishing between the various sails, for instance – constantly reminds the reader that the world of the sea has its own precise language, its own signifying system, with its own grammar, which points to group expertise and distinguishes the landlubber from the initiate. During the insurrection Donkin removes a belaying-pin from its hole in the fore-rigging and throws it at Captain Allistoun. In doing so, he breaches the system of language of which it forms a part: within this nautical grammar, the pin or baton has a specific function – it belays or secures a rope. When Donkin uses it as a weapon he offends this grammar. In forcing Donkin to restore the pin to its proper place and purpose, Captain Allistoun reasserts the claims of order aboard the *Narcissus* by reinstating the language upon which the safety of the ship depends.

> Good-bye, brothers! You were a good crowd. As good a crowd as ever fisted with wild cries the beating canvas of a heavy foresail; or tossing aloft, invisible in the night, gave back yell for yell to a westerly gale. (173)

So ends the novel. But the voyage it recounts begins with old Singleton's warning to Wait: "Ships are all right. It is the men in them!" (24). What transforms these "men" into "brothers"? Mutual dependence, born of collective responsibility, is shown to be, quite literally, a matter of life or death in *The Nigger of the "Narcissus."* Thus the novel dramatises views Conrad expressed in a late essay: "The mysteriously born tradition of sea-craft commands unity in a body of workers engaged in an occupation in which men have to depend upon each other" ("Well Done"; *NLL*: 183). A community, united in duty, and hierarchical in structure, this model comes under strain in the *Narcissus* as the presence of Wait and Donkin exposes divisions and conflicts of allegiances among the crew. Socially and politically, *The Nigger of the "Narcissus"* is identified with the tradition of the late nineteenth-century European social novel. It articulates the tensions between an existing social order and an incipient democracy in terms that recall the clash between the creed of individualism that typifies nineteenth-century liberalism and the pressures for social organisation and regulation deemed necessary for communal as well as individual survival.

From the outset, Wait is associated with confusion and misinterpretation: at the roll-call, Mr Baker misconstrues his name as an instruction to "wait." As Belfast's theft of the officers' pie demonstrates, the confusion Wait introduces is a threat to order in the ship and, by extension, in the body politic where loyalty and rules are required to ensure survival and prevent anarchy. At the heart of this confusion is the problem of whether he is shamming illness or really dying, and thus whether the crew's sympathies are misplaced.

As the narrator says: "All our certitudes were going" (43). After all, Wait confesses to Donkin that he was "Laid up fifty-eight days" (111) in his last ship and still got paid off. The professional consequence of his illness is to leave the crew short-handed and thus to put the ship at risk: their additional workload is graphically illustrated during the storm when he has to be rescued. The albatross in this mariner's tale, Wait claims to "belong to the ship" (18). This proves grimly prophetic: the embodiment of a morally subversive force, he fastens himself onto the conscience of the crew, whose fellow-feeling towards him demonstrates the dangers of unthinking and self-congratulatory sympathy. By contrast, Singleton's terse observation, "get on with your dying … don't raise a blamed fuss with us over that job. We can't help you" (42), signals that the danger to the crew comes when they become introspective, necessarily an individualist act.

The morally seditious Donkin exploits these sympathies for Wait in order to stir up the crew against the officers. Clearly at odds with "sea-craft," he shirks work at every turn during the voyage and, at the pay off, announces: "I'm goin' ter 'ave a job ashore. … No more bloomin' sea fur me" (169). Like Wait, he – and, by extension, the potential threat to order he represents – is intimately associated with the psychology of the crew. When he arrives in the forecastle, he is immediately recognised as a representative "type": "The sympathetic and deserving creature that knows all about his rights, but knows nothing of courage, of endurance, and of the unexpressed faith, of the unspoken loyalty that knits together a ship's company" (11). By providing him with their cast-off clothing when he arrives in the forecastle, the crew symbolically and complicitly constructs Donkin as a composite image of itself. He is a visual testament to the danger of misdirected sympathy. At the heart of their sympathy, once again, lies egoism: "They were touched by their own readiness to alleviate a shipmate's misery" (12). Such self-satisfied and indeed "narcissistic" sympathy anticipates the "latent egoism of tenderness" (138) the crew demonstrate towards Wait. By contrast, Singleton lives "untouched by human emotions" (41), which sets him majestically apart, a counter-balancing icon alone but linked to the ship.

The subversive impact of both Wait and Donkin on crew life in the *Narcissus* is increasingly dangerous in its effect. For example, because Wait objects to a wet floor, the starboard watch refuse to wash the forecastle. Most seriously, during the near-mutiny

the helmsman abandons his post, leaving the ship to drift unattended and bringing about Donkin's reckless desire to let her "Drift an'
be blowed" (108). As well as provoking a contrast with Singleton,
who sticks to the task throughout the storm off the Cape of Good
Hope, this dereliction of duty suggests that this second "storm"
is potentially more dangerous. For his part, Singleton remains the
only crew member unaffected by the combined disruptive influence of Wait and Donkin. He is identified with a bygone age and
older values, with which the present crew are compared unfavourably: "They were the everlasting children of the mysterious
sea. Their successors are the grown-up children of a discontented
earth" (25). Conrad claimed: "I think Singleton with an education is impossible ... he is simple and great like an elemental force.
Nothing can touch him but the curse of decay" (CL1: 423).

As the crew settle down for their first night in the ship, Singleton
tightens the brake of the *Narcissus* as she moves slightly in the
breeze. This image of control and stability immediately identifies
him as an alternative to the new, disruptive forces aboard. Furthermore, Singleton's taciturnity is contrasted with Donkin's "picturesque and filthy loquacity" (101), suggesting that duty is instinctual
rather than intellectual. According to Ian Watt, Singleton is "the
guardian spirit of the *Narcissus*. More than that he is the guardian spirit of the whole tradition of human toil" (1980: 124). Yet
Singleton is repeatedly set apart from the group: not only does he
not share their sympathies but, true to his name, at the end of this
novel he also receives his pay and leaves "without as much as a
glance at any of us" (169).

Singleton's heroism is eulogised in the suitably simple tribute:
"He steered with care" (89). By the time he is relieved, he has
spent "more'n thirty hours" (96) at the wheel, an experience that
brings him "completed wisdom" (99) in the shape of his own mortality about which (unlike Wait) he utters no word. For most of
the storm, however, the *Narcissus* founders on her side under the
weight of water. Only when the danger has passed can Singleton
announce: "She is steering" (87). In other words, until she rights
herself, Singleton's contribution as helmsman is largely redundant – a less heroic act than professional preparedness. But where
does this leave Conrad's celebration of the crew? Does *The Nigger
of the "Narcissus"* perhaps advocate unquestioning adherence to
duty? When silencing the talk of mutiny, Singleton simply appeals
to Captain Allistoun's authority: "Skipper's no fool. He has something in his mind. Look out – I say! I know 'em" (130). To Jeremy

Hawthorn, the novel is divided between "a conservative-paternalist view of the working class and a conservative-reactionary one, oscillating between a sentimental glorification of his 'old chums' and a far more negative view of them as children in need of stern and powerful control" (1990: 70).

At the height of the storm, Captain Allistoun's decision not to cut the masts is taken in direct opposition to the crew's demands, and, although no reason is given for the order, events prove him to be justified. While demonstrating the responsibility that goes hand in hand with authority – what Conrad in "Typhoon" terms "the burden of command" (39) – this episode also reveals the crew's dependence, for both identity and safety, upon the very hierarchy they question. For his part, Allistoun is reluctant to give them the leisure to question their lot. He advocates duty as a distraction and a means of exerting control. After the riot, he instructs the mates: "Keep them on the move tonight, gentlemen; just to let them feel we've got hold all the time – quietly, you know" (126).

Yet, just as the crew are shown to be divided by sympathies that expose tensions between old and new generations of seamen, that prove them child-like and easily led, and, ultimately, in need of sustaining authority, so the representation of authority in the novel is nuanced. Allistoun is not a likeable hero but a martinet who drives his ship "unmercifully" (30) and wants to retire "out of sight of the sea" (31). He points to "luck" rather than skill as the reason for surviving the storm. And his decision to allow Wait to maintain his pretence (to himself at least) and "go out his own way," while believing that he has "no grit to face what's coming to us all" (127), is motivated by sentimental pity, the "weakness" of the crew. When Allistoun confesses that he was driven to this decision by a "Kind of impulse" (127), he allies himself with the idealised image of the unthinking seaman endorsed by the novel. In the light of Donkin's choice of weapon during the riot, it is significant that Allistoun had earlier threatened to "brain" him with a belaying-pin (86). Just as the crew are partially defined by the forces that threaten them, so Captain Allistoun is subtly identified with the threat to his authority.

*   *   *

Conrad's portrait is thus neither entirely romantic, nor entirely realistic; instead, it provides a palimpsest, in which a maritime ideal, the province of tradition, is to be glimpsed below the fractures and fractiousness of contemporary reality. By the end of the novel, the crew, easily led and duty-bound by turns, have survived the storm, Wait, and Donkin. If unquestioning fidelity to the "mysteriously born tradition of sea-craft" renders them susceptible, it is also their bulwark against emotional and ideological threats. As Berthoud has claimed, the codes of the Merchant Service seemed to offer Conrad "the recovery of a dislocated life," but at the same time, "the very uncertainty that made him so responsive to the integrative possibilities of service made him hypersensitive to the disintegrative implications of what he served" (1992: 56).

Although true to the voyage of the actual *Narcissus* in many respects, Conrad patriotically refashions its end. Conrad disembarked from his five-and-a-half month voyage, not in the Port of London, but in France – specifically, in Dunkirk. The fictional *Narcissus* travels home to England, custodian of "priceless traditions," "A ship mother," and "great flagship of the race" (162, 163). This hymn to maritime tradition, sung by a sailor at the end of an arduous voyage, responds to, and helps to formulate an essential constituent of English tradition: the sea as national myth. But this is not the final image: as the *Narcissus* journeys up the Thames to her berth, it is tempered and transformed by social and commercial reality, leading ultimately to the paying-off of the crew: houses seem "to stream down the declivities at a run to see her pass" and "insolent bands" of tall factory chimneys watch her pass, "like a straggling crowd of slim giants, swaggering and upright under the black plummets of smoke, cavalierly aslant" (163). These are images drawn from the world of Dickensian London, or Coketown in *Hard Times*.

The journey upriver, "on the murky stream" (164), is progressively disenchanting. Contact with land systematically denudes the *Narcissus* of her ocean-going romance and emphasises instead her function as a trading vessel: "Between high building the dust of all the continents and soared in short flights; and a penetrating smell of perfumes and dirt, of spices and hides, of things costly and of things filthy, pervaded the space, made for it an atmosphere precious and disgusting" (165). Her unidentified cargo is destined for warehouses whose windows are like the "eyes of over-fed brutes" (165). The contrast between the poetic and prosaic is continued as the crew make their farewells outside The Mint, when they too are commodified by their contact with land. Their experience, however romanticised, occurs in a real world, where the claims of commercialism provide the sole rationale not only for the voyage of the *Narcissus* but also for her existence.

"Typhoon"

First published serially in 1902, "Typhoon" was initially mentioned by Conrad in February 1899 as " 'Equitable Division' (a story of a typhoon)" (*CL2*: 169). The tale, as yet unwritten, was referred to a year later under the title "A Skittish Cargo" (*CL2*: 237). By October 1900, however, Conrad announced to his literary agent, J. B. Pinker, that the story "deals with a lot of Chinamen coolies and a few seamen on board a steamer in a gale of wind in the China Seas. Its title is *Typhoon* and length as far as I can see 12000 words" (*CL2*: 295). In the same letter and with an eye on serial publication of the work, Conrad described "Typhoon" as "quite the thing that finds room in Xmas numbers." The novella, begun in September or October of 1900 and completed in January 1901, would run to 28,000 words. Printed separately in America, in Britain "Typhoon" was the title-story of a volume entitled *Typhoon and Other Stories* (1903). The three Marlow narratives (discussed in Chapter 4) thus belong to the period between *The Nigger of the "Narcissus"* and "Typhoon" in the Conradian *oeuvre*, between complementary portraits of maritime service in sail and in steam.

"Typhoon" recounts a voyage of the steamship *Nan-Shan* in the China Sea, from an unnamed Eastern port to Fu-chau on the south China coast. Her "cargo" includes two hundred Chinese coolies who are returning home to their villages "after a few years work in various tropical colonies" (6). Once at sea and confronted by signs of steadily worsening weather, Captain MacWhirr decides to abandon the received wisdom of textbook "storm strategy," that advocates circumventing the storm, and instead steer his ship through the heart of it: "A gale is a gale, Mr. Jukes," he tells his first mate, "and a full-powered steam-ship has got to face it" (34). The onset of the typhoon occupies the central chapters of the novella and, besides threatening the life of the ship, adds another dimension to the crisis: the Chinamen housed between decks have "fetched away" (51) and are fighting over their hard-won dollars, the currency of the Straits Settlements.

On MacWhirr's instructions, the first mate, Mr Jukes, succeeds in restoring order just as the ship heads towards the height of the typhoon. Tantalisingly, the climax of the storm, which occurs on Christmas Day, is not described. Instead, the narrative jumps forward to the *Nan-Shan*'s arrival in Fu-chau, her voyage having taken her within sight of "the coast of the Great Beyond, whence no ship ever returns to give up her crew to the dust of the earth" (91). The account of how MacWhirr solved the problem of redistributing their dollars to the coolies is presented as a postscript, largely contained in a letter written by Mr Jukes, who concludes that MacWhirr "got out of it very well for such a stupid man" (102).

By contrast with *The Nigger of the "Narcissus,"* "Typhoon" is a tale of captaincy, and whereas the danger to the crew of the *Narcissus* stemmed from excessive introspection, Captain MacWhirr suffers from the opposite vice: a lack of imagination. This removes him at a stroke from the narcissistic self-imaging of the crew of the *Narcissus*. Conrad introduces the hero of the tale and announces the focus of "Typhoon" in the first paragraph:

> Captain MacWhirr, of the steamer *Nan-Shan*, had a physiognomy that, in order of material appearances, was the exact counterpart of his mind: it presented no marked characteristics of firmness or stupidity; it had no pronounced characteristics whatever; it was simply ordinary, irresponsive, and unruffled.   (3)

With no distinguishing traits whatsoever and driven by habit rather than imagination, MacWhirr, whose very name has a mechanical ring, is an unlikely hero. And yet, in "Typhoon", Conrad succeeds in making a virtue of ordinariness and, in the process, revises the heroic stereotype: according to Leavis, Conrad represents "ordinariness" as a form of "heroic sublimity" (1948: 185). Almost contemporaneous with the novel is *The Mirror of the Sea* (composed between 1903 and 1904), containing Conrad's comments on the distinction between sailing ships and steamships, to the disadvantage of the latter. Unromantically, steam offers "not an individual, temperamental achievement, but simply the skilled use of a captured force, merely another step forward upon the way of universal conquest" (31). His later claim in *The Mirror of the Sea* that the "machinery, the steel, the fire, the steam have stepped in between the man and the sea" (72) determines the subject of "Typhoon": this novella is less concerned with the crew than its predecessor for the reason that the *Nan-Shan* is less dependent upon manpower. Thus, at the beginning of Chapter 5 of "Typhoon," at the height of the storm, the narrative focus shifts from men (in Chapter 4) to the engines that drive the *Nan-Shan*. It is steam-power that allows the imperturbable MacWhirr to sail his ship through the typhoon. By contrast with *The Nigger of the "Narcissus,"* the attention here is concentrated not upon the crew but on the ship's officers: Captain MacWhirr, Mr Jukes, the chief mate, and Solomon Rout, the chief engineer.

*   *   *

Conrad's choice of subject matter has a direct bearing on the narrative's style. Given MacWhirr's lack of imagination and literalness, he is necessarily viewed "from without" by a third-person narrator. A man of few words, who "expostulated against the use of images in speech" (25), MacWhirr obviously couldn't narrate this tale, found by its earliest reviewers to contain "the most amazing description of the utter madness of the sea when tormented by a force almost as great as itself that we have ever read" and to offer "the most elaborate storm piece that one can recall in English literature" (Sherry, ed., 1973: 143, 146). An interesting tension thus emerges between the tale and its subject: MacWhirr is resolutely opposed to the very linguistic qualities – vividness, coherence, subtlety – upon which Conrad's tale about him depends.

Conrad saw "Typhoon" as a new departure, describing it in a letter to Pinker as "my first attempt at treating a subject jocularly so to speak" (*CL2*: 304). The slightly mocking description of MacWhirr in "harbour togs" strikes an affectionately comic note at the outset. His ensemble of brown bowler hat and suit "of a brownish hue" is completed by "clumsy black boots" (3) and "an elegant umbrella of the very best quality, but generally unrolled," that he clutches "in his powerful, hairy fist" and calls, in a phrase that recalls Dickens, "The blessed gamp" (4). But this is not comedy for comedy's sake. The adjectival balance (powerful/hairy; elegant/unrolled) that pokes fun at MacWhirr also suggests a broader contrast between appearance and reality. MacWhirr looks comically out of place ashore because he is. Unlike his counterpart in the *Narcissus* whose wish to retire "out of sight of the sea" (*NN*: 31), MacWhirr's vocation is the sea.

Every inch the skipper of a mechanised steamship, MacWhirr is sternly denotative rather than connotative in his response to language. Described as having "just enough imagination to carry him through each successive day and no more" (4), his literal interpretations of the figurative language used by Jukes occasion humour. For example, commenting on the heat in the engine-room, Jukes says: "It would make a saint swear. Even up here I feel exactly as if I had my head tied up in a woollen blanket" (25). Captain MacWhirr, "faithful to facts" (14), views talk of saints swearing as "wild," and the succeeding simile as simply incomprehensible: "D'ye mean to say, Mr. Jukes, you ever had your head tied up in a woollen blanket? What was that for?" (25).

The anecdote concerning Jukes's response to the re-registering of the *Nan-Shan* exemplifies the use to which MacWhirr's literal-mindedness is put in the text. The transfer involves replacing the Red Ensign with the Siamese flag (then depicting a white elephant on a red background). When Jukes remarks that the new flag looks "queer" (10), MacWhirr compares it with the illustration in his International Signal Code-book before pronouncing: "There's nothing amiss with that flag" (10). To his literal imagination the adjective "queer" can only refer to the state of the flag. He thus remains oblivious to the nationalist sentiments behind Jukes's observation. Duty, not the flag, drives MacWhirr. In itself, this is an example of little moment, but it anticipates another: with the sea-swell worsening and Jukes intent on getting his captain to change course, he expresses concern for the comfort of "our passengers" (31). Here, Jukes, who in his earlier dealings with their interpreter "was gruff, as became his racial superiority" (13), is falsely humanitarian, clearly using proclaimed sympathy for the Chinese as a means to an end. Initially confused by Jukes's description ("Passengers? ... What passengers?"), MacWhirr is typically forthright: "Never heard a lot of coolies spoken of as passengers before. Passengers, indeed! What's come to you?" (31). As another advocate of plain language, George Orwell, expressed it in an essay entitled "Politics and the English Language": "The great enemy of clear language is insincerity" (1958: 86).

Beneath the misunderstanding, it is tempting to infer here that MacWhirr is a racist. But this would be mistaken. To the literal MacWhirr, the Chinese are not "passengers" but the "cargo" that he is carrying to Fu-chau. His unimaginative attitude to language is consistent with his attitude to "dirty weather":

> But suppose I went swinging off my course and came in two days late, and they asked me: "Where have you been all that time, Captain?" What could I say to that? "Went around to dodge the bad

weather," I would say. "It must've been dam' bad," they would say. "Don't know," I would have to say; "I've dodged clear of it." See that, Jukes? I have been thinking it all out this afternoon. (34)

Expressed with unconscious humour, his reason for steering his ship through rather than round the typhoon illustrates MacWhirr's philosophy to life: trouble must be faced head-on. The same impulse generates the "equitable division" whereby he resolves the problem of redistributing the coolies' dollars. Far from being racist, MacWhirr is motivated by instinctual fairness unalloyed by false and self-serving intellectualism. Jukes's closing comment, that his captain "got out of it very well for such a stupid man" (102), is not only not borne out by events but is also an implicit warning against the dangers of elevating intelligence above instinct. As Paul Kirschner has astutely observed: "MacWhirr is not only a source of comedy: he is defined and vindicated by it" (1990: 6). MacWhirr rejects the received wisdom of "storm strategy" on the grounds, true enough, that "you don't find everything in books" (34). Instead he asks pragmatically and unanswerably: "How can you tell what a gale is made of till you get it?" (33). In other words, experience, not abstract theory, is his guide, a stance that ultimately justifies his position as captain.

* * *

MacWhirr's lack of imagination makes him dependent upon the facts of life, and only the hard facts of personal experience can teach him about typhoons. Before this voyage, MacWhirr had sailed the seas "without ever having been made to see all it may contain of perfidy, of violence, and of terror" (19). Coming at the end of the opening chapter, this comment constitutes a recognisable fictional formula. It translates as: by the end of this voyage, MacWhirr will have seen these aspects of the sea. The storm sequence, conveyed in prose of impressionist vividness, is designed to convey and replicate MacWhirr's confrontation with reality. To capture something of its flavour, and in particular, of the way the violence of the storm is described in sentences that telescope out their relative clauses to push compositional details further and further apart from one another, here is a single paragraph:

> The sea, flattened down in the heavier gusts, would uprise and over-whelm both ends of the *Nan-Shan* in snowy rushes of foam, expand-ing wide, beyond both rails, into the night. And on this dazzling

sheet, spread under the blackness of the clouds and emitting a bluish
glow, Captain MacWhirr could catch a desolate glimpse of a few
tiny specks black as ebony, the tops of the hatches, the battened
companions, the heads of covered winches, the foot of a mast. This
was all he could see of his ship. Her middle structure, covered by the
bridge which bore him, his mate, the closed wheelhouse where a man
was steering shut up with the fear of being swept overboard together
with the whole thing in one great crash – her middle structure was
like a half-tide rock awash upon a coast. It was like an outlying rock
awash upon a coast. It was like an outlying rock with the water
boiling up, streaming over, pouring off, beating round – like a rock
in the surf to which shipwrecked people cling before they let go –
only it rose, it sank, it rolled continuously, without respite and rest,
like a rock that should have miraculously struck adrift from a coast
and gone wallowing upon the sea.   (43–44)

The relentless force of the storm is presented in the consuetudinal
tense of the opening sentence: "would" suggests repeated action. Its
scale is developed through the description of the sea: first, the sea
covers "both ends of the *Nan-Shan*"; it does so "in snowy rushes
of foam" that, dwarfing the ship, expand "beyond both rails"; and
finally these "rushes" expand even further, "into the night," with
all the connotations of vastness and fear of the unknown that this
conjures up. This mood created, the next sentence provides a vision
of the *Nan-Shan* as seen by Captain MacWhirr (and signalled by the
short third sentence: "This was all he could see of his ship"). The
conjunction with which it begins presents the action as continuous
with the previous sentence while, playfully, extending the havoc
being wreaked by the storm to the grammar used to describe it.
More pertinently, this sentence reduces the *Nan-Shan* to a series
of disjointed impressions. The sequence of fragmentary images –
"a few tiny specks black as ebony, the tops of the hatches, the
battened companions, the heads of covered winches, the foot of a
mast" – simultaneously suggests the potential of the storm to break
up the *Nan-Shan* and mimics MacWhirr's difficulties in seeing his
ship, a perspective that subtly conveys the captain's immediate
responsibility for the safety of his command.

   Once this perspective has been established, the following sentence describing the "middle structure" of the ship extends the
fragmentary impressions from the ship to the crew – and with it
MacWhirr's concern for those in his charge. Instead of describing "Her middle structure" with which the sentence begins, the
focus shifts to the men on this structure: MacWhirr, Jukes, and the

helmsman. Only then does it return to the subject and, in doing so, recommences: "her middle structure was like a half-tide rock awash on a coast." The use of figural language here suggests that this is no longer MacWhirr's perspective but rather the broader vision of the omniscient narrator. The sentence thus strikes a balance between humane concern and the storm's overwhelming force, elevating the fragility of the former to heroic proportions.

The final sentence is a virtuoso performance of movement and vitality whose repetitions and rhythm seem designed to replicate in prose those of the sea. The thrice-repeated simile comparing the *Nan-Shan* to a rock combines the opposed senses of safety and danger: as a rock, she is solid, stable, and safe; but she is not a rock, she is a ship – "only it rose, it sank, it rolled." Likening the *Nan-Shan* to a rock to which shipwrecked people cling also carries this dual implication. The potentially shipwrecked people are presently bound to their rock. Nor should one overlook the obvious here. Even though the ship is described as a rock that has "gone wallowing," rocks do not "wallow," they sink. In other words, as the paragraph dramatises the threat of the typhoon, so its descriptions suggest the expanded knowledge born of experience that MacWhirr acquires.

* * *

On deck and literally confronting the typhoon, MacWhirr exemplifies "the prestige, the privilege, and the burden of command." Indeed, to Jukes it seems that, "simply by coming on deck," his captain had "taken most of the gale's weight upon his shoulders" (39). But the storm scene dramatises the responsibilities of command in other ranks, too. Solomon Rout, the chief engineer, for instance, remains at his post in the engine-room throughout, ensuring that the *Nan-Shan* has the necessary power to confront the typhoon. The intuitive MacWhirr also empowers his chief mate, Jukes, ordering him below decks to settle what is, apparently, a fight among the coolies (and so a human disorder that mirrors the storm). Hardly daring to believe in his own survival, the imaginative and vulnerable Jukes, whose character provides an important contrast with that of his unimaginative, stolid captain, does his duty, leading the crew's efforts to rig up life-lines for the floundering Chinese to cling on to and confiscating their money in order to avoid further trouble between-decks during the storm. Jukes's efforts earn his captain's simple praise. Returning to the bridge, he reports: "We have done it, sir." MacWhirr's response is characteristically direct: "Thought you would" (81). Like his commendation of his chief engineer, "Rout . . . good man" (48), MacWhirr's taciturnity imbues such scant praise with added worth. Jukes's development is signalled more practically a moment later when Captain MacWhirr leaves him in charge of the deck as he goes to read the barometer again.

Explaining his reasons for ordering Jukes below decks, MacWhirr simultaneously reveals his simple humanity: "Had to do what's fair by them" (81). Fairness is a fittingly unambiguous moral creed and consistent with the no-nonsense MacWhirr's literalism. It motivates his solution to the problem of how to return their dollars to the Chinese, by "equitable division," as the original title had expressed it. In this manner, Macwhirr's quiet, self-effacing heroism reveals itself, and Conrad succeeds in treating an unheroic subject heroically.

MacWhirr's taciturnity is elevated to the condition of a structural principle during the storm scene. After the six-hour ordeal, which had "enlarged [MacWhirr's] conception of what heavy weather could be like" (84), the Nan-Shan is becalmed in the eye of the storm where the "darkness ... absolutely piling itself upon the ship" (90) confirms MacWhirr's prediction that "the worst was to come yet" (85). At this point, the narrative is interrupted. Chapter 5 ends thus:

> Before the renewed wrath of winds swooped on his ship, Captain MacWhirr was moved to declare, in a tone of vexation, as it were: "I wouldn't like to lose her."
> He was spared that annoyance. (90)

Chapter 6 opens with the Nan-Shan's arrival in Fu-chau, battered but victorious. As Conrad's decision to elide the "worst" of the storm and leave it to the reader's imagination demonstrates, it is not the typhoon but the doughtiness of the "taciturn man in its path" (90) that is the focus of the story. His firmness in the face of the first phase of the typhoon – like his fairness in dealing with the Chinese – would, in any event, remain unchanged and thus render further description of the storm repetitive. More subtly, the narrative ellipsis echoes something of MacWhirr's own self-effacing, taciturn manner.

*   *   *

"Typhoon" concludes with a medley of voices as MacWhirr, Rout, and Jukes all write letters, the older men to their wives and Jukes to his chum "in the Western ocean trade" (18). These letters, together with the comments of their recipients, extend the narrative's concern with communication by raising such questions as: What is communicated? How factual is this communication? And, how responsive is language to experience? The acts of communication offer parallels and contrasts to humorous effect. For instance, Rout fails to report how his captain solved the problem of the coolies' money to his wife, who is eager to know; while MacWhirr recounts this to his wife who reads uninterestedly and incompletely. Instead, it is Jukes's account of the "equitable division" incident that is communicated. But Rout and Jukes come to different conclusions about MacWhirr's strategy. To the chief engineer it is "something rather clever" (96); the chief mate's verdict is that MacWhirr "got out of it very well for such a stupid man" (102). The reader is left to piece together the meaning of the incident from the three accounts, none of which is wholly reliable: MacWhirr's because of understatement, Rout's because of elision, and Jukes's because he embellishes and misrepresents.

Is MacWhirr really, as Jukes claims, "such a stupid man"? The evidence seems to point the other way. Not only does Rout contradict this, but the opening paragraph of the novella also defines MacWhirr's mind as presenting "no marked characteristics of firmness or stupidity" (3). On the other hand, Jukes is given the final word on MacWhirr, yet his imaginative and loquacious epistolary style – like the descriptive passages in the narrative overall – reveal him to be at odds with his subject. Jukes's judgement, which by implication promotes his own "intelligence," mistakes his captain's stolidity for stupidity, and, in so doing, underscores the narrative's distrust of imagination. Of MacWhirr the narrator says: "To be silent was natural to him" (40). Even the typhoon, "doing its utmost," only manages "to wring out a few words" from him (90). Thus Jukes's words must be seen in the context of the narrative's broader concern with speech and communication. MacWhirr cannot comprehend what "people ashore" find to talk about: "Must be saying the same things over and over again" (18). But this humorously reductive observation conceals the serious point (also made in The Nigger of the "Narcissus") that instinct is allied to taciturnity. During the storm, the helmsman, Hackett, tells his captain: "I can steer for ever if nobody talks to me" (66).

The image of MacWhirr, alone on the bridge of his ship and confronting the typhoon, issuing terse orders to the engine-room by means of a speaking-tube, dramatises his attitude to communication. His literalness extends to his monthly letters home to his wife. Like everything else about MacWhirr, these provide confirmation that the maritime world is his element. The opening chapter of "Typhoon" contains this paragraph:

> The China seas north and south are narrow seas. They are seas full of every-day, eloquent facts, such as islands, sand-banks, reefs, swift and changeable currents – tangled facts that nevertheless speak to a seaman in clear and definite language. Their speech appealed to Captain MacWhirr's sense of realities so forcibly that he had given up his state-room below and practically lived all his days on the bridge of his ship, often having his meals sent up, and sleeping at night in the chart-room. And he indited there his home letters. Each of them, without exception, contained the phrase, "The weather has been fine this trip," or some other form of a statement to that effect. And this statement, too, in its wonderful persistence, was of the same perfect accuracy as all the others they contained.   (15)

The linguistic contours of MacWhirr's world are provided by the "facts" of the sea. (Appropriately, too, his functional language is spoken on a mechanised steamship.) To these facts, this voyage of the *Nan-Shan* adds knowledge of typhoons. And as the narrator cautions at the beginning of the narrative: "facts can speak for themselves with overwhelming precision" (9). The incommunicability – to his mind at least – of such facts in the abstract leads MacWhirr to reject the "storm strategy" and confront the storm head on. But, as the humorous exchanges with Jukes at the beginning of the narrative confirm, the act of communication depends on who speaks, what is said, and who hears. Reading over the shoulders, as it were, of the three recipients of the letters emphasises the collaborative role of the recipient in the act of communication. In particular, Mrs MacWhirr, who lived in "abject terror of the time when her husband would come home for good" (14) and reads her husband's letters only "perfunctorily" (93), demonstrates how the literalness of MacWhirr's language provides a barrier to communication. While this register suffices at sea, it does not translate to land. Instead, finding her husband's letters "so prosy, so completely uninteresting" (93), she skim-reads them, skipping whole pages, and in the process vindicating MacWhirr's taciturnity.

MacWhirr's account of the typhoon is all but obscured by his wife's perfunctory reading. In response, the narrative replicates her reading by reducing MacWhirr's letter to a series of randomly selected fragments caught by "her thoughtless eyes" (93). With symmetrical irony at her expense, this fragmentary style reminds one of nothing so much as the broken sentences that pass between MacWhirr and Jukes in the face of the typhoon. MacWhirr's letter thus offers a palimpsest through which the lineaments of the voyage, though dimly visible, await disinterment by more generous eyes than Mrs MacWhirr's.

It is tempting to see in the references to Lydia's ribbon and the "sale at Linom's" (95), that divert Mrs MacWhirr from her husband's letter, the values of the ephemeral, material world set against those of the sea, with its life-or-death tussle pitting man against the elements. But, as the "equitable division" demonstrates, the *Nan-Shan* is herself inextricably linked to material interests. She is a steamship, run for profit by her owners, Messrs Sigg and Son. One of the reasons that MacWhirr gives for facing the typhoon is financial: avoiding it would result in "Three hundred miles extra to the distance, and a pretty coal bill to show" (33). If MacWhirr, like the steamship he commands, does serve both the mercantile and the maritime worlds, his value as a seaman is unambiguously endorsed by a triumvirate of elder peers: the senior partner of Sigg and Son and "Old Mr. Sigg" himself ashore, and "Old Sol" Rout aboard. Here, as in *The Nigger of the "Narcissus,"* endorsement is the prerogative of age and experience.

Conrad never reveals the identity of the cargo carried in the *Narcissus*, and it is the Chinese coolies who provide the "cargo" of the *Nan-Shan*. That the freight in these ships should be human experience dramatises Conrad's personal and maritime inheritance, while the fact that their settings include both the Atlantic and Indian Oceans points to the international scope of this inheritance.

Works cited

Ackroyd, Peter. *Albion: The Origins of the English Imagination.* London: Chatto & Windus, 2002.

Berthoud, Jacques. "Literature and Drama." *The Cambridge Cultural History: Early 20th Century Britain.* Edited by Boris Ford. 47–99. Cambridge: Cambridge University Press, 1992.

Edel, Leon, ed. *Henry James Letters. Vol. 4: 1895–1916.* Cambridge, Mass.: Belknap Press, 1984.

Hawthorn, Jeremy. *Joseph Conrad: Narrative Technique and Ideological Commitment*. London: Edward Arnold, 1992.

Kirschner, Paul. "Introduction." *Typhoon and Other Stories*. Harmondsworth: Penguin, 1990.

Leavis, F. R. *The Great Tradition: George Eliot, Henry James, Joseph Conrad*. London: Chatto & Windus, 1948.

Levenson, Michael. *A Genealogy of Modernism: A Study of English Literary Doctrine 1908–1922*. Cambridge: CUP, 1984.

Orwell, George. "Politics and the English Language." In *Selected Writings*, edited by George Bott. London: Heinemann, 1958.

Simmons, Allan. "Introduction." *The Nigger of the "Narcissus."* xvii–xxxvii. London: J. M. Dent, 1997.

Smith, Walter E. *Joseph Conrad: A Bibliographical Catalogue of his Major First Editions with Facsimiles of Several Title Pages*. Long Beach, California: Privately printed, n.d.

Watt, Ian. *Conrad in the Nineteenth Century*. London: Chatto & Windus, 1980.

4

The Marlow Trilogy: "Youth," "Heart of Darkness," and *Lord Jim*

After the malleable narrating presence in *The Nigger of the "Narcissus,"* Conrad's next creative phase is marked by the appearance of his most famous narrator, Marlow. His first-person narratives combine the first-hand experience with a dual narrating presence: Marlow both recreates events – of his younger self in "Youth," of his encounter with Kurtz in "Heart of Darkness," and of Jim in *Lord Jim* – and, from the perspective of hindsight, meditates upon their meanings, typically transforming the action of the story into moral and philosophical enquiry. He is simultaneously a character in the tales and their interpreter. As such, Marlow is positioned between the story and the English audience for whom Conrad is writing. Furthermore, each of these first-person narratives creates the illusion of being an oral tale, told to a listening audience, casting the reader in the role of secondary audience, listening over the shoulders of Marlow's dramatised audience, as it were. As Marlow's tales are based upon Conrad's own experiences – "Youth," for instance, draws heavily upon the author's experiences in the ill-fated *Palestine*, and "Heart of Darkness" is modelled upon Conrad's visit to the Congo Free State in 1890 – he has been seen as an autobiographical alter ego.

Conrad himself encouraged posterity to bracket the man and the work, claiming:

> "Youth" is a feat of memory. It is a record of experience; but that experience, in its facts, in its inwardness and in its outward colouring, begins and ends in myself. "Heart of Darkness" is experience, too; but it is experience pushed a little (and only very little) beyond the actual facts of the case for the perfectly legitimate, I believe, purpose of bringing it home to the minds and bosoms of the readers.
> ("Author's Note": *Y*, xi)

The three Marlow tales discussed in this chapter were conceived as a single volume, to which "Youth" would "give the note" and "Heart of Darkness" act as "a foil" for *Lord Jim* (*CL2*: 271). "Youth" was probably written in early 1898, between May and June; *Lord Jim* was begun in May 1898 but only completed in July 1900, during which time Conrad wrote "Heart of Darkness." As this history suggests, the composition of the tales is almost a continuum, further suggesting their interrelatedness. When *Lord Jim* steadily expanded beyond the bounds of a short story into a novel of more than 130,000 words, it thwarted Conrad's plans for a single volume of Marlow tales. *Lord Jim* was published in 1900, with "The End of the Tether" replacing *Lord Jim* as the third tale in the volume, *Youth: A Narrative and Two Other Stories* two years later.

Marlow

Conrad described Marlow as "A most discreet, understanding man" and, as importantly, a "gentleman" (ix–x). Through Marlow, who shares his name with a town on the River Thames, Conrad engages with English culture. Historicized, Marlow's status reflects a central aspect in the widespread contemporary debate about the formalized institutions and structures of Englishness. Mark Girouard (1981), for instance, has shown how the assertion of chivalric codes of honour, bravery, service, and self-sacrifice in English art and culture of the nineteenth century provided models of gentlemanly behaviour up and down the actual social scale. Marlow is a sea-captain, and so not quite the conventional "gentleman." His freedom from strict class codes thus allows him a greater democracy of vision. In *Lord Jim*, particularly, he addresses gentlemanly behavioural codes such as honour, and his designation of Jim and Jewel as "knight and maiden meeting to exchange vows amongst haunted ruins" (312) embeds (and mythologizes) such codes within the context of chivalry. Furthermore, as Jim's experience on Patusan demonstrates, English values and empire-building are intertwined in imperial narratives. While the Marlow trilogy is set, for the most part, in exotic surroundings, its views of colonialism are often censorious. Underlying Marlow's tales is the weakened belief in the right of Empire and, more subtly, a vision or sense of the consequences of this for the definition of Englishness. In short, both Marlow and the tales that fascinate him engage with issues of national identity and belong to a moment when such issues were matters of lively contention.

Perhaps mimicking Conrad's own wariness as an immigrant writing for an English audience, each of the Marlow narratives is mediated by the presence of an anonymous frame-narrator, placing it at one remove from the reader. Thus positioned, between tale and reader, Marlow can be thought of as Janus-faced, seeing and addressing both the British "world" of the tales and the British "island" of the reader. Indeed, his attitude towards England (and Empire) depends upon this perspective: now questioning, now reverent, it enables the charitable irony that defines his poetics. Rooted in the marine and colonial worlds, Marlow's tales blend the facts and myths of Empire, as Great and Greater Britain are brought into critical contiguity and focus.

With his English perspective, Marlow actively seeks for a mirroring nationalism when asking the Russian Harlequin in "Heart of Darkness": "You English?" (Y: 122). His disappointment at discovering that the man is not registers a linguistic and cultural loneliness and alienation. When eulogising "that home distant enough for all its hearthstones to be like one hearthstone" in Lord Jim (221), home is England. John Batchelor reads Lord Jim as "a triple self-portrait" in which Jim is his younger, errant self, Stein the person he has become, and Marlow "the Englishman that Conrad would have liked to have been" (1994: 110).

But just how integrated is Marlow within this group? A shared sea history may bind him to his audience, who may in turn have heard his "inconclusive experiences" before, yet there remains the frame-narrator's parenthetic confession: "(at least I think that is how he spelt his name)" (Y: 3). Linked to the group by shared values and experiences, he nonetheless remains an outsider. Jim first notices him because he "sat apart from the others" (LJ: 32). According to John Galsworthy, Marlow, "though English in name," is "not so in nature" (1927: 78). Despite his prominence, Marlow's biographical roots are almost totally missing – where was he born? Where educated? Does he have a family? Where does he live? Instead, Marlow comes across as less a character than a style, "no more to us than a voice" (*Y*: 83), while his ambiguous Englishness complicates the contract between writer and audience.

"Youth"

"Youth," as its title suggests, is a celebration of youth and adventure in which the older Marlow, reminiscing about his younger self, recounts his first voyage as second mate, which also provided his first encounter with the Far East. The twinned perspectives of the older and younger Marlow ensure that the potency of youth is simultaneously exalted and diminished: "O youth! The strength of it, the faith of it, the imagination of it!" (12). Punctuated by repeated exclamations to "Youth!" made from the vantage point of middle age, the nostalgia that recalls and recreates the experiences of twenty years ago blends celebration and elegy. Garnett called it "a modern English epic of the Sea" in which "the song of every man's youth is indeed sung" (Sherry, ed., 1973: 131, 133). Given the tale's subject matter – the potency of youth tested and the coming into maturity – it is unsurprising that reviewers regarded it as a boys' adventure story. Conrad himself described it thus in a letter of 1902: "Out of the material of a boys' story I've made *Youth* by the force of the idea expressed in accordance with a strict conception of my method" (*CL2*: 417).

Marlow's integration with his English audience in "Youth" is demonstrated by their shared felt experience that his tale describes and, stylistically, by the relationship between the frame narration and Marlow's narrative. The setting for the narration is described in the second paragraph: "We were sitting round a mahogany table that reflected the bottle, the claret-glasses, and our faces as we leaned on our elbows" (3). Marlow's tale is itself a "reflection" upon lost youth, which, in turn, provides a mirror of the lost youths of others. And fittingly, youthful experience is itself seen as a reflection. When, at the end of the voyage, the young Marlow awakens to his first view of the East, in Sumatra, it is to "the wide sweep of the bay, the glittering sands, the wealth of green infinite and varied, the sea blue like the sea of a dream, the crowd of attentive faces, the blaze of vivid colour – the water reflecting it all" (41). These twinned reflections complement the dual perspectives, middle-aged and youthful, of Marlow's narration, and are themselves synthesised in the tale's final paragraph where the evanescence of youth is evocatively conveyed:

> And we all looked at him: the man of finance, the man of accounts, the man of law, we all nodded at him over a polished table that like a still sheet of brown water reflected our faces, lined, wrinkled; our faces marked by toil, by deceptions, by success, by love; our weary eyes looking still, looking always, looking anxiously for something out of life, that while it is expected is already gone – has passed unseen, in a sigh, in a flash – together with the youth, with the strength, with the romance of illusions.   (42)

Walter Benjamin's essay, "Experience," begins on the same note: "In our struggle for responsibility, we fight against someone who is masked. The mask of the adult is called 'experience.' It is expressionless, impenetrable, and ever the same. The adult has already experienced [*erlebt*] everything: youth, ideals, hopes, woman. It was all illusion" (2004: 3). The frame-narrator's closing words, endorsing youth's spontaneity from the vantage of reflective age, reaffirm the men's common experience. The sight-references direct the reader here: those in the past tense convey not sight but hindsight, reinforcing the truism that youth is always what we *had*, never what we *have*; the present participles, however, also suggest the continuity between past and present, that we are partly defined by what we have lost, and, with it, the tale's moral: the impetuous comedy of youth is the reflective tragedy of age.

*   *   *

"Youth" draws heavily upon Conrad's own experiences as second mate of the *Palestine*, which sank off the coast of Sumatra in March 1883 after a troubled and ill-fated voyage to transport her cargo of coal from Newcastle to Bangkok. In the tale, Marlow, lured by the charm of sailing to "Bankok" (as Conrad spells it), signs on as second mate of the *Judea*, whose stern bears the motto: "Do or Die." This is a tale of youth tested. But, as Marlow's voyage ends in Sumatra and not Bangkok, it also demonstrates how youthful anticipation is subject to the compromises of experience. The allegorical names of the chief officers, Beard and Mahon – "he insisted that it should be pronounced Mann" (5) – together with those such as Abraham and *Judea*, contribute to the wider significance of the voyage that "might stand as a symbol of existence" (4).

Successively delayed by gales, collision, repairs, and reluctant seamen, the *Judea* finally sets sail some half way through the tale with her fourth crew. This chronicle of delays and deferrals, each offering a potential first voyage to the East, only heightens the young Marlow's excitement – for instance, he views the buffeting in the Atlantic as "the deuce of an adventure" (12). But behind this youthful perspective can be detected another, from the less self-centred standpoint of the older Marlow. The twenty-two years that separate the Marlow who recounts the tale from his twenty-year-old self, also position him approximately midway in age between that younger self and Captain Beard, who is "sixty if he was a day" (4) and the *Judea* is his first command. Marlow is thus endowed with the dual perspective to which youth is, necessarily, blind: able to recall and recreate the thrill of his "first second-mate's billet" with "the East ... waiting for me," he is equally able to temper this with the benefit of maturity and recognise something of Captain Beard's "worry and humiliation" (15). The narrative is thus composed of two voices, immediate and retrospective, innocent and experienced, a dialogue between emotional fidelity to experience and aesthetic fidelity to memory. And while this dialogue emphasises the myopia of youth, in its tacit suggestion that we are responsible not only for what we do but also for what we see, it also celebrates the irresponsibility of youthful self-glorification.

After the expectation created by thwarted attempts to set sail or get out of British waters, the *Judea*'s entire progress from England, through the Atlantic Ocean, round the Cape of Good Hope, and into the Indian Ocean, steering northwards to Java Head, is con-veyed in less than a page (17–18). Here, narrative summary suggests the uneventful routine of ship life while establishing a rhythmic and ironic counterpoint to both Marlow's excitement and the speed of the ship: "mostly she strolled on at the rate of three miles an hour. What could you expect? She was tired – that old ship. Her youth was where mine is – where yours is – you fellows who listen to this yarn" (17).

Anticipation and memory carry equal weight in this story for, despite its title, "Youth" is also about age. This voyage is as much Captain Beard's as it is Marlow's, and foregrounding Marlow's experience in the tale has the effect of replicating the self-absorbed consciousness of youth. That Marlow completes his journey to the East while the *Judea* founders, affirms the inevitable process whereby youth outwears age. But, with equal certitude, youth is succeeded by experience: it is the "childish rapture, before the long sobriety of serious life," in Benjamin's phrase (2004: 3).

With her "Do or Die" motto and her destruction, the *Judea* symbolically and complicatedly unites youth and age. While her motto is an expression of youthful bravado, for in life one "Does and Dies," the adventurous spirit of youth it conjures up is doubly undercut – ironically, by her speed, and literally, by her "death": "The unconsumed stern was the last to sink; but the paint had gone, had cracked, had peeled off, and there were no letters, there was no word, no stubborn device that was like her soul, to flash at the rising sun her creed and her name" (35). Given their respective ages, the *Judea* and Captain Beard seem made for each other, and, when abandoning ship, it is the captain who wants "to save for the underwriters as much as we could of the ship's gear" (30). The *Judea* thus embodies the pragmatic and the romantic aspects of the Merchant Service: the sea is a late-nineteenth-century business that yet enables the marine dreams of youth, like those of Marlow and Jim.

The spontaneous combustion that destroys the *Judea* provides the tale with its most potent symbol: the fire, simultaneously an image of youthful vigour *and* destruction. In terms of development across the Marlow tales, this flame-image is "answered" by the corresponding emphasis upon light extinguished in "Heart of Darkness." As the *Judea* provides the frame of experience for the young Marlow, the fire that destroys her focuses the trial of youth more narrowly. This is not just Marlow's first voyage to the East, it is his first voyage as an officer, and the incipient adult can be perceived in traces of responsibility and reflection during this narrative sequence. If the untried second-mate is unsure about himself – "what made them obey me" (28) – the ordeal also inspires the reflection about English sailors that has endured: "I don't say positively that the crew of a French or German merchantman wouldn't have done it, but I doubt whether it would have been done in the same way. There was a completeness in it, something solid like a principle, and masterful like an instinct" (28). As Marlow's words here confirm, "Youth" is a narrative of Englishness. Coupled with Conrad's unerring praise for the British Merchant Service, reflected in several celebratory essays, this testament, while proving the degree to which fiction and autobiography flow in and out of each other, mirrors the author's own cultural absorption.

If the explosion adds to the sense of maritime adventure that the young Marlow craves, restoring order amid the chaos in its immediate aftermath is a testament to professionalism and duty. Mahon immediately insists upon "having the foreyard squared" (24). Captain Beard's return to the deck – extending the time-theme in the tale, the moment of combustion finds the captain "in his own berth winding up the chronometers" (24) – is even more emphatic: "And, mark, he noticed directly the wheel deserted and his barque off her course – and his only thought was to get that miserable, stripped, undecked, smouldering shell of a ship back again with her head pointing at her port of destination. Bankok!" (25). For their part, the crew's endeavours on behalf of the crippled ship earn Marlow's enduring tribute to British seamanship while simultaneously confirming, with the benefit of hindsight, an evident and existential paradox: "Do you see the lot of us there, putting a neat furl on the sails of that ship doomed to arrive nowhere?" (28).

* * *

The *Judea*'s end is strikingly pictorial. With her three lifeboats launched and loaded with what can be salvaged of the ship's gear "for the underwriters" (30), Marlow eagerly awaits the rest of the crew. In another of the tale's inversions, Marlow, who had earlier and contradictorily proclaimed "there was also my youth to make me patient" (18), grows impatient and returns to the ship to see what is keeping the others and is greeted by the sight of the rest of the crew taking their last meal aboard her as the exhausted Captain Beard sleeps. Providing the most potent symbol of the tale, the fire around which the sailors are sitting is fed by the ship herself.

When, after the *Judea* has sunk, the three lifeboats, under the respective commands of Beard, Mahon, and Marlow, do set sail for Java, Marlow disobeys the Captain's instructions to "keep together as much as possible" (36) and instead views the voyage in the open boat – an extension of the "Do or Die" theme – as a race. That Marlow is first to arrive is certainly a celebration of youthful vigour – "the feeling that I could last for ever, outlast the sea, the earth, and all men" (36). Even when he sights a sailing ship on the horizon, he conceals it for fear that she might be homeward bound and so turn him back from "the portals of the East" (36). But this "race" is also a testament to youthful insensitivity, as Captain

Beard's "murmured" words upon arrival prove: "I had a terrible time of it" (38).

The reader is left with the problem posed by the story's focus: what stance should we take towards youthful egoism and self-absorption? It is not Marlow the subject but Marlow the narrator who, along with the privileged reader, is granted this dual perspective and can appreciate the justice of Melville's claim in *Moby-Dick*: "Be sure of this, O young ambition, all mortal greatness is but disease" (71). In this respect, the tribute to youth in "Youth" remains ambiguous, leaving the reader to wonder at how little Marlow learns about life and the degree to which his first "command" is ironic, accidental, and even wasted on him.

This need to view the youthful self within wider perspectives is finally asserted in a reversal of the colonial gaze at the end of the voyage. When Marlow wakes to look upon his destination for the first time, having spent the night sleeping in the lifeboat, it is to find himself the object of an Eastern gaze: "And then I saw the men of the East – they were looking at me" (40). Marlow's fascination with the East is thus realised in the reversal whereby "the tired men from the West" (41) themselves appear fascinating to their Oriental counterparts. The description of the sleeping sailors in "the careless attitudes of death" (41) is appropriate: the end of the voyage – and the end of the narrative – it is also the end of this phase of Marlow's youth. Once seen, the East can no longer remain unknown, that essential quality of youth – its innocence – has been lost.

But a further reversal remains, for the older Marlow confesses: "I have known its fascination since; I have seen the mysterious shores, the still water, the lands of brown nations, where a stealthy Nemesis lies in wait, pursues, overtakes so many of the conquering race, who are proud of their wisdom, of their knowledge, of their strength" (41–42). Within this "knowledge" of the East lies the historical awareness of adventurers as colonisers, "the conquering race," and that for every Western narrative of colonial adventure a parallel narrative exists in which it is the Westerner who is perceived as "Other." This is explored more fully in the two later Marlow tales. Situated at the confluence of lived and meditated experience, the narrative of "Youth" anticipates these in the sense of dislocation Marlow feels, both the young Marlow upon his arrival in the East and the older Marlow, capable of a multiplicity of perspectives, looking back on his youth with a degree of self-reproach.

"Heart of Darkness"

"And this also has been one of the dark places of the earth." (48)

With this seemingly simple phrase, Marlow's tale in "Heart of Darkness" begins. And yet nothing in this richly textured narrative is simple, for the phrase is consistent with the age's clichés about itself. Biblical in inspiration – "for the dark places of the earth are full of habitations of cruelty" (Psalms, 74:20) – it is contemporaneous with Henry Stanley's *In Darkest Africa* and the provocatively titled *In Darkest England* by William Booth, founder of the Salvation Army, both published in 1890, the year in which Conrad journeyed to Africa, the so-called "dark continent." Appropriately, Conrad recalled his first impressions of London (in the essay "Poland Revisited") in terms that resonate with Marlow's impressions of Africa in "Heart of Darkness": "I had walked into the great city with something of the feeling of a traveller penetrating into a vast and unexplored wilderness. No explorer could have been more lonely" (*NLL*: 150).

The boundaries between fact and fiction in Conrad's most famous story are porous. Its narrative draws both factually and impressionistically upon Conrad's own experiences in Africa from June to December in 1890, where he served as an officer and, for a short while, commander in a steamboat on the Congo River, in the employ of the Société Anonyme Belge pour le Commerce du Haut-Congo. This era of late-nineteenth-century imperialism is often dubbed "the scramble for Africa" and pictorially lampooned in caricatures of greedy Western European leaders carving up what King Leopold II of Belgium called "this magnificent African cake" (Pakenham, 1991: 22). Having seen the excesses of colonialism at first-hand, Conrad would later describe this venture as "the vilest scramble for loot that ever disfigured the history of human conscience and geographical exploration" (*LE*: 17).

Although there are sufficient historical and factual clues to identify the Congo Free State as the setting for Marlow's narrative in the novella, Conrad stops short of explicitly naming it, thereby ensuring that the critique of colonialism offered in "Heart of Darkness" is generalised. At the time of Conrad's visit, the Congo, an area of approximately one million square miles, was administered not by the Belgian Government but by King Leopold II as his personal property. The Charter of the Congo State was granted by the Berlin Act of 1885 and subsequently endorsed by the Brussels Act of 1890. The Berlin Conference's decision to recognise Leopold's sovereignty over the Congo was, in essence, a compromise based on self-interest: none of the major colonial powers represented at the conference was prepared to see an area of this size fall into the hands of a rival, and all saw the danger of becoming embroiled in a free-for-all in the Congo. Leopold, who in any case was acting individually rather than as representative of the Belgian Parliament (which had little enthusiasm for his colonial schemes), was regarded as a neutral.

In a letter of 31 December 1898, Conrad described his new story thus: "The title I am thinking of is 'The Heart of Darkness' but the narrative is not gloomy. The criminality of inefficiency and pure selfishness when tackling the civilizing work in Africa is a justifiable idea" (*CL2*: 139–40). "The Heart of Darkness" was first published in *Blackwood's Magazine* between February and April 1899. The title was changed to the more evocative "Heart of Darkness" when the tale was included as one of the "other stories" in *Youth: A Narrative and Two Other Stories* in 1902. The title-change is immediately more ambiguous (does "darkness" qualify "heart" or is it the other way round?) and alerts the careful reader to the many inversions that ensure that this protean tale resists easy definition. Despite its relative brevity, "Heart of Darkness" is daunting for the first-time reader. Not an easy read – since, to Marlow, "the meaning of an episode was not inside like a kernel but outside, enveloping the tale which brought it out only as a glow brings out a haze, in the likeness of one of these misty halos that sometimes are made visible by the spectral illumination of moonshine" (48) – but a powerful experience, the story's multiple meanings and paradoxes are symptomatic of Modernity itself and have exercised generations of interpreters. Travelogue, fiction, historical document, and polemic are but some of the literary categories into which this story falls.

* * *

In "Heart of Darkness," Marlow recounts his journey as captain of a steamboat on the Congo River. It is a rescue mission (partly like Stanley's famous quest for Livingstone), to find and bring back one of the Company agents, Mr Kurtz, an ivory trader in the Interior, who according to reports received downriver at the Central Station is ill. But this particular quest-narrative acquires general, parabolic, and mythical dimensions. Marlow's is a voyage of self-discovery: a voyage not to prove himself and so become a man, as, say, Jason does in Greek mythology, but, paralysingly, to know who he is, to truly understand the limitations of self.

Kurtz is a protean figure whose qualities seem to represent the apogee of civilized man: a journalist, a painter, "essentially a great musician" who would equally have been "a splendid leader of an extreme party" (153, 154), he is variously described by his peers as "a first-class agent" (69), "the best agent ... an exceptional man, of the greatest importance to the Company" (75), "a prodigy ... an emissary of pity, and science, and progress, and devil knows what else" (79), "a 'universal genius'" (83), and "a gifted creature" (113). His background and parentage are similarly extensive: "The original Kurtz had been educated partly in England, and – as he was good enough to say himself – his sympathies were in the right place. His mother was half-English, his father was half-French. All Europe contributed to the making of Kurtz" (117). But Kurtz's identification as a representative of civilized Western Europe has an important consequence: if he can "go wrong," then who, in Hamlet's words, "shall scape whipping?" (II.ii.525). The literal journey into the heart of the jungle to find Kurtz is, thus, simultaneously a metaphorical journey into the heart of man: confronting Kurtz's excesses is analogous to the revelation of the inexpungible capacity for evil that lurks repressed in human nature.

Marlow's river journey is a journey of disenchantment: the deeper he travels into the wilderness, the more disillusioned he becomes with the imperial process. Far from being the civilizing mission that involves "weaning those ignorant millions from their horrid ways" (59), as envisioned by his idealistic aunt fed on clichés, the European presence in Africa is demonstrably motivated by nothing finer than greed and characterised by brutality towards the Africans on whom the supply of ivory depends. Signalling the relativity of European values, the imported trappings of Western civilisation are shown to be inoperative once dislocated from their European context. At the first river station, for instance, Marlow finds "a boiler wallowing in the grass," "an undersized railway truck ... with its wheels in the air" that "looked as dead as the carcass of some animal," and "decaying machinery" (63–64). But these concrete images prefigure a more crippling redundancy: the moral values of the ironically named "pilgrims" are also discarded once displaced from their European context. While the image of, say, "undersized" railway trucks conveys the inefficiency of the colonists, it also conveys their inapplicability outside a European context. The cruelty meted out to the Africans extends this suggestion: European "civilized" behaviour, too, is a relative matter, and culturally untranslatable.

The consequences of this realisation are as unsettling as they are profound and provide the deepest "darkness" that Marlow discovers in "Heart of Darkness." If moral goodness is itself fragile and dependent upon the arbitrariness of circumstance, wherein lie the confirming associations with others on which civilized society depends? Furthermore, if contingency determines ethical practice, what are the implications for human self-conception? Confronting Kurtz's madness and megalomania, Marlow as interlocutor reflects upon the nature of "moral" action constrained by the threat of punishment and guaranteed by regulatory mechanisms:

> He had taken his seat among the high devils of the land – I mean literally. You can't understand. How could you? – with solid pavement under your feet, surrounded by kind neighbours ready to cheer you or to fall on you, stepping delicately between the butcher and the policeman, in the holy terror of scandal and gallows and lunatic asylums – how can you imagine what particular region of the first ages a man's untrammelled feet may take him into by the way of solitude – utter solitude without a policeman – by the way of silence – utter silence, where no warning voice of a kind neighbour can be heard whispering of public opinion? These little things make all the great difference. When they are gone you must fall back upon your own capacity for faithfulness. (116)

In "Heart of Darkness" moral values are shown to be relative rather than absolute.[1] Freed from the restraints of European society and driven by avarice, the colonists degenerate into unrestrained barbarity, leading Marlow to conclude that, at its most extreme, morality reduces to simple cowardice or hypocrisy – the fear of being found out and the consequent punishment – and that the belief in human development as progressively civilized is illusory.

As in "Youth," "Heart of Darkness" depicts an older, sadder, wiser, and – since, like Coleridge's Ancient Mariner, he is driven to re-tell his story – perhaps haunted Marlow looking back at incidents in his life. In both tales, he is presented as a figure of disillusion who yet harbours illusions. Instead of the consolations of the bottle as in "Youth," Marlow here retreats into Buddha-like silence – the novella concludes with him "in the pose of a meditating Buddha" (162) – but even this is ambiguous: is his withdrawal indifference or wisdom? The atrocity he witnesses in Africa leads Marlow to equate colonial reality with Dantean Hell. Slaves of an exploitation from which there is no escape, Africans are literally worked to death, reduced to "Black shapes ... clinging to the earth, half coming out, half effaced within the dim light, in all the attitudes of pain, abandonment, and despair" (66). Unsurprisingly, Marlow feels as if he has "stepped into the gloomy circle of some Inferno" (66). This lends an added dimension to his quest: is there any substance behind the idea of colonisation as a "civilizing mission," or is this idea merely a glib alibi for the uncivilized practice of the Europeans?

In the face of the brutality Marlow witnesses on his journey upriver, Kurtz comes to represent the last hope to redeem the imperial ideal. But this expectation is dashed when Kurtz is discovered to provide the ultimate expression of unrestrained brutality. Having assumed a god-like status among his followers, Kurtz ornaments his hut with the human skulls of his enemies. In a narrative that provides a rich thesaurus of symbols of inhumanity, Kurtz's actions extend to presiding "at certain midnight dances ending with unspeakable rites, which ... were offered up to him" (118). While the other Europeans whom Marlow meets in Africa are identified as mere functionaries of the Company, described in terms of their roles as "the Manager" or "the Accountant" for instance, Kurtz is dignified with a name, suggesting that one of the novella's unsettling themes is the incoherence of Western identity itself.

More than simply an exotic location to provide local colour or a locus for colonial excess, the wilderness offers a site of resistance and revenge, taking "a terrible vengeance for the fantastic invasion" (131). It visits illness upon the Europeans in "playful paw-strokes" (105) and transforms them into grotesque caricatures of their own obsessions. Kurtz, for instance, is transformed into "an animated image of death carved out of old ivory" (134). In response to Kurtz's assertion of ownership – " 'My Intended, my ivory, my station, my river, my –' everything belonged to him" – Marlow expects to hear "the wilderness burst into a prodigious peal of laughter that would shake the fixed stars in their places" (116). The African jungle adds the theme of revenge to such familiar standbys of adventure stories as deception, romance, and loot, while serving the broader relocation of the quest-motif by raising questions about the socio-psychological substratum out of which such colonisation sprang. As Marlow becomes increasingly wary of the rhetoric of civilization, so "Heart of Darkness" recasts the tale of imperial adventure in terms of a psychological quest in which the jungle, though it still retains the trope of "Darkest Africa" so central in late nineteenth-century exotic romance, helps to explicate the darkness within the European adventurer.

If the jungle helps to explain Kurtz to the reader by analogy, it also helps to explain Kurtz to himself: "I think it had whispered to him things about himself which he did not know, things of which he had no conception till he took counsel with this great solitude" (131). Kurtz's darkness is the darkness of moral vacancy rather than of evil. He is described as "hollow at the core" (131). This emptiness renders him susceptible to the influence of, and vampire-like possession by, the wilderness: "it had taken him, loved him, embraced him, got into his veins, consumed his flesh, and sealed his soul to its own by the inconceivable ceremonies of some devilish initiation. He was its spoiled and pampered favourite" (115). While Marlow's tale makes us re-see the world through analogy and metaphor, his is, of course, a European view of the jungle: one less interested in Africa and Africans than Kurtz and European identity. However, the fact that this European identity is both threatened and reformulated by contact with Africa recognises the necessity of including the story of the colonised in any grand narrative of colonialism.

Marlow recounts his African adventure to the anonymous frame-narrator, a Director of Companies, a Lawyer, and an Accountant – the same audience who had heard his tale in "Youth." Marlow thus tells his story of Belgian colonialism to an English audience, but its criticism also extends to British imperialism, although this criticism is often oblique and sometimes so implicit as to be evasive. As the Cambridge historian J. R. Seeley noted in 1884, Empire was "the great fact of modern English history" (1909: 16). The Director of Companies, Lawyer, and Accountant all have potential counterparts in the story: underscoring the material basis of the "civilizing mission" is the Accountant whom Marlow meets at the first river-station, keeping his books "in apple-pie order" (68) as a distraction from the brutality outside; the Lawyer is evoked in "all the legality of time contracts" (66) by which the unsuspecting

Africans are reduced to slaves of the Company; while the Director of Companies is evoked in the "impression of pale plumpness in a frock-coat. The great man himself" (56) who interviews Marlow at the Company's offices in the "sepulchral city" (152).

In this manner, the consoling distance between the frame and the narrative, between British and Belgian imperialism, is reduced to an unsettling similarity. That some of Marlow's audience probably fall asleep during his tale – "The others might have been asleep, but I was awake" (83) – only emphasises the reluctance of imperialism to recognise the dark truth about itself. (More subtly, as the disciples who fall asleep in the Garden of Gethsemane remind us, to be human is to be weak.) As Marlow says: "The conquest of the earth, which mostly means the taking it away from those who have a different complexion or slightly flatter noses than ourselves, is not a pretty thing when you look into it too much. What redeems it is the idea only" (51). The disjunction between the colonial ideal and colonialism in practice, between "philanthropic pretence" (78) and "imbecile rapacity" (76), provides Marlow with what he calls "a choice of nightmares" (138).

Marlow's tale is told aboard the *Nellie*, a cruising yawl moored at the mouth of the Thames, as the five men await the turning of the tide to set sail. Symbolically, this narrative of colonial conquest, which in the period equated with a nation's maritime power, occupies the space between flood and ebb tides. The silence that succeeds Marlow's tale is broken by the Director's seemingly incongruous observation: "We have lost the first of the ebb" (162). It seems appropriate that these men, linked by "the bond of the sea" (45), should miss the tide, for the Thames, initially portrayed in terms of its endless possibilities, "an interminable waterway" (45), now appears to lead only "into the heart of an immense darkness" (162).

The importance of the Thames to British imperialism, conjured up in the frame-narrator's Kiplingesque roll-call of the nation's adventurer-explorers and their ships, concludes with the observation:

> Hunters for gold or pursuers of fame, they all had gone out on that stream, bearing the sword, and often the torch, messengers of the might within the land, bearers of a spark from the sacred fire. What greatness had not floated on the ebb of that river into the mystery of an unknown earth! . . . The dreams of men, the seeds of commonwealths, the germs of empires.
>
> The sun set; the dusk fell on the stream, and lights began to appear along the shore.   (47)

Ominously here, the "sword" precedes the "torch," rendering ambiguous – like the "germs" which bear both disease and generation – the "greatness" of British expansion. Equally damning is the paragraph break where the proximity of "empires" to "The sun set" recalls and undermines the late-Victorian truism: "The sun never sets on the British Empire." The frame narration thus provides a national and patriotic context for the story to follow, but is simultaneously undermined by a more knowing, ironical perspective that prepares for Marlow, leading the reader towards the Marlow narrative in a manner already designed to question any simple certitude.

*   *   *

To Marlow, the upriver journey is "like travelling back to the earliest beginnings of the world" (92). But if he feels like a wanderer "on prehistoric earth," his destination is clear: for him, the steamboat "crawled towards Kurtz – exclusively" (95). The atavistic sense that Marlow has of the Africans as "prehistoric" seems disparaging and designed to confirm nineteenth-century racial theories about evolution that, at their crudest, lent support to the belief that certain races are destined to be subjugated by others. However, this belief is overturned through a "thrilling" identification:

> They howled and leaped, and spun, and made horrid faces; but what thrilled you was just the thought of their humanity – like yours – the thought of your remote kinship with this wild and passionate uproar. Ugly. Yes, it was ugly enough; but if you were man enough you would admit to yourself that there was in you just the faintest trace of a response to the terrible frankness of that noise, a dim suspicion of there being a meaning in it which you – you so remote from the night of first ages – could comprehend. (96)

*   *   *

"Heart of Darkness" daringly annihilates time and space. As the contemporary colonisers are seen as counterparts of the Romans in the story's prologue, and the Thames and Congo Rivers are seen as comparable, so the difference between the Africans and the Europeans is replaced – "if you were man enough" to admit it – by a fundamental "kinship." Yet significant differences remain. For example, the sterility of the European, given its most potent expression in the figure of Kurtz's Intended, whose fidelity to Kurtz reflects the faked authorisation of colonialism, is unfavourably contrasted with the "wild and passionate" vitality of the Africans.

Marlow's contradictory response to Africa – he is repelled and fascinated – is symptomatic of the novella's presentation of colonialism generally. For instance, Kurtz's outbursts are now self-indulgent, now self-loathing, while his African mistress inspires both desire and disgust. Described as "a wild and gorgeous apparition of a woman" (135), she is simultaneously real and unreal ("apparition") to Marlow. Adorned with ivory ornaments she adds an erotic dimension to the commodification of Africa while at the same time embodying and reflecting its essence: "the colossal body of the fecund and mysterious life seemed to look at her, pensive, as though it had been looking at the image of its own tenebrous and passionate soul" (136).

In order to address the issue of race and racism in "Heart of Darkness" the text needs to be placed within its own historical moment. To accuse as "racist" a text whose racial terms were the common, if demotic coin of its age, is wilfully to overlook any notion of social progress that expects the present to have learned from the past. Rather, it is necessary to consider the text in relation to contemporaneous attitudes and publications. An insight into the racial climate of the time is provided in a recent book entitled *Professional Savages: Captive Lives and Western Spectacle* (2004), in which Roslyn Poignant draws on documentary sources to describe how showmen like P. T. Barnum (1810–91) exhibited "ethnic strangers" for the entertainment of fee-paying European and American publics. "The Heart of Darkness" was published in the same year as Rudyard Kipling's "A Song of the White Man," which argues that it is "well for the world when the White Men drink / To the dawn of the White Man's day" and speaks of colonial expansion in terms of White Men going "to clean a land." By contrast, the condemnation of imperial exploitation in "Heart of Darkness" is bravely interrogative, and ideologically and culturally subversive.

Marlow's narrative clearly subverts the colonial distinction between Europeans and Africans by reducing the civilized–savage opposition to a fundamental similarity that renders the distinction redundant. Similarly, "civilized" traits such as the Victorian work ethic are recast as non-European, while the moral codes upon which

European society rests are shown to be, at best, illusory. Against this could be set the stark representation of Africans as wild, superstitious, and primitive. It clearly falls to Marlow both to transcend his age through criticism and at the same time represent its views, hence his status as implicated outsider in the Congo. (His own journey, and that of the narrative, replicates Kurtz's "invasion" of Africa, albeit in a minor key.) Here is his description of "the savage who was fireman" aboard the steamboat:

> He was an improved specimen; he could fire up a vertical boiler. He was there below me, and, upon my word, to look at him was as edifying as seeing a dog in a parody of breeches and a feather hat, walking on his hind-legs. A few months of training had done for that really fine chap. He squinted at the steam-gauge and at the water-gauge with an evident effort of intrepidity – and he had filed teeth, too, the poor devil, and the wool on his pate shaved into queer patterns, and three ornamental scars on each of his cheeks. He ought to have been clapping his hands and stamping his feet on the bank, instead of which he was hard at work, a thrall to strange witchcraft, full of improving knowledge.   (97)

The passage is condescending, paternalistic, and resonates with ethnocentric clichés, yet it consistently upsets our expectations through qualifications and tonal shifts that undermine the proclaimed "improvement" worked by European contact, despite the scientific register ("specimen") and the appeal to Western knowledge and mechanisation. Marlow's racist canine comparison seems designed to echo Samuel Johnson's equally contentious reference to women preachers: "A woman's preaching is like a dog's walking on his hinder legs. It is not done well; but you are surprised to find it done at all" (Boswell 1791; 1924; 285). Cultural and gendered "othering" resort to comparably crude codes of diminution. Whether or not Conrad had Johnson in mind, the degeneration of Kurtz into madness certainly poses a challenge to European aspirations to rationalism, a tradition towards which Johnson contributes in no small measure.

Even Marlow's claim that the fireman has been diminished by contact with Europeans is double-edged. Couched in the language of morality – "He *ought* to have been" – it nonetheless rests on a traditional assumption: that culture is what separates humans from nature. A more analytical approach recognises the culture of a society as the product of learned behaviour passed down across the generations. Marlow's sympathy for the Africans exists at the expense of this insight. Furthermore, if the "strange witch-craft" of machinery in the above passage conveys something of Marlow's expectations of African understanding – also perceived, for instance, in his speculation that the "bit of white worsted" worn by one of the Africans in the Grove of Death as "an ornament – a charm – a propitiatory act" (67), or indeed their veneration of Kurtz, whom the pilgrims also regard with awe – then the interpret-ation of the gauges as "witchcraft" equally subverts the great West-ern panjandrum of science as a secular Victorian substitute religion, a "fetish" of the age, as Conrad calls it in *The Secret Agent* (31).

* * *

Marlow's mission to rescue Kurtz is unsuccessful: Kurtz is found, but he dies on the journey down river, to be buried (with thematic and symmetrical appropriateness) "in the mould of primeval earth" (147). Instead of returning with Kurtz, Marlow returns with his papers and with destabilizing knowledge of human nature that robs him of his naïve faith in society – whose knowledge of life now seems to him "an irritating pretence" (152) – and relativizes his own moral behaviour, to the point where he can be seen as the victim of a contradiction he doesn't acknowledge. Having asserted earlier, "I hate, detest, and can't bear a lie" (82), his narrative ends with him lying to Kurtz's Intended, allowing her to believe that Kurtz's last words were her name. Consolatory and perhaps patronising as this lie seems, it adds a private dimension to the political delusion about itself that Europe continues to harbour – in the face of which, one suspects, Marlow's truthful account of his experience would appear, like the invasion of the jungle itself, "fantastic." In the moral universe of "Heart of Darkness," it is egoism rather than altruism that motivates human behaviour, and the alienation that Marlow experiences confirms one of the novella's starkest pronouncements: "We live, as we dream – alone" (82).

Although his presence dominates Marlow's narrative, Kurtz is only actually present for less than twenty of the novella's pages. One implication of this is to reduce Kurtz to less a character than an incarnation of the quality of evil, although the word "evil" is not used in the narrative. Typical of Conrad's fictions is their fascin-ation with how man copes, or fails to cope, *in extremis*. Through Kurtz, "Heart of Darkness" demonstrates that evil is human in ori-gin and beggars explanation. Whereas tragedy offers some moral consolation in the revelation of an underlying logic to death or suffering, this narrative offers no such comfort. To the Africans, evil strikes without warning and has its origins in the psychological makeup of the invaders.

The lengthy withholding of Kurtz and the horrors associated with his reign means that the reader of "Heart of Darkness" is made to share Marlow's increasing sense of unease. In this manner, the interplay between structure and subject matter influences the dynamic between the reader and Marlow. In his tale of the Roman commander, Marlow identifies the "fascination" that "goes to work on him" as the "fascination of the abomination" (50). This combination of fascination and repulsion also impinges upon Marlow's narrative technique. Elliptical and evasive, Marlow's narrative seems motivated by a reluctance to confront the dark truths it contains.

However far "utter solitude" and "utter silence" (116) may go towards explaining his actions, Kurtz's brutality and rapacity demolish any lingering faith that Marlow has in colonialism as a civilizing enterprise. So wherein does Kurtz's greatness for Marlow rest? To answer this we need to address his final words: "The horror! The horror!" (149). This famous valediction, distinctly un-English verbally, is capable of myriad interpretations. It might, for instance, simply provide a comment upon Africa and the Africans. After all, it resonates with the desire to "Exterminate all the brutes!" (118), the words of that "valuable postscriptum" Kurtz adds to his report for the "future guidance" of the International Society for the Suppression of Savage Customs (117). However, given the dramatic significance of the phrase – it haunts Marlow during his conversation with the Intended – more seems to be intended.

A second, and deeper, interpretation is that Kurtz's final words testify to the fact that, at the bottom of his soul, is something recognisably horrific. According to Marlow, "his soul was mad. Being alone in the wilderness, it had looked within itself, and, by heavens! I tell you, it had gone mad" (145). The problem with this reading is that the phase states the obvious (although it has not been obvious before that Kurtz can recognise and judge his own part in the debacle); and since the manifestations of this human capacity are everywhere, there is really no need to spell it out. Rather, we need to look to a third interpretation: that "The horror! The horror!" constitutes a moral judgement. Not only does Marlow claim that

98   JOSEPH CONRAD

Kurtz "had summed up – he had judged. 'The horror!'" (151), but he
also views this summing-up as "an affirmation, a moral victory paid
for by innumerable defeats, by abominable terrors, by abominable
satisfactions" (151). In other words, in the depths of his degradation,
Kurtz has preserved a sense of moral judgement, thereby ensuring
Marlow's loyalty: "But it was a victory! That is why I have remained
loyal to Kurtz to the last, and even beyond" (151). Behind this judgement there seems to be an almost Jansenist conception of the primacy
of evil, and the implication that the "criminal" hero discovers in the
ultimacy of evil redemptive possibilities not open to average pilgrims
of the world, like Marlow who can't follow Kurtz "over the threshold
of the invisible" (151).

Thus, paradoxically, Marlow becomes another of Kurtz's "disciples." However shocking and unpalatable are the vitiating
excesses that Kurtz embodies, what he reveals about the dark truth
of human potential provides Marlow's quest with its goal. That
this insight about human nature erodes Marlow's faith in society
upon his return to Europe forms part of the interplay between the
individual and the group in the novella, to which the communal act
of story-telling contributes. Kurtz confirms something unacknowledged at the heart of the society he has simultaneously represented
and abandoned. Released from social constraints, Kurtz's individualism has been allowed unrestrained and free play. But while this
individual experience can be turned into an encapsulation of the
collective experience, it challenges the cohesiveness and constitu-
tion of society. As Marlow's feeling of alienation demonstrates,
once such truths about human nature are realised, there can be no
homecoming. In the words of T. S. Eliot: "After such knowledge,
what forgiveness?" ("Gerontion").

Lord Jim

Upon its publication in 1900, *Lord Jim* was described as "a book
to make the world wider and deeper" (Sherry, ed., 1973: 113), and
ever since has maintained its high place in the reading public's affec-
tions. On publication, the novel earned comparisons with Henry
James, one critic claiming: "If Mr. Henry James had a consum-
mate knowledge of life at sea and in the Pacific Coast towns and
settlements, he would write a novel very like *Lord Jim*" (Sherry,
ed., 1973: 126). Responding to contemporary reviews, Conrad
declared himself "the spoiled child of the critics" (*CL2*: 313). To

Albert J. Guerard, the secret of the novel's "universality" lies in human fallibility, "since nearly everyone has jumped off some *Patna* and most of us have been compelled to live on, desperately or quietly engaged in reconciling what we are with what we would like to be" (1958: 127).

Building upon the early discoveries of Norman Sherry in *Conrad's Eastern World* (1966), researchers have convincingly established a number of prototypes for the incidents and characters that contribute to *Lord Jim*. Chief among these is the infamous *Jeddah* affair of 1880. This Singapore-based steamship plied her trade carrying Muslim pilgrims bound for Mecca for the hajj from her home port to Jeddah. On 8 August 1880, carrying over nine hundred pilgrims, and having developed boiler-trouble and begun to leak, she was abandoned by her European officers, who were picked up and taken to Aden, where, on 10 August, they reported her lost with all passengers. Notoriety could hardly wait to get at Captain Clark and his officers: the following day, the *Jeddah* was towed into Aden with the pilgrims on board, having been discovered foundering off Cape Guardafui by the S. S. *Antenor*.

The maritime scandal that ensued echoed from London, where it occasioned a question in the House of Commons, to Singapore, where it was the subject of an official inquiry. Two comments from the pages of the daily press will serve to illustrate the public outrage – and, by implication, the degree to which Conrad's novel responds to it. *The Times* of 12 August 1880 reminded its readers of maritime professionalism: "to the honour of sailors, nothing is more rare than that, in a disaster at sea, the captain and the principal officers of the vessel should be the chief or the sole survivors"; while the *Daily Chronicle* of the same day gave the incident a national inflection: "We sincerely trust that no Englishman was amongst the boatload of cowards who left the *Jeddah* and her thousand passengers to shift for themselves" (Sherry, 1971: 321, 322). The *Jeddah* incident provides the basis for the fictional tale of the *Patna* in *Lord Jim*, which unites such concerns as professional seamanship with the gentlemanly code of honour in the figure of the *Patna*'s first mate, Jim.

Aesthetically, a work of fiction cannot be reduced to and judged on its sources, yet, as Berthoud argues, "to disregard the world out of which linguistic art emerges ... is to run the risk of receiving it in impoverished terms" (1992: 244). Awareness of the factual basis for *Lord Jim* involves recognition of the degree to which Conrad historicizes and politicises the sea and British imperialism in the novel, and thus the degree to which the novel both reflects and critiques its age.

* * *

Serving in the British merchant marine, Conrad was part of the great trading network that assimilated remote areas of the world into the British economy. Set in the colonial world, *Lord Jim* was published at a moment when the Boer War and increasing international competition on the seas, particularly from America and Germany, raised doubts about the sustainability of Empire. Conrad may have chosen to redraw the *Jeddah*'s English captain as a "New South Wales German," and so provide a national counterpoint to Stein in this elegantly structured novel, but his subject is Jim, the *Patna*'s first mate, an Englishman, and in Marlow's repeated phrase "one of us" – that is, according to a contemporary reviewer: "an Englishman and a gentleman" (Sherry, ed., 1973: 121). Seen in this light, the protocols of professional and social inclusion examined in *Lord Jim*, through the respective subjects of maritime conduct and the English gentleman-adventurer, are freighted with political and personal anxieties.

The cast of characters in *Lord Jim* is truly multinational. The European characters surrounding Jim are drawn from and reflect a remarkably wide range of nationalities. For instance, besides the various Englishmen, whose number includes Jim, Marlow, Brierly, Brown, Denver, and Bob Stanton, there are the Scots Alexander M'Neil and the captain under whom Jim serves when disabled by a falling spar, the French Lieutenant, the Germans Stein and, by way of national contrast, the "renegade" (14) captain of the *Patna*, the Scandinavian Egström, the Swiss Siegmund Yucker, the (probably) Italian Mariani, the Danish lieutenant, the Alsatian Schomberg, the (probably) Dutch De Jongh, and the Malacca Portuguese Cornelius. While this cast-list conveys the historical fact of European presence in the region, it also ensures that, to adapt Marlow's comment upon Kurtz in "Heart of Darkness" (117), all Europe contributes to the making of Jim.

Equally important is the cast of non-Europeans who are grouped around Jim and who also, whether by complement or contrast, add to our perception of him. Indeed, since Jim regains his self-respect through the trust of Patusan's inhabitants, they are integral to his identity – although post-colonial critics would point out that the natives have an integrity of their own that is not always acknowledged by the narcissistic Jim. Representatives of the non-European world include Chester, a West Australian; Brown's Solomon Islander and American; and the host of characters who reflect a rich racial and cultural mix, among them: Chinese; Javanese; the Arab pilgrims; a cast of Malays that embraces the helmsman on the *Patna* and Rajah Allang, Sherif Ali, and their followers; and Doramin and his Bugis, immigrants to Patusan from Celebes. As Marlow claims: "The thing was always with me, I was always eager to take opinion on it, as though it had not been practically settled: individual opinion – international opinion – by Jove!" (159).

The international scope of *Lord Jim* is everywhere – often present in the hybrid form of the half-caste, such as the brigantine captain – and resulting in complex cultural configurations: Gentleman Brown's Solomon Islander has deserted from a Yankee ship; Brown's French schooner is captured by a Spanish patrol cutter and taken into a Philippine bay; Stein & Co. trade in Patusan, thanks to a permit from the Dutch authorities; the *Patna* is Chinese owned, Arab chartered, skippered by a German, plies her trade between Singapore and Jeddah, and, after the collision, is rescued by a French gunboat and towed to the British port of Aden. Although unmentioned by name, scenes also occur in India and Penang. In this manner *Lord Jim* transcends the specific context of Eurocentric values during the age of Empire to engage with the wider cultural dialogues from which they emerged.

* * *

The novel's epigraph is a slight rewording of an aphorism by Novalis, the pen name of the German Romantic author Friedrich von Hardenberg (1772–1801): "It is certain my conviction gains infinitely the moment another soul will believe in it." This introduces the important themes of communication and community that shape the narrative. Jim's impulse to confess to Marlow – "You don't know what it is for a fellow in my position to be believed – make a clean breast of it to an elder man" (128) – is replicated in

Marlow's willingness to recount the tale to his after-dinner audience: "I am telling you so much about my own instinctive feelings and bemused reflections because there remains so little to be told of him. He existed for me, and after all it is only through me that he exists for you. I've led him out by the hand; I have paraded him before you" (224).

Recounted by a frame-narrator, the first four chapters of *Lord Jim* offer a selective synopsis of Jim's life up to the period of his success on Patusan. The fact that this summary omits the tale's conclusion – the invasion of Patusan by another European, Gentleman Brown, and his desperados – is, on the one hand, a result of the story's expansion into a full-length novel, but it also playfully suggests that the omniscient "frame" cannot contain the whole story, reminding one of Samuel Beckett's claim about Proust's *Remembrance of Things Past*: "The whisky bears a grudge against the decanter" (1965: 21–22). In a sense, this cannot be otherwise, for *Lord Jim* is, in effect, two stories: one tells of Jim's private attempt "to save from the fire his idea of what his moral identity should be" (81) and the other of Marlow's social need to affirm "the sovereign power enthroned in a fixed standard of conduct" (50). This dualism persists in the broader outline of *Lord Jim* that, as the reader discovers, is, generically, two novels: the *Patna*-sequence offers a psychologically intense Modernist narrative about the nature of self while the Patusan-sequence is more akin to a reworking of exotic romance.

Professing himself "always eager to take opinion" (159) on Jim's story, Marlow's narrative includes encounters with a host of characters, including Captain Brierly, the French Lieutenant, and Stein, each of whom contributes to and complicates his understanding of Jim. The shape of the novel complements the dilemmas posed by Jim's story: is the "self" public or private property, and is the story concerned with interior disgrace or public shame? Marlow's role as narrator is thus linked to the possibilities of understanding another individual. Coexistent with the social act of storytelling, whereby Marlow seeks to reclaim and reaffirm Jim as "one of us," is Jim's individual sense of himself, as measured by his personal ideals.

* * *

Lord Jim is famously divided into two "halves," that of the *Patna*, in which he transgresses the professional code of seamanship and undermines his conception of himself as honourable, and that of

Patusan, where he directs the affairs of a native state and regains a sense of self-worth. This comparative construction is sustained through a network of analogies and dramatised inlays that blur generic boundaries (between psychological and imperial adventure tales) as Jim's failure in the *Patna* sequence prefaces his success in Patusan, including his romance with Jewel. The resulting hybrid narrative engages, often problematically, with the tradition of the novel as *Bildungsroman* as Jim attempts to reconstitute his lost sense of honour. Conrad described "The division of the book into two parts" as its "plague spot" (*CL2*: 302). With the benefit of hindsight, however, this bifurcation reveals Conrad's sensitivity to both the ideological spirit of his age – *Lord Jim* shares its year of publication with Sigmund Freud's *The Interpretation of Dreams* – and the practicalities of a marketplace in which exotic literature reflected the new imperialism. As the critic, Andrew Lang, remarked in 1891: "people have become alive to the strangeness and fascination of the world beyond the bounds of Europe and the United States" (Kucich, 2003: 3).

The novel's title combines an honorific with a diminutive. "Jim" gains by association, while "Lord" is familiarly reduced. Furthermore, the honorific is a translation of a Malay term of deference: "They called him Tuan Jim: as one might say – Lord Jim" (5). In this manner different cultural perceptions of Jim coexist: his status as a gentleman, inspired by a code of honour and realised in his status as a naval officer, exists alongside an aristocracy of colour. In his "Author's Note," Conrad identifies the subject of the novel as "the acute consciousness of lost honour" (ix). The Lord/Tuan translation implicitly questions whether honour lost in one "world," that of the *Patna*, can indeed be redeemed in another, that of Patusan.

Jim's dereliction of duty in the *Patna* is also formulated in terms of gentlemanly conduct by the ensuing Court of Inquiry. According to one of the judges, Captain Brierly, Jim has failed to "preserve professional decency" (68). Marlow's interest in Jim's case stems from the broader challenge it poses to the tacit gentlemanly agreement, the code of "decency," that binds the profession: "I thought to myself – well, if this sort can go wrong like that..." (40). As Dickens' *Great Expectations* (1860–61) demonstrates, the status of a gentleman, together with the porousness of the British class-system, increasingly exercised nineteenth-century authors. Set in the masculine realm of the merchant marine and colonial adventure,

Lord Jim provides a study of an officer who has failed to behave like a gentleman – and, in consequence, called into question "the honour of the craft" (46).

The old saw connecting "an officer and a gentleman" takes on various guises in *Lord Jim*, with Jim being accused by the *Patna*'s crew of thinking himself "too much of a bloomin' gentleman" (117) to lend a hand during the desertion of the ship. Jim confesses to Marlow during their conversation at the Malabar House: "Of course I wouldn't have talked to you about all this if you had not been a gentleman. I ought to have known . . . I am – I am – a gentleman, too" (131), to which Marlow's reaction is: "'Yes, yes,' I said hastily" (131). The mirroring identification Marlow seeks in his "younger self" thus extends to their shared status as gentlemen, whose definition is intimately linked to social comportment.

Jim's leap from the *Patna* alienates him from both marine and domestic traditions. Following the trial, his rootlessness dramatises this double detachment. Described by the frame-narrator as "a seaman in exile from the sea" (4), Jim's "exile" extends beyond his profession to his personal life. Professionally, the price of Jim's crime is to have his certificate cancelled by the Court of Inquiry; privately it severs his ties with home. He is the son of a parson whose church "had stood there for centuries" and whose "living had belonged to the family for generations" (5). As Jim tells Marlow, his father "has seen it all in the home papers by this time . . . I can never face the poor old chap" (79). In this context, Marlow's paean to England and home, that "reward" that can only be touched "with clean hands, lest it turn to dead leaves, to thorns, in your grasp" (222), serves as a reminder of what Jim has lost. For his part, Jim remains haunted by what he has lost, whether taunting Marlow "all the same, you wouldn't like to have me aboard your own ship – hey?" (306) or struggling to communicate with the outside world: " 'Tell them . . . ' he began" (335). To Marlow, this residual commitment to spheres of influence from which his actions have alienated him demonstrates Jim's worth: "in virtue of his feeling he mattered" (222).

It is, moreover, this "feeling" – and Marlow also says: "those who do not feel do not count" (222) – that ensures the narrative's dual focus whereby Jim's actions in the present are continuous and contiguous with those in his past, and the codes by which he is ostracised from the group remain those to which he adheres. As the broad division of *Lord Jim* into the *Patna* and Patusan sequences suggests, the novel relies upon the art of juxtaposition to achieve this dualism, while Jim's proclaimed need to "feel – every day, every time I open my eyes – that I am trusted" (247) preserves, in the form of a palimpsest, traces of the *Patna* incident that led to his exile in Patusan.

Relational logic is a key concern of the Marlow narrative in particular, and of Modernist aesthetics, in general. In Cubist art, for instance, the subject is simultaneously fragmented (analysed) and synthesised (reconstructed), with the result that discontinuity becomes as important as continuity. The formal fragmentation and disrupted chronology of Marlow's narrative emphasises impressionism and subjectivity, ensuring that connections between present and past multiply in unexpected ways as the tale unfolds. His account of Jim takes the form of a collage that deliberately disturbs the reader's perspective. Interpolating the account of Jim's trial with their conversation at the Malabar House, for instance, entangles objective fact and subjective impression: what is foreground, and what background? A consequence of such construction is that the objective case against Jim is presented alongside his emotional understanding of the incident and Marlow's professional, but increasingly sympathetic, interest.

For example, the evidence presented to the Court of Inquiry by the Malay helmsman, "this extraordinary and damning witness," although described as "*the* sensation of the second day's proceedings" (99), is compressed into less than a page of text and framed between Marlow's confession ("Frankly, had I been there, I would not have given as much as a counterfeit farthing for the ship's chance to keep above water to the end of each successive second" [97]), and the persuasive contrast between Jim's apparent willingness "to sink with the ship ... stiffened in the idea of some sort of heroic discretion" (99) and the frenetic attempts of the rest of the crew to desert.

The picture of Jim that Marlow presents emerges through a succession of encounters, with characters as diverse as the French Lieutenant, who avers that "Man is born a coward" (147), Chester, to whom Jim is "no good" (166), and Stein, whose diagnosis is: "He is romantic" (212). Apart from Stein, who Marlow actively seeks out, each of these encounters occurs by chance. By implication, the impression of Jim would be subtly altered were Marlow to happen upon someone else connected with the *Patna* affair. Similarly, the tale we receive is one of many such tellings: "many times, in distant parts of the world, Marlow showed himself willing to remember Jim" (33). Crafted from a mass of recollected and rearranged material into a form, the narrative of Jim's identity emerges as the result of contingency, emphasising the impossibility of final knowledge about him and, more generally, the elusiveness, multiplicity, and contradictoriness of human nature.

In essence, Jim's crisis stems from his inability to reconcile his imaginative vision of the world, "his adventurous fancy" (151), with brute reality. His idealised vision of himself, "always an example of devotion to duty, and as unflinching as a hero in a book" (6), is shattered when the *Patna* strikes an unidentified object – probably a submerged wreck – in the sea. Convinced that she is sinking, Jim's will to survive overcomes his self-ideal and he joins the rest of the feckless European crew in jumping ship, abandoning the pilgrims to their fate.

To Marlow, Jim is "protected by his isolation, alone of his own superior kind, in close touch with Nature, that keeps faith on such easy terms with her lovers" (176). And, despite his insistence upon Jim as representative – "He stood there for all the parentage of his kind" (43) – Marlow concludes to the Privileged Man that "of all mankind Jim had no dealings but with himself" (339). Significantly, when Jim rescues his sense of self it is in Patusan, where he sees himself as "alone of his kind" (254).

Jim's leap from the *Patna* can be construed as a leap out of the idealised world of the subjective imagination and into the world of objective fact. Marlow's sympathetic identification with Jim ensures that the facts of the Inquiry are mediated through a growing awareness of Jim's romantic nature, and thus that the social codes by which he is judged as a sailor are revealed alongside an understanding of his private self. However, while this ensures that the report of what Jim did is palliated by the account of what Jim felt, Marlow is, first and foremost, a merchant seaman, with a vested interest in defending the "honour of the craft" (46), admitting: "Perhaps, unconsciously, I hoped I would find that something, some profound and redeeming cause, some merciful explanation, some convincing shadow of an excuse" (50).

This sensitivity to Jim's public and private selves directs his actions. Recognising that Jim requires more than "merely opportunities to earn his bread" (202) that he can provide, Marlow consults Stein, whose decision to send Jim to Patusan provides an alternative opportunity, to "Slam the door" (235) on his past and reassert the claims of his romantic temperament: "He left his earthly failings behind him and that sort of reputation he had, and there was a totally new set of conditions for his imaginative faculty to work on" (218). It is thus inevitable that the psychological intensity of the novel's first half should diminish here, since the social implications of Jim's actions, formulated in such comments as Marlow's claim that "We exist only in so far as we hang together" (223), have been construed within an objective code of conduct, here configured as maritime tradition. In this light, at least, the appearance of Gentleman Brown and his desperados in Patusan is a structural necessity: their invasion realigns Jim with social tradition by forcing the imaginative and real worlds into contiguity.

According to Marlow, "The real significance of crime is in its being a breach of faith with the community of mankind" (157). But complicating the perception of "crime" is the French Lieutenant's judgement that "one is no cleverer than the next man – and no more brave" (146). As Marlow recognises, this locates the sphere of moral action in a world of accident. When he puts this point to the French Lieutenant – "but couldn't it reduce itself to not being found out?"– the latter declares it "too fine for me" (149).

* * *

In *Lord Jim*, human frailty is intimately linked to chance. This is reinforced by the narrative's emphasis upon contingency: Marlow meets the former *Avondale* officer "by the merest chance" (137); when the second engineer turns up at Denver's, it is "One chance in a hundred!" (189); the final part of the tale stems from Marlow discovering Brown "most unexpectedly" (344); and "luck" (357) brings Brown to Patusan. Such incidents complement the central "accident" of the *Patna* herself, an incident "rare enough to resemble a special arrangement of a malevolent providence" (159). Jim's *Patna* ordeal thus poses a moral test determined by factors that are seemingly beyond his control. How then can he be said to be morally responsible? To Thomas Nagel such actions constitute moral luck: "Where a significant aspect of what someone does depends on factors beyond his control, yet we continue to treat him in that respect as an object of moral judgement, it can be called moral luck" (1979: 26). Deserting the *Patna*, Jim is removed from the world of idealised imagination and cast headlong into the world of actions for which he will be judged and yet that are themselves contingent upon chance.

While it is true to say, as Nagel does, that "We judge people for what they actually do or fail to do, not just for what they would have done if circumstances had been different" (1979: 34), the paradoxical nature of moral luck renders understandable Jim's interpretation of the judgement of the Court: "he made so much of his disgrace while it is the guilt alone that matters" (177). Recasting objective transgression (guilt) as subjective failure (disgrace), Jim eschews the moral relativism of the Court of Inquiry in favour of "the impossible world of romantic achievements" (83).

The degree to which the "fanciful realm of recklessly heroic aspirations" (83) is divorced from the reality of abandoning "eight hundred pilgrims (more or less)" (14) can be measured in Jim's egotistical and morally inadequate response to his crime: "'Ah! What a chance missed! My God! What a chance missed!' he blazed out" (83). And yet, while Stein's decision to send Jim to Patusan certainly provides "another sort of reality" (230), it does not remove Jim from the social codes by which he has been judged and found wanting. Instead, his actions in Patusan adhere to the tradition of chivalry that underpins the "professional decency" (68) to which Brierly appeals. The qualities of the ideal knight are well known: he was brave, loyal, true to his word, courteous, and merciful. Death was preferable to dishonour. *Mutatis mutandis*, these are the same qualities that Jim exhibits in Patusan.

Jim stands at the point of intersection between two mutually defining codes of conduct: personal honour and public duty. The issue of lost honour that provides a mainspring of the plot is consequent upon Jim's feeling of disgrace at having betrayed a code of behaviour in which he continues to believe – a different thing from the guilt at failing in his professional duty, for which he is duly punished by having his certificate cancelled.

* * *

The Stein interview occupies a pivotal place in the narrative of *Lord Jim*, between the *Patna* and Patusan sequences. Fittingly, and as his own history confirms, Stein has succeeded in uniting the claims of the romantic temperament to those of heroic action. The French Lieutenant is concerned with the realm of action – "And so that poor young man ran away along with the others" (145) – but can offer no solution to the problem of lost honour: "What life may be worth when ... when the honour is gone – *ah ça! par exemple* – I can offer no opinion. I can offer no opinion – because – monsieur – I know nothing of it" (148). To the pragmatic Chester, the solution is obvious: because Jim takes "to heart" his failure, "he's no good" (161). Chester therefore proposes that Jim manage a waterless guano island in the Walpole Reefs, starkly confirming the public perception of Jim's public worth in the wake of his trial. But, to Marlow, "in virtue of his feelings [Jim] mattered" (222).

Stein is an entomologist, whose trading history in the Archipelago combines exotic adventure and romance. He thus brings to Jim's "case" the combined authority of natural science and romantic achievement. Through him the moral problem of Jim's actions acquire a philosophical dimension as the focus shifts from what Jim did to who Jim is. His pronouncement on Jim's case is gnomic and oracular:

> A man that is born falls into a dream like a man who falls into the sea. If he tries to climb out into the air as inexperienced people endeavour to do, he drowns – *nicht war?* ... No! I tell you! The way is to the destructive element submit yourself, and with the exertions of your hands and feet in the water make the deep, deep sea keep you up.   (214)

Jim's temperament, his "destructive element," is romantic, which Stein paradoxically acknowledges to be "very bad – very bad.... Very good, too" (216). Unlike Marlow, whose practical assistance subordinates this romanticism within the sphere of day-to-day living, Stein's solution is to give free play to Jim's romanticism. Fittingly, the analogy that Stein employs to describe Jim's romantic nature recalls the claim of the frame-narrator: "he was a seaman in exile from the sea" (1). This "exile" is ended in Patusan, simultaneously an image of and a locus for the romantic imagination, and where, until the arrival of Gentleman Brown, Jim is exiled from the outside world.

The degree to which Stein's perception informs the narrative can be measured in the transformation of Marlow's attitude towards Jim. His initial view is voiced in the first chapter of his narration, where he sees Jim as "outwardly so typical of that good, stupid kind we like to feel marching right and left of us in life" (44). That this is the prevailing opinion is proved when he summarises the views of the Privileged Man in the narrative's final movement: "we must fight in the ranks or our lives don't count" (339). But, now possessed of the end of Jim's story, Marlow proceeds to counter:

"The point, however, is that of all mankind Jim had no dealings but with himself, and the question is whether at the last he had not confessed to a faith mightier than the laws of order and progress" (339). In other words, Stein's experiment reorients Marlow's view of Jim – he is no longer a type but an individual – and in the process questions how far an individual can be made to carry collective significance. As Stein's collection of beetles and butterflies remind us, the natural sciences look to contrast and sequence for their taxonomy, and, as he demonstrates when describing his own "rare specimen" (208) to Marlow, that beauty is found in the individual specimen as much as in its relation to the rest of the species.

* * *

Patusan offers a site of Western imperial fantasy, complete with the European gentleman-adventurer winning the trust of the natives, instituting a system of government, and, indulging in an exotic romance. It is less historical fact (although, as ever in Conrad, rooted in geographical and historical realities, specifically the reign of Rajah Brooke in Sarawak) than a country of the literary imagination. As Marlow says: "three hundred miles beyond the end of telegraph cables and mail-boat lines, the haggard utilitarian lies of our civilization wither and die, to be replaced by pure exercises of imagination" (282). Readers who consider *Lord Jim* a flawed masterpiece point to the diminution of psychological intensity after the *Patna* narrative. One reason for this must be that, for the most part, the Patusan sequence self-consciously replicates the stereotypical and formulaic representation of exotic space in colonial fiction, where the European succeeds to "greatness as genuine as any man ever achieved" (244). However, this representation fails to account for Conrad's sheer audacity in *Lord Jim* in forcing the colonial narrative to encounter alien ways of thinking that undermine its assumptions and threaten its coherence.

Patusan provides Jim with the refuge he seeks: "Once he got in, it would be for the outside world as though he had never existed" (232). Both a refuge from and a counterbalance to the world of the *Patna*, Patusan is repeatedly described as hermetically isolated from the outside world, bearing out Marlow's claim: "to Jim's successes there were no externals" (226). According to the master of the brigantine in which Jim sails, Patusan town is "situated internally" (240). The very blossoms seem "not grown in this world" (322), and the inhabitants "exist as if under an enchanter's wand" (330). On his departure, Marlow declares: "I had turned away from the picture and was going back to the world where events move, men change, light flickers, life flows in a clear stream, no matter whether over mud or over stones" (330). Even the spectral, moonlit settings in the Patusan scenes suggest less an actual place than a realm whose topography charts contours of the romantic imagination.

Thus, while the pursuit of honour through heroic action remains a motivating force, the question of causal relationship between the worlds of the *Patna* and Patusan persists. Put simply, how much weight does the reparation Jim makes for lost honour in Patusan carry in the world of the Court of Inquiry that has judged Jim and found him wanting? The suggestion that Jim has escaped from reality into a symbolic world even threatens the logic of colonial adventure to which his Patusan adventure belongs.

Despite – or perhaps because of – remaining "one of us," in Patusan Jim prevails militarily, administratively, socially, and romantically. He redeems himself, in his own eyes, through success-ful action that brings peace to the region, and with more than a hint at the tradition of chivalry, rescues Jewel, the damsel in distress, from the clutches of her step-father, Cornelius. In keeping with this idealised portrait, the "moral effect of his victory in war" (269) over Sherif Ali is stressed while the human cost, "the half-consumed corpses" (271), is glossed over. In contrast to the myopic Euro-centrism of colonial fiction, this novel creates a demand for Brown through whose "demonstration of some obscure and awful attrib-ute of our nature" (404) the unforeseen consequences of action once again bedevil Jim's fate.

* * *

If Jim has brought peace and prosperity to Patusan, the arrival of Gentleman Brown – significantly while Jim is away in the Interior (361) – exposes the essential fragility of this apparent stability. For instance, the Rajah's confidant, Kassim, quickly opens negotiations with the invaders, implying that Jim has interrupted rather than resolved the local struggle for political dominance. Similarly, while Jim's influence had been sufficient to deflect the Bugis from "pay-ing off old scores" (273) after the defeat of Sherif Ali, who is to prevent the Rajah seeking revenge following Jim's death? That such questions remain points to the transient nature of colonial influence – and hence serve to unsettle claims of beneficial European interference.

In terms of the plot, Gentleman Brown's arrival in Patusan is the beginning of the end of Jim's benign paternalism. It also reasserts the claims of the outside world, rescuing the narrative for realism. The reputed "son of a baronet" (352) but described as a "blind accomplice of the Dark Powers" (354), Brown has his place within the chivalric scheme of *Lord Jim*. Their honorific titles seem designed to allegorise the contest between Jim and Brown. But where Jim's conception of honour is sustained by clichés of the gentleman-imperialist, Patusan is simply a source of plunder to Brown. His is also an aristocracy of colour and race, as when he seeks identification with Jim: "You have been white once, for all your talk of this being your own people and you being one with them" (381).

Brown's invasion is a mistake, as he quickly realises. Finding himself surrounded and hopelessly outnumbered, Brown agrees to Jim's demand to leave Patusan. Himself the recipient of charity, Jim extends the same to Brown and his men by promising them a safe passage. The ensuing massacre of Doramin's son, Dain Waris, and his men is a vengeful act of spite. It makes Jim's position in Patusan untenable, especially as he proclaimed himself "responsible for every life in the land" (394). But in this crisis Jim's heroic self-ideal triumphs over his will to live, and he surrenders himself to Doramin and certain death. His act is a supreme expression of the chivalric code: Jim seeks death before dishonour. This is not to discount the human cost of Jim's action, which, as Marlow's closing words remind us, can equally be read as an example of "his exalted egoism" (416), and involves his betrayal of Jewel, perhaps *the* life-promoting force in *Lord Jim*. Rather it is a question of emphasis that relates directly to the novel's concern with fundamentally different ways of perceiving reality: *logos* and *mythos*. While the former is rational, scientific, practical, and views the world in terms of logical explanation, the latter finds meaning in the atemporal and intuitive, and its expression in art and ritual. Succeeding the factual world of the *Patna*, Patusan is depicted through images and motifs that belong to the fictional province of magical realism, a narrative form combining the domestic and the supernatural, often incorporating fairytale and myth. As such, the broad structural arrangement of *Lord Jim* juxtaposes *logos* and *mythos* to demand that Jim be judged in terms of such ritualised and romantic codes as chivalry.

The Patusan sequence is, then, itself generically divided between the claims of Jim's real "bride," Jewel, and the "opportunity" that "like an Eastern bride, had come veiled to his side" (416). Asserting his idealism, Jim's death elevates him above the novel's unimaginative or self-seeking characters, but, in the process, Jewel is marginalised by a panoply of archetypal symbols fashioned in the literary tradition of the death of the hero, such as the sunset imagery, that promote the counterclaims of elegy, tragedy, and the fated hero (Simmons 2003: 199–200). The structural and rhetorical arrangement of the novel, that begins with the replacement of the frame-narrator by Marlow, leads one to expect an answer to the enigma of Jim's character that the conclusion configures in terms of aestheticism and openness: to Marlow, Jim "passes away under a cloud, inscrutable at heart, forgotten, unforgiven, and excessively romantic" (416).

Works cited

Batchelor, John. *The Life of Joseph Conrad*. Oxford: Blackwell, 1994.

Beckett, Samuel. *Proust*. London: John Calder, 1965.

Benjamin, Walter. *Selected Writings. Volume 1: 1913–1926*. Edited by Marcus Bullock and Michael W. Jennings. Cambridge, Mass.: Belknap Press, 2004.

Berthoud, Jacques. *Joseph Conrad: The Major Phase*. Cambridge: Cambridge University Press, 1978.

——. "Appendix: *Almayer's Folly* and the East." 241–44. In *Almayer's Folly*, edited by Jacques Berthoud. "Oxford World's Classics." Oxford: Oxford University Press, 1992.

Boswell, James. *The Life if Samuel Johnson, LL.D.* Vol. 1. [1791] Edited by Percy Fitzgerald. London: George Allen & Unwin, 1924.

Firchow, Peter Edgerley. *Envisioning Africa: Racism and Imperialism in Conrad's Heart of Darkness*. Lexington: University Press of Kentucky, 2000.

Galsworthy, John. *Castles in Spain and Other Screeds*. London: Heinemann, 1927.

Garrod, H. W. ed. *The Poetical Works of John Keats* (Second Edition). Oxford: Oxford University Press, 1970.

Girouard, Mark. *The Return to Camelot: Chivalry and the English Gentleman*. New Haven & London: Yale University Press, 1981.

Guerard, Albert J. *Conrad the Novelist*. Cambridge, Mass.: Harvard University Press, 1958.

Kucich, John, ed. *Conrad, Kipling, Stevenson: Fictions of Empire*. Boston: Houghton Mifflin, 2003.

Melville, Herman. *Moby-Dick*. Edited by Harrison Hayford and Hershel Parker. New York: Norton, 1967.

Nagel, Thomas. *Mortal Questions*. Cambridge: Cambridge University Press, 1979.

Najder, Zdzisław, ed. *Conrad under familial eyes*. Translated by Halina Carroll-Najder. Cambridge: Cambridge University Press, 1983.

Pakenham, Thomas. *The Scramble for Africa*. London: Weidenfeld and Nicolson, 1991.

Poignant, Roslyn. *Professional Savages: Captive Lives and Western Spectacle*. New Haven: Yale University Press, 2004.

Seeley, J. R. *The Expansion of England: Two Courses of Lectures*. [1884]. London: Macmillan, 1909.

Sherry, Norman. *Conrad's Eastern World*. Cambridge: Cambridge University Press, 1966.

——, ed. *Conrad: The Critical Heritage*. London and Boston: Routledge & Kegan Paul, 1973.

Simmons, Allan H. "The 'craftiest arrangement of words': *Lord Jim* and the Art of Juxtaposition" in *Lectures d'une oeuvre: Lord Jim*, edited by Nathalie Martinière. Nantes: Editions du Temps, 2003.

5

Political Novels: *Nostromo, The Secret Agent,* and *Under Western Eyes*

After the early-Malay, sea, and Marlow novels, Conrad embarked on his most audacious creative period. The decade after the publication of "Typhoon" saw the publication of *Nostromo* (1904), *The Secret Agent* (1907), and *Under Western Eyes* (1911), three masterpieces whose combined subject-matter is national and international politics: *Nostromo*, which Conrad described in his "Author's Note" as "the most anxiously meditated" (vii) of his longer novels, recreates the history of the fictional South American country of Costaguana and the forces of "material interests" that shape its modern destiny; set in London against a backdrop of anarchist activity, *The Secret Agent* is a novel of counter-espionage that charts the destruction of a *petit bourgeois* family caught up in the intrigues of foreign extremists; while *Under Western Eyes*, the most autobiographical of the political novels, portrays a promising young Russian scholar isolated between the Tsarist authorities and revolutionaries, and, in its study of "the very soul of things Russian" (*CL4:* 8) allows Conrad to explore topographies long suppressed in his Polish consciousness. The prevailing impression is that, having established himself as an English author, addressing such national concerns as Empire and the sea from the viewpoint of an increasingly integrated outsider, his confidence now afforded him the perspective to look outwards and engage with international politics.

Nostromo

Set in the 1880s and 1890s, *Nostromo* charts the inexorable power of foreign financial investment in Costaguana, a country on the Pacific coast of South America. Lured by the prospective wealth of the San Tomé silver-mine, the American financier Holroyd underwrites the restoration of the derelict mine inherited by Charles Gould, a young Englishman. Gould's family history in Costaguana is bound up with the history of the mine: both his father and grandfather worked and died in Costaguana, their efforts to manage the mine overwhelmed by rapacious governments and political instability. Despite the failures of his predecessors, Charles Gould "had, in his turn, fallen under the spell of the San Tomé mine" (59) and, newly married to Emilia, the counterbalancing force of sympathy and humanity in the novel, he returns to Costaguana to take up what he sees as his destiny, the Gould Concession. Thanks to a combination of his own determination, foreign investment, a period of relative political calm, and a host of allies drawn into the orbit of the mine for reasons as diverse as greed, vanity, love, and nationalism, Gould succeeds – to the point where the mine becomes a force in the land, an "Imperium in Imperio" (135) whose continued prosperity demands and occasions the succession of the Occidental Province from the rest of the country.

Focusing upon the San Tomé mine, Conrad presents a broadly Marxist vision of Costaguana's history as the product of economic forces. Where unscrupulous politicians and rapacious army officers once flourished in a political culture of malfeasance and corruption, American capital has now transformed those associated with the mine into the country's powerbrokers, buying and selling politicians and making its own security arrangements. The history of the mine itself reflects the commercial exploitation and foreign involvement that shape the country's fortunes. Initially worked by Indian slaves, the mine closes during the War of Independence, during which Gould's grandfather fights with Bolivar and through which Sulaco becomes part of the Federation of Costaguana. It then reopens briefly under English management before the miners revolt and massacre its owners, and is then confiscated by one of the succession of governments that succeed Guzman Bento, a strong man of Costaguana politics whose dictatorship unites the country and who kills Gould's uncle, the President of Sulaco. There follows a period when the mine lies dormant before "the fourth government in six years" (53) forces it upon Gould's father. Bound by "the infamous Concession," he is "robbed under the forms of legality and business" (57, 56) and dies a broken man, begging his son not to return to Costaguana.

The novel's present-tense action deals with the Monterist revolution in Sulaco – by which time Charles Gould has earned the nickname *El Rey de Sulaco* ("King of Sulaco") and the San Tomé silver mine has become the dominant political force in the province, financing the Blanco government of Don Vincente Ribiera in Costaguana, necessitating the National Central Railway, and, inevitably, attracting the avaricious attention of the Monteros. Intricately woven into this political tapestry are the tales of the individuals, mainly Europeans or Costaguaneros of European descent, whose diverse personal motives combine to ensure the secession of the Occidental Province. Thus *Nostromo* conforms to the historical view proposed by Tolstoy in *War and Peace* (1865–69):

> Each man lives for himself, using his freedom to attain his personal aims, and feels with his whole being that he can now do or abstain from doing this or that action; but as soon as he has done it, that action performed at a certain moment in time becomes irrevocable and belongs to history, in which it has not a free but a predestined significance....
>
> Man lives consciously for himself, but is an unconscious instrument in the attainment of the historic, universal, aims of humanity. A deed done is irrevocable, and its result coinciding in time with the actions of millions of other men assumes an historic significance. (1977: 665 66)

To name but some of the principal characters implicated in Costaguano's history: Charles Gould's motivation stems from the desire to right a family wrong; Monygham's from a desire to rehabilitate himself and protect Mrs Gould, a victim of her husband's obsession with the mine; Martin Decoud's from his love for Antonia Avellanos, despite his sceptical commitment to the country; and Nostromo's from overweening vanity that finds its outlet in public reputation. Underscoring all of these individual histories are groups such as "the miners of San Tomé, all Indians from the Sierra" (476), attracted by the prospect of work and implicated in the armed struggle to save the mine, and whose very invisibility identifies their servitude under various political castes, regardless of hue. In its combination of individual characters and the unindividuated masses *Nostromo* engages with the problem of how to represent the sovereignty of collective action. The focus on individual experience obscures the force of the collective – to the point where the novel's conclusion narrows its focus to concentrate upon the personal fate of Nostromo, for so long an instrument in San Tomé's history and now its victim, leading Albert J. Guerard to wonder: "What indeed of the essential *Nostromo* would be lost if we simply lopped off those last two hundred and sixty pages?" (1958: 204). But this interleaving of individual and collective action endorses the Tolstoyan view of history and is a feature of Conrad's sceptical pessimism, his implicit questioning of the capacity of an essentially bourgeois form – the novel – to represent revolutionary activity.

* * *

The time-shifts in *Nostromo* are notoriously treacherous for the first-time reader and, together with rapid and unexpected changes in perspective, create a vertiginous narrative that is an expression of the individual's instability and entrapment within the forces of history, as stressed by an opening that emphasises legend and myth. Its temporal dislocations and continuities, together with the rapidly alternating individual and collective points of view, mean that the narrative mimics the confusion of forces out of which the Occidental Republic itself emerges. The time-shifts, zigzagging between different historical moments and veering between historical reality and literary creation, support both the sense that everything is happening at once and the novel's encyclopaedic interest. One consequence of eschewing a linear chronology is that the narrative undermines any simple view of history, be it comprehensive or progressive and developmental. Instead, history is portrayed as a tragic cycle of repeated error. In fact, by the end of *Nostromo*, prominent Sulacans are planning a war to "Annex the rest of Costaguana to the order and prosperity of Sulaco ... There is no other remedy" (509). The sense that each phase of history contains the seeds of its own obsolescence while becoming a recognisable variant of its predecessor is inescapable.

Nowhere is the individual's entrapment within the broader forces of history more apparent than during the Sulaco riots:

Knots of men ran headlong; others made a stand; and the irregular rattle of firearms came rippling to his ears in the fiery, still air. Single figures on foot raced desperately. Horsemen galloped towards each other, wheeled round together, separated at speed. Giorgio saw one fall, rider and horse disappearing as if they had galloped into a chasm, and the movements of the animated scene were like the passages of a violent game played on the plain by dwarfs mounted and on foot, yelling with tiny throats, under the mountain that seemed a colossal embodiment of silence. (26–27)

Here, dwarfed by events, are ranged the confused forces that will determine Costaguana's future. Overlooking the mêlée is the snow-capped Higuerota Mountain – part of the Cordilleras that divide the Occidental Province from the rest of Costaguana – providing a reminder that geography, too, is instrumental in fashioning history. As Martin Decoud, the Journalist of Sulaco and apostle of succession, claims: "Look at the mountains! Nature itself seems to cry to us 'Separate!' " (184). The impact of geographical setting upon the tale was noted by Conrad's contemporaries: to Cunninghame Graham "the book ought to have been called 'Costaguana' "; while Arnold Bennett confessed: "I always think of that book as *Higuerota*, the said mountain being the principal personage in the story" (Watts, ed., 1969: 159; Sherry, ed., 1973: 161).

Costaguana is acutely historicized, and its historical reality is a testament to the evolving form of colonialism: from the anterior reference to "the time of Spanish rule" (3) in the opening sentence, supported by the high incidence of Spanish words in the text, to Holroyd's prescient observation that "some day" the United States "shall run the world's business whether the world likes it or not. The world can't help it – and neither can we, I guess" (77). Behind all lies the shaping force of "material interests," given its most succinct expression in the silver mined by native labour for foreign profit. The San Tomé silver is both a tangible object and an abstract idea: the recurring phrase "material interests" combines this dualism of the tangible and the intangible, posing the difficulty of defining with precision the silver's influence upon people while textually mimicking its pervasive influence. With its sheltered natural harbour, and standing at the intersection of land and sea-borne trade routes, the coastal town of Sulaco is of strategic importance to Costaguana and an inevitable focus for international economic aspirations.

This tale about the impact of silver upon Costaguana is simultaneously a tale about material obsession. The keynote is struck in the

novel's opening chapter with the legend about two gringo fortune
hunters who perished in their search and whose ghosts are locally
believed to haunt the Azuera Peninsula. (Like the gringos, their
successors, who provide the novel's cast of central characters, are
dislocated peoples.) Different manifestations of this fixation delineate the political history of Sulaco, as successive governments and
Europeans fall under the same spell of the silver, crudely motivated
by avarice. The intertwined lives depicted in *Nostromo* represent
subtle variations of the same Azuera legend. For example, to Emilia
Gould, Holroyd's is the "religion of silver and iron" (71), while
Charles Gould's obsession with the San Tomé mine – "His father
had not desired it. The son would never surrender it" (402) – is
such that he is prepared to destroy it by dynamite, "to send half of
Sulaco into the air" (204), rather than surrender his claim.

* * *

The "unapproachable style" of the aloof Capataz de Cargadores,
the Genoese sailor for whom "to be well spoken of" is the "only
thing he seems to care for" (246), includes his silver-grey mare with
"silver plates on headstall and saddle," "enormous silver buttons"
on his embroidered jacket, and a row of "tiny silver buttons" down
the seam of his trousers (125). When toying with a pretty Morenita,
and the centre of public attention, he plays to the gallery and invites
her to "cut all the silver buttons off my coat" (129). Yet, through
his involvement in the attempt to save the cargo of silver from
Sotillo, himself a perfect study of naked greed, Nostromo, too,
becomes "a faithful and lifelong slave" of the silver (501). For,
after Decoud has purloined four ingots to weight his body down
in the water, Nostromo realises that his own reputation would
be compromised were he to return the remainder of the silver.
Thus compelled to keep the entire cargo, Nostromo enters upon a
duplicitous life, "growing rich very slowly" (523), with the result
that this subterfuge destroys his own faith in his public image.
It is fitting that he should choose to revert to his original name,
Giovanni Battista Fidanza, at this point – and equally fitting that the
name of Captain Fidanza, with its connotations of trustworthiness,
the very quality that made him "invaluable … a man absolutely
above reproach" (12–13) to Captain Mitchell, should now provide
an ironic and persistent reminder of his enslavement.

No longer the dashing Capataz de Cargadores, Giovanni Fidanza appears mutely dressed in "the vulgarity of a brown tweed suit" (527) that conceals and renders inaccessible his identity and true purpose. Cedric Watts notes the irony in the name "Gian' Battista" (John the Baptist): "John the Baptist prepared the way for Jesus Christ and was thus the inaugurator of the Christian era; Nostromo prepares the way for the control of Sulaco by the economic imperialists and is thus an inaugurator of its capitalist era" (1993: 195). Nostromo's name is both the Italian word for "bosun," which is what he is when he first arrives in Sulaco, and an abbreviation of the phrase *nostro uomo*, meaning "our man," which is what he becomes to his employers. Changing it to Captain Fidanza has the effect of highlighting the degree to which individuality is subordinated to and perverted by the material interests that provide the novel's central and unifying theme. The myth of the gringos extends into the lives of each of the central characters and to the political determination of Costaguana itself. No life remains untouched, but, equally, each life adds its commentary to the central theme of materialism. Thus, when Father Roman and Don Pépé, "spiritual and temporal pastors of the mine flock" (102), attempt to identify "some small, staid urchin met wandering, naked and grave, along the road with a cigar in his baby mouth, and perhaps his mother's rosary, purloined for purposes of ornamentation, hanging in a loop of beads low down on his rotund little stomach" (102), the description of the child is composed of emblems – cigar, rosary – that reveal competing colonial claims.

* * *

Looking back on *Nostromo*, in a letter to Edmund Gosse of 11 June 1918, Conrad described the novel as "an achievement in mosaic" (*CL6*: 231). This structural principle, whereby discrete, individual perspectives and different historical moments coexist, simultaneously ensures that no single view of Costaguana is authoritative and suggests that all attempts to engineer her fate are, at best, limited, and subordinate to the broader workings of historical inevitability. For example, the successful defence of the San Tomé silver from the Monterists that provides the central action in the narrative appears to confirm a victory for the systematic workings of capitalist imperialism: the triumph of the mine strengthens the secessionist desire for sovereignty and self-determination. But while victory provides a heightened sense of internal credibility within the province, it lacks moral authority. The capitalist counter-revolution does not implicate everyone in its purpose and vision. Instead, it is shown, in the novel's closing stages, to have unconsciously spawned an anti-capitalist backlash. Fittingly this is presented only fleetingly, in references to "secret societies," and in the figure of the unidentified "pale photographer, small, frail, bloodthirsty, the hater of capitalists," sitting at Nostromo's deathbed intent upon securing further donations for the cause: "The rich must be fought with their own weapons" (562). The narrative "mosaic" that juxtaposes private and social life thus works to collapse psychological, social, and political structures through the competing demands of self-interest and collective governance.

Any attempt to form a coherent view of the birth of the Republic of Sulaco from the disparate lives of the central characters, whose immigrant status is itself testament to international involvement in the country, soon reveals the intricate web of connections that link them to the silver. Nostromo's countryman, Giorgio Viola, "one of Garibaldi's immortal thousand in the conquest of Sicily" (20), had accompanied his leader to South America forty years ago to fight "for the cause of freedom" (30) in Uruguay. His "austere contempt for all personal advantage" (31) would seem to render him immune to the silver's influence. Yet, with his daughters, Linda and Giselle, by the end of the novel he has forsaken his inn, the Casa Viola, rechristened the "Albergo d'Italia Una" in the wake of the revolution, to administer the new lighthouse on the Great Isabel and thus, unwittingly, become the guardian of Nostromo's hoard of silver buried on the island.

To Viola, the old Garibaldino, now "too old to wander any more" (124), the Monterist revolt is symptomatic of the end of humanitarian revolutions: "These were not a people striving for justice, but thieves. Even to defend his life against them was a sort of degradation ... He had an immense scorn for this outbreak of scoundrels and leperos, who did not know the meaning of the word 'liberty' " (20–21). If this attitude suggests Viola's political alignment with Sulaco aristocrats like Don Pépé, for whom the country is "the land of thieves and sanguinary macaques" (113), then it equally and sceptically voices the failure of liberal idealism in the continent which Viola had served and from which he is finally, and symbolically, detached on the Great Isabel. As he comes to recognise: "Too many kings and emperors flourished yet in the world which God had meant for the people" (31). Viola himself is a puppet of history in the novel. The Casa Viola is "the Italian stronghold" into which "No native of Costaguana intruded" (32).

* * *

To Charles Gould, the San Tomé mine is intimately linked to a vision of Costaguanan politics, as he explains to his wife: "What is wanted here is law, good faith, order, security. Any one can declaim about these things but I pin my faith to material interests. Only let the material interests once get a firm footing, and they are bound to impose the conditions on which alone they can continue to exist. That's how your money-making is justified here in the face of lawlessness and disorder. It is justified because the security which it demands must be shared with an oppressed people" (84). The consequences of adapting the population to the needs of a competitive market economy, however, question Gould's "justification." For instance, as he observes during the fiesta: "All this piece of land belongs now to the Railway Company. There will be no more popular feasts held here" (123). The unrestrained disorderliness of carnival is supplanted by the orderliness that Charles Gould demands; a comparable example of restraint lies in the designation of the mining villages: primero, segundo, and tercero.

The barometer of political power in Costaguana, the San Tomé silver is similarly attended by a Nemesis that taints the lives of everyone who comes into its orbit. Mrs Gould, the "Never-tired Señora" (89), with her "humanizing influence" (45), hospitality – "kindness personified" (42) – and empathetic capacity to see "the man under the silent, sad-eyed beast of burden" (89), is a victim of her husband's obsession: "She had watched it with misgivings turning into a fetish, and now the fetish had grown into a monstrous and crushing weight. It was as if the inspiration of their early years had left her heart to turn into a wall of silver-bricks, erected by the silent work of evil spirits, between her and her husband" (221–22). Such is Gould's monomania that "his wife was no longer the sole mistress of his thoughts" (365) and, symbolically, the Gould marriage is childless. Instead, with "a prophetic vision," Mrs Gould anticipates "surviving alone the degradation of her young ideal of life, of love, of work – all alone in the Treasure House of the World" (522).

By moving swiftly between scenes and eras, the narrative acquires a multivalent perspective capable of registering ambiguities that evade official ideologies. First, while individuals are implicated in Sulacan political machinations, brief reminders of their desires and motives predispose the novel towards an implied ethical foundation: Mrs Gould's imaginative understanding of others poses an important, if fragile, challenge to political commitment. Secondly, the prodigiously expansive handling of time that represents the changing face of foreign involvement in South America, from the Spanish conquistadors to American capitalist imperialism, also makes of Costaguana an allegorical place. While emphasising the multiple resemblances between phases of her history, the legend of the Azuera ghosts sets the notion of causal, historical progress against a concept of time as mythological and circular, and in the process invites analogies between them.

Thirdly, the use of multiple viewpoints and time-shifts generates an ironic perspective that renders political machinations, in Decoud's phrase, a "tragic farce." For instance, the humorous description of President-Dictator Ribiera fleeing "the lost battle of Socorro" and ignominiously arriving in Sulaco on a lame mule that "expired under him at the end of the Alameda, where the military band plays sometimes in the evenings between the revolutions" (11) precedes Sir John's designation of him as an instrument of the National Central Railway: "After all he was their own creature" (38). Ribiera's instrumentality is dramatised by the fact that he disappears from the narrative after this. Similarly, Don José Avellanos' *History of Fifty Years of Misrule*, which, in a further blurring of fictional boundaries, Conrad cites as his "principal authority for the history of Costaguana" ("Author's Note," x), is never published: printed on the *Porvenir* presses, the pages, that detail the "untold indignities" (50) suffered by this aristocratic patriot under the tyrannical Guzman Bento yet also generously affirm that "this monster, imbrued in the blood of his countrymen, ... too, loved his country" (142), are used as gun-wadding during the Monterist revolt. Thus the fires of present revolution are, literally, fed by the past, and the "silvery" haired (141) Don José's liberal idealism is bathetically placed in the service of his country's revolutionary reality.

Because of his apparent blindness to the real significance of events taking place around him, it is easy to scoff at Captain Mitchell's description of, say, Nostromo's rescue of Ribiera, as: "It was history – history, sir!" (130). But in charting the incidents that result in Sulacan independence, *Nostromo is* history – and on a grand scale. The novel has been compared with *War and Peace* (Baines 1959: 297), and if its thesis about the historical process is less formally composed than Tolstoy's, it is also a more nuanced study for being distributed among individuals who represent widely divergent views of history.

These different perspectives, together with the numerous digressions, asides, and qualifications, exhibit an anxiety about the adequacy of any single viewpoint. In a narrative that advertises itself as history, it is fitting that the dominant viewpoint should be that of an omniscient narrator, but this does not mean that the text is free from other voices, challenging the view of history being described. Virtually every page of the novel contains some comment or aside that calls attention to the fact that, even as we're listening to a single voice, other ironic commentaries are being smuggled into the narrative. For example, early in the novel we read of

> the great body of strong-limbed foreigners who dug the earth, blasted the rocks, drove the engines for the "progressive and patriotic undertaking." In these very words eighteen months before the Excellentissimo Señor don Vincente Ribiera, the Dictator of Costaguana, had described the National Central Railway in his great speech at the turning of the first sod. (34)

Here, the practical importance of international investment in Costaguana is emphasised by the complex first sentence. Complementing this, the second sentence is overloaded with superlatives and titles that capitalise upon political sloganeering, quoted in Ribiera's actual words, while ironising his self-importance through their cumulative effect. Now grave and serious, now playful and cynical, in *Nostromo* the history of Costaguana emerges through the intersection of imperial "grand narrative" and popular language, composed of political slogans (like "Fifty Years of Misrule") and titles (like "Capataz de Cargadores" or "El Rey de Sulaco"), and by constantly juxtaposing moments in the past with moments in the present.

* * *

Among the central characters implicated in saving the San Tomé silver are Don José's godson, Martin Decoud, and Dr Monygham, both of whom explicitly assume a sceptical disengagement from the larger political designs in which they reluctantly find themselves participating. Decoud, the "idle boulevardier" who imagines himself "Parisian to the tips of his fingers" (152–53), returns to the country of his birth to deliver a consignment of rifles. A combination of his reawakened feelings for Antonia Avellanos and the welcome he receives as "the brilliant defender of the country's regeneration" makes it impossible for him to confess his intention "to go away by the next month's packet" (156), and he stays to take up his role in what he calls *"une farce macabre"* (152), as the Journalist of Sulaco. Surprising even himself at the degree to which he becomes involved in Sulacan public life, Decoud is the first to advocate independence from the rest of Costaguana.

Together with Nostromo, Decoud is entrusted to smuggle the current shipment of silver out of Sulaco when the Monterist revolution erupts. Their collision with Sotillo's rebel troopship prevents any thoughts of leaving the Golfo Placido to secure the help of a passing ship, and the silver is landed and concealed on the Great Isabel. (This accident also thrusts the hapless hide-merchant, Hirsch, into the brutal world of revolution, suggesting once more the corrosive effect of the San Tomé silver on those who stray, even unwittingly, under its influence.) Left alone on the island by Nostromo, Decoud is placed in a familiar Conradian predicament of a man tested to the limits of his endurance through isolation and forced to confront his own moral toughness. With grim irony, the sceptic Decoud proves unable to live without the social comedy he derides and commits suicide: "A victim of the disillusioned weariness which is the retribution meted out to intellectual audacity, the brilliant Don Martin Decoud, weighted by the bars of San Tomé silver, disappeared without a trace, swallowed up in the immense indifference of things" (501).

As an outsider, unwillingly drawn into and increasingly implicated in the political processes from which the new republic will emerge, Decoud is yet another foreigner determining Sulaco's identity; by contrast, Doctor Monygham's similarly unwilling involvement in the country's fate brings the spectre of Costaguana's past to bear on her present. Monygham, like so many of the Costaguaneros, identified and unidentified, could echo the words of Stephen Dedalus in *Ulysses*: "History ... is a nightmare from which I am trying to awake" (1986: 28). An English medical doctor who has lived in Costaguana for many years, Monygham's physical disfigurement, psychological scars, and misanthropic demeanour bear witness to his torture under the cruel regime of Guzman Bento and his henchman, the sadistic army chaplain, Father Beron, whose "inquisitorial instincts" (372) finally broke his victim. Having betrayed friends, wholly understandably, under these conditions, Monygham is nevertheless left with "an ideal conception of his disgrace" (375) that manifests itself in his corrosive sense of failure and of being "not fit for confidences" (379). (In this, Monygham's experience is analogous to Jim's in *Lord Jim*.) His personal experience has left him a rambling, dislocated figure, emblematic of the country's brutal past, with the memory that "makes truth, honour, self-respect, and life itself matters of little moment" (373).

It is Emilia Gould who rehabilitates Monygham, securing for him the post of chief medical officer for the mine. From this vantage, he comes to love Mrs Gould from afar. Recognising her abandonment by her husband's absorption in the mine, he casts himself in the role of protector and, unusually in the novel, idealises a person rather than the silver, settling the "great fund of loyalty" in his nature "on Mrs. Gould's head" (376). Positive and regenerative though this is, his private feelings for Mrs Gould none the less implicate him in the political intrigues of Sulaco. He both inspires Nostromo to undertake his "famous ride to Cayta" (473) to recall General Barrios to Sulaco and, by convincing Sotillo that the silver has been sunk and can be reclaimed by dredging the harbour, provides the necessary diversion to buy time for Barrios' return.

With symmetrical elegance, Monygham's "game of betrayal with Sotillo" (410) recalls his earlier "betrayal" to Father Beron. He himself views it as "the work I was fit for" (507), yet Mrs Gould recognises the sacrifice for what it is: "You faced the most cruel dangers of all. Something more than death" (507). Public prestige follows Monygham's private bravery: he is advanced to the status of "Inspector of State Hospitals, chief medical officer of the Consolidated San Tomé mines" (481). But, to the end, he remains clear-eyed about the corrosive impact of material interests. Amid the expansionist aims to "Annex the rest of Costaguana to the order and prosperity of Sulaco" (509), he responds to Mrs Gould's desperation – "Will there be never any peace? Will there be no rest? ... I thought that we –" (511) – in words that affirm the futility of humane endeavour caught up in the self-perpetuating logic of economic, political, and historical forces:

> There is no peace and no rest in the development of material interests. They have their law, and their justice. But it is founded on

> expediency, and is inhuman; it is without rectitude, without the con-
> tinuity and the force that can be found only in moral principle. Mrs.
> Gould, the time approaches when all that the Gould Concession
> stands for shall weigh as heavily upon the people as the barbarism,
> cruelty, and misrule of a few years back. (511)

As her husband becomes increasingly more fixated with the San
Tomé mine, so Mrs Gould occupies a more marginal position in
his life. One consequence of this detachment is that she acquires
a critical distance from which to judge the European venture in
this South American country. Initially accepting of her husband's
political vision, she becomes progressively more critical of it. An
alternative voice to "material interests," Mrs Gould exemplifies
in her increasingly sterile marriage the damage caused by such a
philosophy.

* * *

In *Nostromo*, the various and shifting viewpoints emphasise the
impossibility of ever seeing the whole picture of Costaguaga while
simultaneously calling attention to the limitation of any one interpretation. Instead, the picture of the country emerges through
fragmentary glimpses, each promoting its own vested interests.
This fragmentation has consequences for the portrayal and development of character. To take just one example, our impression
of Mrs Gould is partly filtered through the views of others: her
husband, Doctor Monygham, Nostromo, and so on. While such
varied perceptions construct her social reality, they emphasise the
difficulty of making sense or coherence of her life, suggesting the
tensions that threaten an easy, unambiguous view of her.

The novel's title directs us towards the issue of identity in
Nostromo, not only the identity of individuals like Nostromo
or Mrs Gould but also nations. After all, what does it mean
to be a Costaguanero? On first reading, her sympathies identify
Mrs Gould with a humane, gentler imperialism to set against the
triumphalist creed of "material interests," of which she becomes
increasingly critical. Insofar as *Nostromo* can be read as an anti-
cipatory allegory of the workings of twentieth-century capitalism,
her function is to offer an opposing voice. Watching the plight of
those Don Pépé refers to as "Poor people! Pobrecitos!" (97), while
her husband's obsession with the silver drives a wedge between
them, her own fortunes offer a critique of the imperialist enterprise.

But she, too, is "cursed" by the silver: put bluntly, Mrs Gould has benefited nicely from the exploitation of Costaguana, living in a luxurious house maintained by the labour of others. In a novel that pits need against greed, and in a plot driven by economics, she can *afford* not to be as materialistic as her husband. At the end of the novel, Nostromo tells her accusingly: "You are all alike, you fine people" (559).

It is a question of scale, but, like Marlow in "Heart of Darkness," she is acutely of her age: Marlow's sympathy for the Africans coexists with his racism that marks him out as a product of the "Scramble for Africa"; for her part, Mrs Gould appreciates the picturesque culture that her husband is changing forever. If this tarnishes her image, it also renders her recognisably Conradian in character, attended by the forces of economic and social reality. Expanding the "Heart of Darkness" parallel still further, Mrs Gould offers another study of failed idealism. Setting the pattern for the three political novels, *Nostromo* blends the microcosmic and macrocosmic, the little society of the family with the larger society of the nation. Unable to speak his love for her, Doctor Monygham instead forces her to consider whether what she and her husband have done might have caused more harm than good in Sulaco. One reading is that Mrs Gould's idealism acts as a cover for Charles Gould's capitalism.

The Secret Agent

In 1907, Conrad published his great metropolitan novel, *The Secret Agent*. Set in London, the novel has as its factual basis in what became known as the "Greenwich Bomb Outrage": on 15 February 1894, the anarchist Martial Bourdin accidentally blew himself up in Greenwich Park with a home-made bomb that he was carrying towards the Greenwich Observatory. The physical setting and the theme of anarchism combine to provide the focus for Conrad's study of "a mankind always so tragically eager for self-destruction" ("Author's Note," ix).

To state the obvious, it is easy to see why Conrad, as an ex-sailor, should have been creatively inspired by the apparent attempt to blow up the Greenwich Observatory. The very sea-charts by which he had navigated depended upon Greenwich for the mapping of the globe into lines of longitude. The attempt to destroy the Observatory was simultaneously an anarchic attempt to destroy the symbolic order of established society, an attack on time and place, the equivalent of blowing up the known world.

When dedicating *The Secret Agent* to H. G. Wells, whose own fictions brought scientific scepticism to bear on social questions, Conrad described the novel as a "simple tale of the XIX century," while his "Author's Note" refers to "the dynamite outrages in London, away back in the [eighteen] eighties" (xi). The choice of historical setting is acute for, according to George Woodcock, it was during this decade that "Anarchism as a movement began in Britain" (1986: 371). As Continental anarchism spread into the awakening socialist movement in the clubs for foreign workers in London's Soho and in the East End, "The discreetly blind eye of Scotland Yard usually allowed expatriate political activities in London to go unmolested; by a tacit gentleman's agreement most of the foreign revolutionists refrained from dabbling in English affairs or embarrassing the British government internationally" (1986: 371).

In common with many European cities, London had seen its share of bombings in the closing decades of the nineteenth century as Anarchists, Fenians, and other revolutionary groups tried to disrupt the social and economic order through violence. As the Professor says: "Nothing would please me more than to see Inspector Heat and his likes take to shooting us down in broad daylight with the approval of the public. Half our battle would be won then; the disintegration of the old morality would have set in its very temple. That is what you ought to aim at" (73). Social revolution was in the air: the Socialist movement, inspired by Karl Marx, and the International Anarchist Movement, founded by Michael Bakunin, led to such partially successful revolts as the Paris Commune of 1871 and the Russian uprising of 1905. The sheer scale of anarchist activities is evident in the popular press of the day. For instance, *The Times* of 20 February 1894 carries consecutive reports headed "Another Explosion in Paris," "Anarchist Newspapers Seized in Brussels," and "Anarchism in Austria" (5). The spectre of the mad dynamiter, intent upon wreaking havoc, haunted the late-Victorian and Edwardian imagination.

While understandable government hostility led anarchists "to think in terms of underground organization and spectacular deeds" (Woodcock, 1986: 213), England's liberal tradition made it a natural haven for European revolutionaries. The list of political refugees whose revolutionary principles had led to persecution and imprisonment abroad, and who consequently sought sanctuary in

Britain, reads like a who's who of anarchists and revolutionary socialists, and includes Bakunin, Kropotkin, and Marx, who wrote *Das Kapital* in the Reading Room of the British Museum. On 14 July 1881, shortly before the assassination of Tsar Alexander II, the International Anarchist Congress was held in London and attended by such celebrated figures in revolutionary circles as Kropotkin and Malatesta. The Congress declared its aim of revolution through terrorism, with the Mexican delegate advocating a "military academy" for anarchists and the need for "education in chemistry" (Woodcock 1986: 213). *The Secret Agent* pits the potential threat from anarchists against the British liberalism that harbours them, and, as Berthoud argues: "The central issue in the novel is not how anarchism should be judged, but what anarchism reveals about the England of the time" (Stape, ed., 1996: 106).

* * *

Conrad wrote *The Secret Agent* in 1906. Initially conceived as a short story entitled "Verloc," it was begun during a two-month family holiday in the South of France. While extending the political focus initiated in *Nostromo* to the domestic politics of England, *The Secret Agent* also represents a new departure for Conrad. Between these two novels, he published a volume of reminiscences, anecdotes, and historical reflections on sea-life, entitled *The Mirror of the Sea* (1906), which he described as "an unreserved attempt to unveil for a moment the profounder intimacies of the sea and the formative influences of nearly half my life-time" (*SA*, "Author's Note," ix). With the benefit of hindsight, this order of publication suggests that Conrad's critical engagement with English politics in *The Secret Agent* – that constitutes an ironic condition-of-England novel – is balanced by his celebration of the county's maritime tradition: *The Mirror of the Sea* concludes with an essay entitled "The Heroic Age," a centennial paean to the British Navy and Lord Nelson.

Conrad's recollections of the novel's genesis, set out in his "Author's Note" (1920), are described in scientific metaphors that would be realised in the Professor's home-made bomb-making, while the setting, London, is introduced in terms of an alienation that will find tragic expression in the domestic tragedy of the Verlocs:

And then ensued in my mind what a student of chemistry would best understand from the analogy of the addition of the tiniest little drop of the right kind, precipitating the process of crystallization in a test tube containing some colourless solution.

It was at first for me a mental change, disturbing a quieted-down imagination, in which strange forms, sharp in outline but imperfectly apprehended, appeared and claimed attention as crystals will do by their bizarre and unexpected shapes. One fell to musing before the phenomenon – even of the past: of South America, a continent of crude sunshine and brutal revolutions, of the sea, the vast expanse of salt waters, the mirror of heaven's frowns and smiles, the reflector of the world's light. Then the vision of an enormous town presented itself, of a monstrous town more populous than some continents and in its man-made might as if indifferent to heaven's frowns and smiles; a cruel devourer of the world's light. There was room enough there to place any story, depth enough there for any passion, variety enough there for any setting, darkness enough to bury five million lives.   (xi–xii)

The description of London as a place of "darkness" obviously recalls the "brooding gloom" that characterised the metropolis as the source of the colonial "darkness" that Marlow encounters in "Heart of Darkness." But while colonialism is inherent in the establishment here – the Assistant Commissioner's career "had begun in a tropical colony" (99) – Conrad's concern with London in *The Secret Agent* is more aesthetically ambitious, seeking to convey what we may term the poetics of the modern city. English Literary Modernism was a city art; to Holbrook Jackson it was "not a product of England but of cosmopolitan London" (1913; 1966: 58).

In *The Secret Agent*, London emerges, in a series of vivid descriptions and visceral images, as a variegated reflector of human feeling. To Verloc, on his way to the Embassy where he will receive his anarchist mission to blow up the Greenwich Observatory, the city represents "the majesty of inorganic nature" whose "very pavement ... had an old-gold tinge" (14, 11); after his interview, it has been transformed into "the enormity of cold, black, wet, muddy, inhospitable accumulation of bricks, slates, and stones" (56). The pathology of modern man is thus inscribed on his urban environment. To the Assistant Commissioner, London is both "a slimy aquarium from which the water had been run off" and "a jungle" (147, 150), to Verloc it is "a vast and hopeless desert" (179), and to Ossipon an "enormous town slumbering monstrously on a carpet of mud under a veil of raw mist" (300). Having murdered her husband, Winnie Verloc steps out into a "town of marvels and mud, with its maze of streets and its mass of lights ... sunk in a hopeless night, rested at the bottom of a black abyss" (270–71).

As the example of Dickens demonstrates, Conrad was not alone in locating contemporary unease and alienation in urban space. Henry James also linked London with anarchism, in *The Princess Casamassima* (1886). Describing London as "the great grey Babylon" (v), James identifies his intentions with his setting in terms that anticipate *The Secret Agent* some twenty years later: "My scheme called for the suggested nearness (to all our apparently ordered life) of some sinister anarchic underworld, heaving in its pain, its power and its hate" (1977: xxi).

* * *

The story begins when Adolf Verloc, the secret agent of the title, answers a summons from an unidentified foreign embassy, presumably Russian, by whom he is employed to spy on the activities of London anarchist groups, with such names as The Future of the Proletariat. But behind his ostensible profession as a purveyor of "shady wares" (5) – pornography, mainly – Verloc is in fact a double agent, also acting as a police informer for Chief Inspector Heat of the Special Crimes Department. During his interview with the First Secretary of the Embassy, Mr Vladimir, Verloc's activities are derided, and he is instructed that "The proper business of an 'agent provocateur' is to provoke" (25). Vladimir denounces the British liberalism that makes the country attractive to foreign anarchists and a haven in which to plot their revolutionary acts abroad: "The imbecile bourgeoisie of this country make themselves the accomplices of the very people whose aim is to drive them out of their houses to starve in ditches" (29). Identifying the present as "the psychological moment" for action, Vladimir instructs Verloc to undertake an anarchist attack that must have "the shocking senselessness of gratuitous blasphemy" (29, 33). Verloc is trapped: a self-styled "protector of society" (5), he is called upon to unsettle the very fabric of British social life that assures his material comfort, modest as it is.

Having married his former landlady's daughter, Verloc has also adopted her mother and brother, the simpleton Stevie for whom Winnie feels a "quasi-maternal affection" (8). The political secrecy that underpins the tale acquires its domestic expression in the Verloc marriage: unbeknown to Verloc, Winnie only married him in order to provide for and protect her hypersensitive brother. Loyal and unquestioning wife though she is, Stevie not Verloc is the centre of Winnie's emotional life. In *The Secret Agent* Conrad's broad survey of English society presents it as a web of parasitical relationships, that extends from the cabman, for whom "This ain't an easy world" (167), at one extreme, to Sir Ethelred, the Secretary of State, at the other.

The members of Verloc's anarchist circle are, contradictorily, all dependent for their existence upon the society they threaten: Michaelis, the obese "ticket-of-leave apostle" (41), gains access to high society through the protection of a Lady Patroness who is a close friend of the Assistant Commissioner's wife; Karl Yundt, the self-styled "terrorist" (42) who resembles "a senile sensualist" (43), is nursed by and dependent upon "a blear-eyed old woman" (52); while Comrade Alexander Ossipon "was sure to want for nothing as long as there were silly girls with savings-bank books in the world" (53). Their clandestine meeting in the Verlocs' parlour in Chapter 3 of the novel locates the tale within the prevailing discourse of anarchism and revolutionary socialism – which is exposed as rhetorical clap-trap. Despite voicing their theories, there is little in the way of consensus and, reinforcing the novel's theme of human isolation and alienation, the revolutionaries appear to speak not to but past each other, each preoccupied with his own agenda. To Michaelis, "History is dominated and determined by the tool of production – by the force of economic conditions. Capitalism has made socialism, and the laws made by the capitalism for the protection of property are responsible for anarchism" (41); the nihilistic Yundt dreams of a band of "destroyers" with "No pity for anything on earth, including themselves, and death enlisted for good and all in the service of humanity" (42); and the ex-medical-student-turned-propagandist Ossipon invokes the Italian pseudo-scientist Lombroso's belief that social "degenerates" are recognisable by such physical features as their ear lobes (46–47). Within a month of the novel's publication, Conrad told Cunninghame Graham: "I don't think that I've been satirizing the revolutionary world. All these people are not revolutionaries – they are shams" (*CL3*: 491).

Overhearing the revolutionaries' conversation, Stevie interrupts his drawings of circles that suggest "a rendering of cosmic chaos, the symbolism of mad art attempting the inconceivable" (45). Emotionally traumatised by what he hears, he imaginatively identifies with Yundt's graphic visions of state-inflicted pain. After his guests have left, Verloc discovers Stevie in this distracted state and wakes Winnie to attend to him. She in turn wakes her mother to sit with Stevie until he goes to sleep. Trivial in itself, this sequence foreshadows the disruptive consequences of anarchism on the Verloc household. Verloc's anxiety about his orders from Vladimir clearly exercises him, as his reaction to the word "science" during the revolutionists' discussion, together with his sleeplessness, demonstrates. The first three chapters thus establish both the public and the private threat posed by the would-be revolutionists.

According to Todorov, detective fictions contain "not one but two stories: the story of the crime and the story of the investigation" (1992: 44), and the sequential narrative is disrupted at this point: Chapters 4–7 look back upon the Greenwich Observatory affair. For instance, Chapter 4 dramatises a meeting between Ossipon and The Professor considering the breaking news about an explosion in Greenwich Park, involving "a man's body blown to pieces" (70). The Professor embodies Conrad's depiction of "a mankind always so tragically eager for self-destruction" ("Author's Note," ix): obsessed with developing the perfect detonator, he walks the streets of London, quite literally carrying a bomb in his pocket, a symbol of an inert society primed to explode. The Professor confesses to supplying dynamite for the explosion to Verloc, who is thus assumed to be the victim. Similarly, Chapters 5–7 chart the beginnings of the police investigation into the incident during which the body of the dead man is traced back to Verloc's shop by means of an address label sewn onto his coat.

The disrupted narrative chronology, whereby the reader is left to rearrange the order of events in order to understand their place in the scheme of the tale, means that, rather than the Royal Observatory, the concrete embodiment of abstract time, it is the narrative sequence that is exploded. The novel's fractured chronology represents the destabilizing effect of anarchism upon both the form and substance of the tale while lending a grimly ironic note to retrospective accounts of Verloc's preparations to carry out Vladimir's orders, during which it gradually becomes clear that the dead man is not Verloc but Stevie. For instance, the police constable who collects the remains of the body – "He's all there. Every bit of him" (87) – describes the victim to Heat as: "Fair. Slight" (89). The lengthy withholding of circumstances surrounding Stevie's death produces a sudden change in the reader's perception of events that reflects the shock experienced by Winnie, whose discovery of and reaction to the truth provides the novel's tragic conclusion. Before this, however, such comments as Winnie's "I wish you would take that boy out with you, Adolf" (185) or "You could do anything with that boy, Adolf. ... He would go through fire for you" (184) acquire devastating ironic force once the reader knows of Stevie's fate. Similarly, the self-sacrificing decision taken by Winnie's mother to leave Brett Street and enter an almshouse, so as to ease the family burden on Mr Verloc and thus further protect Stevie, is invested with a tragi-comic sense of futility. While extending the sphere of anarchist influence into the realm of human emotions, Stevie's fate also demonstrates that it is the simple-minded who are made the dupes of political revolution.

But if the anarchists constitute a subversive and secret underground society, the authorities are depicted as no less intriguing and parasitical. As the narrative bifurcates into twin tales, of the crime and its detection, such parallels identify anarchy as the condition of society at large. Chief Inspector Heat correctly identifies Verloc as the perpetrator of the outrage, but in order to protect his informant, he tries to pin the blame upon Michaelis. Heat's superior, the Assistant Commissioner of the Special Crimes Department, who has his own personal motives for protecting Michaelis, detects the cover-up and decides to conduct his own investigation. Disguising himself, he visits Brett Street and interviews Verloc, who accepts the offer of police protection in return for turning state witness against Vladimir. Having reported to the Home Secretary and clearly relishing his success, the Assistant Commissioner is able not only to rebut Vladimir's "immense contempt for the English police" (224) by announcing that the mystery has been solved, but, having listened to his fulminations against British liberalism – "we suffer greatly from their [the anarchists] activity, while you ... suffer their presence gladly in your midst" (224) – also to hint at Vladimir's own impending exposure: "We can put our finger on every anarchist here ... All that's wanted now is to do away with the agent provocateur to make everything safe" (228).

*   *   *

Although Verloc is the "secret agent" of the novel's title, he is only one of many characters whose behaviour stems from secret motives: all of the other major characters practise concealment and are secret agents. Why does Winnie marry Verloc? Why does Ossipon not sit with Winnie on the train? Why does the Assistant Commissioner not want Michaelis arrested? Wherever one looks in this novel, one finds characters motivated by reasons known to them alone. Both the anarchists and the forces of law and order ranged against them depend upon secrecy and double-dealing. To Chief Inspector Heat, the relationship between the policeman and the burglar is symbiotically determined by the state of society: "Products of the same machine, one classed as useful and the other as noxious, they take the machine for granted in different ways, with a serious-ness essentially the same" (92). Yet, significantly, he excludes the anarchists from this relationship: "There were no rules for dealing with anarchists" (97). To Heat, the anarchists threaten the very relationship between law and lawlessness upon which the security of British society is shown to depend. By contrast, his anarchist adversary, the "Lunatic" (97) Professor, insists upon their mutual definition and identification: "The terrorist and the policeman both come from the same basket. Revolution, legality – counter moves in the same game" (69).

The Assistant Commissioner may dismiss the incident as a "sham" (227), but its public and potential political ramifications are extreme: a bomb outrage on British soil perpetrated by the representative of a foreign government. No less extreme is this incident's private impact: by the end of the novel the entire Verloc household – Verloc, Winnie, and Stevie – are dead. Reporting to Sir Ethelred, the Assistant Commissioner offers the opinion that "From a certain point of view we are here in the presence of a domestic drama" (222). The collocation of public and private dimensions of anarchism ensures that it becomes a metaphor for Conrad's social vision in *The Secret Agent*.

If the revolutionary threat posed by the anarchists in *The Secret Agent* fails to achieve its public end, its effect is felt instead in the havoc wreaked in the private sphere of the Verloc family, the domestication of the outrage. Secrecy characterises the marriage: Winnie's belief that "things do not stand much looking into" (177) means that her husband's clandestine activities remain unques-tioned and unexamined. Similarly, Winnie's ulterior motive for marrying Verloc, like her mother's decision to leave the family home, is motivated by concerns for Stevie of which Verloc remains ignorant. No less than the women who variously support Michaelis, Yundt, and Ossipon, Winnie and her mother demonstrate the para-sitic nature of human relationships through self-sacrificing gestures.

Such gestures acquire dramatic form in the cab-ride that takes Winnie's mother to the almshouse in Chapter 8 and provides the novel with one of its most enduring and bleakest metaphors of human destiny. Synthesising many of the novel's social themes, the dilapidated hackney-carriage travels past the Treasury and Palace of Westminster (called by its old name, St Stephens), on a journey that implicitly anatomises English society through the institutions of British government. *The Secret Agent* is a political novel not simply because it deals with diplomats and members of Parliament, but also in its treatment of the individual's place in politically organised society. With its maimed and alcoholic driver and infirm horse – "the steed of apocalyptic misery" (167) – the journey provides a pitiless exposure of the plight of the poor, leading to Stevie's recognition that this is a "Bad world for poor people" (171). Defending his treatment of the horse, the driver says: "I am a night cabby, I am ... I've got to take out what they will blooming well give me at the yard. I've got my missus and four kids at 'ome" (166).

In his essay on *The Secret Agent*, Thomas Mann wrote: "the striking feature of modern art is that it has ceased to recognise the categories of tragic and comic or the dramatic classifications, tragedy and comedy. It sees life as tragi-comedy, with the result that the grotesque is its most genuine style" (1933: 240–41). The cab-ride epitomises this claim. Poverty and degradation coexist with countervailing sympathy and sacrifice, but the sentiment behind human action is rendered ironic by the chronological arrangement of the narrative. Winnie's mother's belief that Stevie's life will be made more secure by her removal from the home occurs after the reader suspects that his may well be the body that was blown to bits by the explosion in Greenwich Park, emphasising the futility of altruistic sentiment behind human action in a macabre comedy of inevitability.

The violence of Stevie's dismemberment prefigures the end of the Verloc household as, first, Winnie murders Verloc and, then, takes her own life in a closing sequence in which the anarchic impulse is domesticated. Listening at the keyhole, Winnie overhears her husband's conversation with Chief Inspector Heat and discovers that Stevie was the victim of the Greenwich Park bomb. The delayed revelation of this suspected truth means that the reader shares the full force of its explosive impact upon Winnie. Haunted by "the supreme illusion of her life," that Verloc and Stevie "Might have been father and son" (244), Winnie is traumatised by the news.

At this point, the crime has been solved and all the central characters apprised of its details. The focus now remains resolutely fixed upon its domestic implications, revealing the personal investment in political action. The scene in which Verloc faces his wife's grief in Chapter 11 provides a minute study of the lack of communication and secrecy that lies at the heart of the domestic tragedy: his self-absorbed account of how he came to be embroiled in the outrage is balanced by her bewildered reaction to it and to the secret sacrifice of her married life. Thus, events leading up to the trauma are presented after it has happened, and, in this sense, Vladimir's intention of blowing up time is fulfilled. The disrupted narrative chronology in *The Secret Agent* ensures that innocent, contingent remarks are transfigured, with hindsight, into precursors of inevitable fate.

Exemplifying the "moral nihilism" (13) attributed to him by the narrator, Verloc appears supremely unaware of the enormity of what he has done. Rather, he blames Winnie for "shoving" Stevie onto him (257) and believes himself magnanimous for not criticising her for sewing the address label into Stevie's coat: "It is you who brought the police about our ears. Never mind, I won't say anything more about it" (247). As a grim extension of the lack of communication, Winnie discovers that, despite her willed detachment from her husband's affairs, she is implicated in them. By cultivating the bond between Verloc and Stevie, she has unwittingly contributed to her brother's death. Not merely a victim of anarchy, she is also an unwitting collaborator.

With Stevie's death, Winnie realises that the secret bond that tethered her life to Verloc is dissolved: "Her contract with existence, as represented by that man standing over there, was at an end. She was a free woman" (251). Oblivious to her husband's attempts to explain his actions, Winnie, in what seems an automatic, unmeditated action, stabs her husband when he calls her to join him on the sofa. The pervading sense of social alienation in *The Secret Agent* is here configured as personal loss, and the veneer of domestic functionality beneath which such loneliness has been suppressed is violently shattered. In a supreme example of the entrapment of humanity within a matrix of destruction, Winnie's brief moment of freedom is dashed as she becomes a murderess. Escaping from the house she encounters Ossipon and throws herself upon his mercy, aware of and even playing upon his previous erotic interest in her. He promises to aid her escape but takes her money and abandons her just as the boat-train is departing for the Continent. In an epilogue to the novel, Ossipon visits The Professor a week later, obsessed with a newspaper report of the mysterious suicide of a female passenger on a cross-Channel ferry.

Conrad admitted that *The Secret Agent* was "a new departure in genre," explaining its "technical intention" as "a sustained effort in ironical treatment of a melodramatic subject" (*CL3*: 491). Now accepted as one of his greatest novels, early reviewers were exercised by what they perceived as its gratuitous bleakness. The *Country Life* reviewer, for instance, claimed: "it is as indecent to exhibit a murder done in this slow and tedious manner as it would be to have the shambles of a butcher in the public streets" (Sherry, ed., 1973: 189). That Conrad was unprepared for this reaction is demonstrated by comments in his "Author's Note" to the novel, written in 1920: "I must conclude that I had still preserved much of my pristine innocence in the year 1907. It seems to me now that some criticisms would be based on the ground of sordid surroundings and the moral squalor of the tale" (vii).

In *The Secret Agent*, the threat from foreign anarchists raises concerns about national security and summons into action the state intelligence apparatus. Added to this, the depiction of London's poor, acutely registered in the consciousness of the compassion-ate Stevie or the cabman, provides such politically revolutionary doctrines with a basis in social experience. What matter could be more serious? And yet the tone that Conrad adopts is one of cor-rosive irony. Verloc's death provides a good example of Conrad's method. As Verloc calls his wife to come and join him on the sofa, he does so "in a peculiar tone, which might have been the tone of brutality, but was intimately known to Mrs Verloc as the note of wooing" (262). The brutality/wooing ambiguity is typical of the tonal deception that characterises the narrative and sustains Conrad's "ironical treatment." Just before this, overcome by the "sensation of unappeasable hunger," Verloc had dined:

> The piece of roast beef, laid out in the likeness of funereal baked meats for Stevie's obsequies, offered itself largely to his notice.... Mr. Verloc partook ravenously, without restraint and decency, cut-ting thick slices with the sharp carving knife, and swallowing them without bread. (253)

Verloc, of course, does not make the connection between Stevie and the carved meat, the British national dish – less a case of his callous-ness than proof of his self-absorption – but the narrator ensures that the reader does, and this connection stimulates a host of further correspondences that conflate Winnie's murderous action with its cause. Like the beef, Stevie's body, as seen by Chief Inspector Heat in Chapter 5, was reduced to pieces of meat, "an accumulation of raw material for a cannibal feast" (86). Numerous parallels sustain the grotesque connection between Stevie and the meat on which Verloc dines. For example, Heat resembles "an indigent customer bending over what may be called the by-products of a butcher's shop with a view to an inexpensive Sunday dinner" (88). It is a cruel irony that Winnie's last conversation with Stevie concerns his appearance: "You know how you do get yourself very untidy when you get a chance, Stevie" (189).

With macabre, poetic justice, the carving knife that Verloc uses to cut the beef provides Winnie's weapon – and we recall her telling Verloc at the end of Chapter 3 of how she had to take the carving knife away from Stevie after he had become so incensed by a story of military cruelty in one of Ossipon's pamphlets that he "would have stuck that officer like a pig if had seen him then. It's true, too! Some people don't deserve much mercy" (60). Once recognised, the complex of associations – that extends to the narrator's early description of Verloc as "Undemonstrative and burly in a fat-pig style" (13) – confers a sense of tragic inevitability upon the individual lives while dramatising Conrad's view of "a mankind always so tragically eager for self-destruction" (ix). As Winnie demonstrates, it is not merely the bomb-carrying Professor who is primed to explode in *The Secret Agent*: anarchism has become a metaphor for social and private vision.

In the supreme instance of communication at cross purposes in the novel, Winnie responds to her husband's invitation to "Come here" (262), only to murder him. Moving past the dinner table on her way to the unsuspecting Verloc, she arms herself with the carving knife, and as she approaches "the resemblance of her face with that of her brother grew at every step, even to the droop of the lower lip, even to the slight divergence of the eyes" (262). Again, it is the reader and not Verloc who appreciates the grim appropriateness of his nemesis.

The murder is represented indirectly and from Verloc's perspective: "He saw partly on the ceiling and partly on the wall the moving shadow of an arm with a clenched hand holding a carving knife. It flickered up and down. Its movements were leisurely enough for Mr Verloc to recognize the limb and the weapon" (262). Such stylised indirectness heightens the detachment between the couple, while the presentation of the murder in slow motion comically recalls that the origins of this tragedy lay in an attempt to blow up time itself.

Under Western Eyes

Conrad's declared intention in writing *Under Western Eyes* was "to capture the very soul of things Russian – Cosas de Russia" (*CL4*: 8). Unsurprisingly, the confrontation with the spectre of Russian autocracy that had blighted his family proved painful. This most autobiographical of his political fictions, "the most deeply meditated novel that came from under my pen" (*CL5*: 695), was begun in December 1907 and only completed in January 1910. It contributed to a physical and psychological breakdown, during which, Jessie Conrad recalls, her husband "spoke all the time in Polish" and repeated "snatches of orders in an Eastern language" (1935: 143).

Under Western Eyes was originally conceived as a short story, entitled "Razumov," after the novel's protagonist. It is first mentioned in a letter of 4 December 1907 as being "about the revolutionist who is blown up with his own bomb" (*CL3*: 513). The echo of *The Secret Agent* in this outline is obvious, and even though Conrad's conception of the plot altered as the writing proceeded, *Under Western Eyes* recalls its predecessor in important ways, including its atmosphere of surveillance and conspiratorial visions, the atrocities committed in the name of utopia, and its twin narratives that combine a psychological thriller with a witheringly critical account of the anarchist milieu in which the action takes place.

The cause of Polish independence from Russia dominated the lives of Conrad's parents. When he left Cracow in 1874, Conrad took with him, as part of his intellectual and emotional inheritance, memories of Russian autocracy that made him sceptical about any concept of freedom that presumed to impose itself through political coercion. The novel draws upon recognisable clichés and identifiable prototypes of Russianness for its sources. For instance, Fleishman (1967) notes how the arc of Peter Ivanovitch's life traces that of Michael Bakunin's. In his "Author's Note" (1920) to *Under Western Eyes* Conrad confessed: "I had never been called before to a greater effort of detachment: detachment from all passions, prejudices and even from personal memories" (viii). Although he described the novel as "an attempt to render not so much the political state as the psychology of Russia" (vii), the narrative demonstrates the degree to which psychological states are linked to political situations.

* * *

The narrative emerges as "something in the nature of a journal, a diary" (4) written by Kirylo Sidorovitch Razumov and charting his tragic implication in politics, that has been translated by and filtered through an English teacher of languages. Obtuse at times, acute at others, distancing and interventionist, the Teacher of Languages is more than simply a framing device: he is the persona of the Occidental with a substratum of sympathy for the Russians. His presence invests the narrative with a double authority, juxtaposing Eastern and Western ideas, while his mediation between the Russians and the reader foregrounds the problem of adequately conveying the sensibilities of a foreign culture. As the novel's heroine, Natalia Haldin assures him, it is the Russians' "*mouvements d'âme*" – literally, the movements of their souls – that are beyond Westerners (105).

Listening to the political idealism of Natalia Haldin, with whom he is engaged in "a course of reading the best English authors" (101), the English teacher confesses: "I suppose ... that you will be shocked if I tell you that I haven't understood – I won't say a single word; I've understood all the words ... " (106). In his attempt to convey the "psychology of Russia," Conrad uses the Teacher of Languages to dramatise his conviction that there is something definitively different about the Russian and Western European imaginations. As the "heroic fugitive" (125) Peter Ivanovitch puts it: "In Russia it is different" (119).

The Teacher of Language's narrative begins with a disclaimer about his fitness for the task: "Words, as is well known, are the great foes of reality" (3). This stark pronouncement is borne out by a narrative in which revolutionary atrocities are committed in the name of utopia and the search for the ideal in the midst of misery becomes a recurrent motif in Russian experience. Translating Razumov's "strange human document," the Teacher of Languages perceives his task as the accurate rendering of "the moral conditions ruling over a large portion of this earth's surface" and, intent upon discovering some "key-word" that will "hold truth enough to help the moral discovery which should be the object of every tale," he settles on "cynicism":

> For that is the mark of Russian autocracy and of Russian revolt. In its pride of numbers, in its strange pretensions of sanctity, and in the secret readiness to abase itself in suffering, the spirit of Russia is the spirit of cynicism. It informs the declarations of her statesmen, the theories of her revolutionists, and the mystic vaticinations of prophets to the point of making freedom look like a form of debauch, and the Christian virtues themselves appear actually indecent. (67)

Razumov views cynicism as an ineluctable aspect of his national inheritance: "We are Russians, that is – children; that is – sincere; that is – cynical" (207). The Teacher of Languages partially endorses this view when he claims: "Russian simplicity often marches innocently on the edge of cynicism for some lofty purpose" (125–26). However, he fails to adopt the connection of sincerity with cynicism, with the result that he sometimes seems to be "othering" what he does not immediately understand.

To the narrator, Russian psychic reality is pervaded by a language of cynicism that always looks for base motives, never seeing the good in people, and finds its expression in contempt for the joys of everyday life. While Razumov is caught in a political trap in *Under Western Eyes*, the Teacher of Languages is caught in a rhetorical trap: acknowledging the Russians as unintelligible, he yet seeks to translate their words and feelings that fall under his "Western eyes" for the Western reader.

Everything in the novel is double-edged. Russian autocracy creates a fraught political situation that gives rise to heroic revolutionary struggle, yet the revolutionists are ambiguously presented. For instance, Peter Ivanovitch's reputation as "the great feminist" is demonstrably undermined by his treatment of Tekla, his long-suffering secretary; in turn, sympathy for Tekla is qualified due to her self-abasement. Even the alternative to autocracy, Western democratic stability and orderliness as exemplified by Geneva, is presented as sterile. Describing Geneva as "the heart of democracy," Razumov declares that it is "A fit heart for it; no bigger than a parched pea and about as much value" (205–06). The suspicion that the Russians engage in a kind of double-think, in impossibilities where contrary extremes are compatible, rendering them unknowable, supports the Teacher of Language's repeated emphasis upon his and the reader's remoteness from them.

Compounding the problem of Russian officialdom's cynicism – seen in its "sublime contempt for truth" (306) – is the language of mysticism with which the revolutionists couch their aspirations, claiming for their actions a spiritual authority beyond the practical and pragmatic world. One is reminded of Michaelis' claim in *The Secret Agent*: "All idealization makes life poorer" (41). In this light, Conrad's choice of central character is both politically and aesthetically acute. A philosophy student, Razumov distrusts the relevance of revolutionary rhetoric to real life, while, historically, Russian universities were purged of their philosophy departments by, for instance, Tsar Nicholas I in response to the Decembrist attempt on his life in 1825 and by Lenin after the Bolsheviks seized power in 1917.

Razumov, a third-year student at St Petersburg University, without family, although apparently the natural son of Prince K–, dreams of making his way in the world by winning the silver medal offered as an essay-prize by the Ministry of Education. These dreams are shattered when he returns to his lodgings one day to discover Victor Haldin, an older student and "not one of the industrious set" (14–15), in his room. Haldin announces that he has just killed a Minister of State and has turned to Razumov, whom he knows only slightly, expecting shelter and help with his escape.

Thus Razumov, whose name draws upon the Russian word for "reason," *razum*, is undone – as he sees it – by the merciless logic of fate:

> Fatality enters your rooms while your landlady's back is turned; you come home and find it in possession bearing a man's name, clothed in flesh – wearing a brown cloth coat and long boots – lounging against the stove. It asks you, "Is the outer door closed?" – and you don't know enough to take it by the throat and fling it downstairs. You don't know. You welcome the crazy fate. (84)

The ambiguities and complexities of the political and psychological thriller to follow develop from this basic situation. Razumov's desperate attempts to stave off the collapse of his rational and circumscribed world lead only to his implication in the workings of the state – beginning with the betrayal of Haldin and continuing with his role as police spy. Action itself is rendered compensatory as he faces up to the monstrous reality that has overtaken him.

Haldin's sister, Natalia, expresses the standard Russian view of the West when she refers scornfully to "nations that have made their bargain with fate" (114). However much "fate" is cheapened by this "bargain" – and the Teacher of Languages reminds her that "the terms men and nations obtain from Fate are hallowed by the price" (114) – as Razumov's experience demonstrates, fate is equated with politics for Russians because free will and self-determination do not exist.

While the novel exploits the traditional alienation between the Russian state and the intelligentsia, Razumov considers himself apolitical. Nonetheless it is to the state that he looks for definition: "His closest parentage was defined in the statement that he was Russian. Whatever good he expected from life would be given to or withheld form his hopes by that connexion alone" (10–11). But Razumov's real life is duplicitous: seeking the potential rewards of the silver medal that he hopes will "convert the label Razumov into an honoured name" (14), he needs the recognition of a ruthless tyranny. His belief that "A man's real life is that accorded to him in the thoughts of other men by reason of respect or natural love" (14) involves Razumov in a contradiction, for this "real life" is circumscribed and inhibited by the autocracy personified by de P–, "President of the notorious Repressive Commission," and driven by a "mystic acceptance of the principle of autocracy" (7).

* * *

Confessing to Razumov, Haldin says: "It was I who removed de P– this morning" (16). But how does Razumov – or the reader – receive the euphemism "removed"? This "removal" is a crude, calculated act, carried out with precision: it leaves a "small heap of dead bodies lying upon each other near the carcasses of the two horses" (10) – and in this heap, both Haldin's target and his fellow assassin. Compounding the Teacher of Language's translation of Razumov's document are other, ideological "translations." How should one judge Haldin's action: is it inherently loathsome, or defensible under this particular regime?

Initially, at least, there is no falsity of position in Razumov's decision to betray Haldin. Motivated by self-preservation, Razumov recognises that, as a Russian, "for him to be implicated meant simply sinking into the lowest social depths amongst the hopeless and the destitute – the night birds of the city" (25–26). Similarly, his reason rejects the idealism behind Haldin's action: "A murder is a murder" (26), he claims. Yet even while dismissing Haldin as a "sanguinary fanatic" intent upon "disruption," he acknowledges the misery of Russian life: "Better that thousands should suffer than that a people should become a disintegrated mass, helpless like dust in the wind. Obscurantism is better than the light of incendiary torches" (34). If Razumov had assisted rather than betrayed Haldin, he would have become an accomplice in the crime, and the issue confronting the reader would be that of endorsing one position rather than another. By including a political dimension, however, *Under Western Eyes* complicates judgement, not least because of the titular and narratorial emphases placed upon how Russians appear to Western eyes: as the characters are not Westerners, how do our value judgements apply?

In betraying Haldin, Razumov has sought to free himself from implication in the political crime. But his self-preserving action has made him an instrument of the state, with the consequence that, in betraying Haldin, he has simultaneously betrayed himself. Far from negotiating his own future by means of his studies, Razumov has the role of state-spy imposed upon him as Councillor Mikulin, director of "general police supervision over Europe," decides to make use of the "tool" that "the revolutionists themselves had put into his hands" (307).

The satire on Russians and their use of language, whereby words are deprived of fixed meanings, extends to the moral ambiguity of Razumov and the revolutionaries: in the fraught atmosphere of autocratic Russia, it would appear, no one and no action emerges untainted and unambiguous. Razumov is at the mercy of impossible twentieth-century forces: the act of betraying Haldin to the state leads to his own entrapment within the workings of the state. As he confesses late in the novel: "In giving Victor Haldin up, it was myself, after all, whom I have betrayed most basely" (361). The degree to which Razumov is implicated in state surveillance is expressed with forceful simplicity when he attempts to leave Councillor Mikulin's office at the end of Part I: " 'Where to?' asked Councillor Mikulin softly" (99). The consequent implications for the notion of the "self" – is it private or state property? – provide the narrative with its tone of self-alienation and psychological intensity. In Carabine's formulation, Razumov "incarnates the dissensions that are tearing his nation apart" (Stape, ed., 1996: 126).

* * *

In Part 2, the action shifts to Geneva. The revelation that Razumov is in the city as a spy for the Russian government, reporting upon the revolutionary circle he has infiltrated, is long delayed. The narrative deception complements the lie that his life has become: his studies abandoned, he is officially but secretly an instrument of tyranny; and, further illustrating how the narrative's penchant for opening up dual perspectives populates the work with alter egos and doubles, the revolutionaries on whom he is spying believe him to have been Haldin's accomplice in the murder of de P–. The chain of circumstances by which his life is bound to the state is extended by this enforced identification with Haldin, while personal drama is added to the ideological contest at the heart of this novel of ideas when Razumov meets and is struck by Miss Haldin, Victor's sister.

The Teacher of Language personifies stereotypical English reserve in his detachment from the emotionally volatile Russians. To his bewildered Western eyes they shade into grotesquerie and their actions into tragic folly. Ironically cast in the role of bumbling swain in his relationship with Natalia Haldin: he is by turns teacher, family friend, distant admirer, and confidant in an unlikely romantic triangle involving Miss Haldin, Razumov, and himself.

As Kirschner (1988) has shown, Conrad's use of Geneva as locale in *Under Western Eyes* not only draws upon his memories of the city for mimetic effect (the novel was begun shortly after his fourth and final visit to the city), but his alertness to the geography of the city creatively underscores the novel's central themes. For instance, the Haldin women occupy a house in the Boulevard des Philosophes, an address whose name recalls Razumov's abandoned studies while teasingly stressing that Western philosophy can offer no consolation to Mrs Haldin on the death of her son. But the Boulevard des Philosophes is also midway between Geneva's Russian Orthodox Church, to the north, and the quarter known as "La Petite Russie," to the south. Thus Conrad has located the women between the old religion and the new, topographically reflecting the narrative debate between faith and reason. In response to his portrayal of the city, when the Genevese erected a plaque on the Hôtel-Pension de la Roserie to commemorate Conrad's four visits, it included the inscription: "Geneva Despecta Suscipiens" [Geneva is scorned giving shelter].

Conrad's early outline of the Geneva scenes that dominate the rest of the narrative are expressed in a letter of 1908:

> The student Razumov meeting abroad the mother and sister of Haldin falls in love with that last, marries her and after a time confesses to her the part he played in the arrest and death of her brother....

The psychological developments leading to Razumov's betrayal of Haldin, to his confession of the fact to his wife and to the death of these people (brought about mainly by the resemblance of their child to the late Haldin) form the real subject of the story.
(*CL4*: 9)

Although it contains the seeds of the tragic love story Conrad originally envisioned, the relationship between Razumov and Natalia Haldin is neither realised nor exploited for its potential romantic interest. Instead, it provides a further dimension of his dealings with Russian émigrés in Geneva, and is characterised by this contest between trust and deception, ensuring that the focus of *Under Western Eyes* remains the ideological contrast between East and West.

Natalia Haldin's presence ensures that the private and public sides of Razumov's nature are comparably compromised. Both romantically and politically he is living a lie. Summarising Natalia's views on her brother's death, the Teacher of Languages says that she "was disposed to think that her brother had been betrayed to the police in some way" (193). Razumov's reactions to such observations are understandably hysterical. Sincerity is the central term in his notion of what it is to be Russian – "children; that is – sincere; that is – cynical" (207) – yet concealment, whether his betrayal of Haldin or his role as a state spy or his emergent feelings for Natalia Haldin, has robbed him of the confidence of this sincerity. Symbolically, when the teacher of Languages leaves Razumov at the end of Part 2, the latter is leaning over the parapet of a bridge, staring into the rushing waters of the Rhone, half-attracted by the abyss.

In Geneva, Razumov enters the orbit of Peter Ivanovitch, "Europe's greatest feminist" (205), and it is noticeable how women now dominate his dealings with the revolutionaries. Whereas women are cast in supporting roles as regards the revolutionaries in *The Secret Agent*, in *Under Western Eyes* they appear to have followed Ivanovitch's injunction to "descend into the arena" (131) of political action. At one extreme stands the grotesque Madame de S–, "a galvanized corpse out of some Hoffman's Tale" (215), whose revolutionary aim is to "spiritualise the discontent" of the Russians (221) and to whom the revolutionaries look in vain for a financial bequest. At the other extreme stands Sophia Antonovna, Peter Ivanovitch's "right hand" (253), whom Razumov recognises as "the personal adversary he had to meet" (261) and regards as "un-Russian" (264) in appearance.

Sophia Antonovna is elevated above the "the visionary and criminal babble of revolutionists" (248) that Razumov encounters in Geneva: "Stripped of rhetoric, mysticism, and theories, she was the true spirit of destructive revolution" (261). Like that of Tekla, Peter Ivanovitch's *dame de compagnie* and long-suffering secretary, Sophia Antonovna's history under Russian autocracy, which she describes as "the great social iniquity of the system resting on unrequited toil and unpitied sufferings" (262), charts her inevitable recruitment to the cause of revolution. Tekla's story of how she was converted to the cause, awakened "to the horrors from which innocent people are made to suffer in this world, only in order that governments might exist" (150), graphically conveys the human misery in Russia that has inspired her self-sacrifice, while her mistreatment at the Château Borel, a dilapidated *bourgeois* villa on Geneva's outskirts and the centre of the revolutionary cell Razumov infiltrates, damns the revolution as similarly autocratic.

When, echoing Marlow's words in *Lord Jim*, Peter Ivanovitch calls Razumov "one of *us*" (208), Razumov responds with vehemence: "I don't want any one to claim me. But Russia *can't* disown me. She cannot! ... I am *it!*" (209). The realignment of his contact with the revolutionaries on the grounds of gender has important consequences. In particular, his meeting with an actual mother, Mrs Haldin, asserts the power of claims beyond those of reason, for which his kinship with "Mother Russia" provides no guidance. To Razumov, the fifteen minutes he spends alone with Mrs Haldin are "like the revenge of the unknown" (340). Both politically and emotionally Razumov proves to be, in the Teacher of Languages' words, "the puppet of his past" (362). It is when Razumov emerges from this interview to find Natalia Haldin in the anteroom that, "tottering suddenly on the very edge of the precipice" (349), he confesses to betraying her brother. His diary includes the accusation directed at her: "You were appointed to undo the evil by making me betray myself back into truth and peace. You! And you have done it in the same way, too, in which he ruined me: by forcing upon me your confidence" (358). Intriguingly, his caveat to this – "Only don't be deceived, Natalia Victorovna, I am not converted" (361) – combines political allegiance and mystical sentiment in the word "converted."

The psychological and emotional distance that Razumov travels in *Under Western Eyes* is confirmed by the *volte-face* he performs. His "atrocious confession" (355) includes his Mephistophelian intention to revenge himself upon Haldin through his sister: "And do you know what I said to myself? I shall steal his sister's soul from her" (359). Perhaps as a vindictive replacement for the silver medal he hoped to win, Natalia herself becomes Razumov's "prize" (360) within the scheme of the novel. But, in one of a number of comparisons with Dostoevsky's *Crime and Punishment* (1866), love proves the redemptive force for change: "I felt that I must tell you that I had ended by loving you" (361). The portrait of Razumov in *Under Western Eyes* combines the development of his political consciousness with a study of the moral complexities of choice and betrayal. In the process his right to privacy is subordinate to the protection of existing structures of domination, ensuring that any dream of love is dispelled by circumstance and the machinations of the state.

* * *

In his complex process of self-excoriation, Razumov epitomises what Malcolm Bradbury has called "the self-alienating modern imagination" (1989: 52). He is a spy who, in a world of adversaries and doubles, is always spying on himself as he struggles with the contradictions in his own sensations that lead, through a psychological crisis, to his confession. While describing himself as "just a man. ... A man with a mind" (61), Razumov is unable to connect his mind with the randomness of the world that surrounds him. His taciturnity contrasts with the loquacity of the revolutionists who, more often than not, condemn themselves out of their own mouths: now inadvertently creating his alibi by interpreting the death of Ziemianitch as proof of Haldin's betrayer, now unknowingly determining his role as state spy. When Julius Laspara urges Razumov to write, he takes it as his cue to draft his first report for the Russian authorities – with ironic appropriateness, while sitting on the Ile Rousseau, beneath a statue of the author of *The Social Contract*. For his own part, he recalls the epigram that "speech has been given to us for the purpose of concealing our thoughts" (261).

Having confessed privately to Miss Haldin, Razumov then visits the house of Julius Laspara to make a public confession to the assembled revolutionists. Betrayed into truth by the conventional power of love and the impossibility of continuing to live a lie, Razumov unmasks himself not because he is conscience-stricken but as an act of self-assertion over the revolutionists he derides. Retribution is swift: grimly extending the narrative's theme of communication, the brutal Nikita deafens him by bursting his eardrums, "with an excited, gleeful squeak" (369). But in this world of espionage and counter-espionage, Nikita himself is a double agent and is subsequently betrayed to Peter Ivanovitch by Mikulin. To the Teacher of Languages, who hears the story from Sophia Antonovna, this is a further instance of his detachment from "things Russian, unrolling their Eastern logic under my Western eyes" (381).

References to sight punctuate the narrative, including Miss Haldin's "trustful" eyes, Peter Ivanovitch's dark glasses, or the fact that assignations between Mikulin and Razumov take place at an oculist's. In playful opposition to this, Razumov's actions in Geneva provide a solemn version of a standard comic situation: a comedy of frustrations in which he is unable to reveal the obvious. With "the misfortune to be born clear-eyed" (345), Razumov is a tragic character not simply because he betrays himself but also because he is conscious of this betrayal.

In consequence of his deafening, Razumov is knocked down by a tram and rendered "a hopeless cripple" (373). But, once again, this incident draws him into the world of revolutionaries. He returns to Russia to eke out the rest of his life being accompanied by and cared for by the self-sacrificing Tekla who, in Sophia Antonovna's words, "had found work to do after her own heart" (379). The fate of the Haldin family, too, provides both a testament to Russian autocracy and an index to the call to revolution: after her mother's death, Natalia, in "a characteristically Russian exploit in self-suppression," returns to her homeland in order to answer "the stifled cry of our great distress" (375, 376).

Terry Eagleton identifies the central concern of the novel as "the relations between English and foreign experience" (1970: 32). Presented through the filter of the English Teacher of Languages, the Russians are unknowable. This sense persists to the final words, uttered by Sophia Antonovna: "Peter Ivanovitch is an inspired man" (382). Thus she confirms the Russian penchant for "mysticism" and the narrative's preferred tone for their revolutionary thinking. Within this fated context, language itself is debased. For instance, when Natalia Haldin emphasises that the Russian experience cannot be understood in Western terms, she says: "You think it is a class conflict, or a conflict of interests, as social contests are with you in Europe. But it is not that at all. It is something quite different" (104). To the Teacher of Languages such comments are essentially "Russian": "That propensity of lifting every problem from the plane of the understandable by means of some sort of mystic expression, is very Russian" (104). So, not only is politics reducible to fate in *Under Western Eyes*, but the language of reason is pitted against the language of faith. The revolutionaries' mysticism thus alienates them from both the Language Teacher and Razumov. Michael Ignatieff's conclusion in *The Language of Strangers* is salutary here:

> We need justice, we need liberty, and we need as much solidarity as can be reconciled with justice and liberty. But we also need, as much as anything else, language adequate to the times we live in. We need to see how we live now and we can only see with words and images which leave us no escape into nostalgia for some other time and place.   (1990: 141)

* * *

In *Under Western Eyes*, the political is the personal, with ordinary Russians caught in a world hopelessly divided between an inherited autocracy, marked by brutality and corruption, and new, revolutionary forces demanding to be heard. To appreciate the scale of Conrad's achievement in the novel, both in creating a Russian perspective and as an extension of the political impulse that began with *Nostromo* nearly a decade earlier, one might compare Razumov with another Conradian hero who betrays himself through circumstances beyond his control, Jim. Marlow's insistence that Jim is "one of us" in *Lord Jim* offers a conventional code of values with which we can identify to pose the question: how can one of *us* do such a thing? By contrast, *Under Western Eyes* seeks to explain the inexplicable Russian character, offering no "us," with which to identify.

Founded upon the belief that there is an underlying truth, a completeness, against which moral behaviour can be measured, *Lord Jim* contains a moral quest that ends in Stein's gnomic experiment. The novel is thus based upon a paradox: Marlow's appeal to an underlying moral truth implies the belief that this urge can be answered, but, to Marlow, Jim remains elusive in important respects. Consequently, the reader admires commitment that can never be justified. Although *Under Western Eyes* contains a greater degree of complexity because of its political dimension, at its heart is a very ordinary moral problem: Razumov's betrayal of Haldin is understandable, even inevitable. While Jim appears to have a moral being separate from that illustrated by his actions – he is both Jim and Lord Jim – the different Razumovs are just different perspectives, there is no comparable falsity of position. Put another way, we cannot imagine Marlow in *Under Western Eyes*.

Under Western Eyes begins with a potentially rich moral situation, juxtaposing images of Russian tyranny with those of a heroic struggle for liberty. As in *Hamlet*, "the time is out of joint," but Razumov makes the reverse choice from Hamlet, he acts rather than procrastinates, thereby shifting the emphasis away from the anxiety to understand him. In large part the distinction between Jim and Razumov centres on the nature of their "crimes." Marlow sympathises with Jim but does not become his accomplice: under Marlow's eyes, Jim's crime of abandoning the *Patna* remains a crime. Placed in a situation where his only choices are illusory – he must either accept or betray Haldin – Razumov would have become an accomplice had he helped the young revolutionary to escape. Instead, in an act that approximates to Jim saving himself by jumping ship, he saves his skin by turning Haldin in to the authorities. So, the focus of attention shifts to how we are to interpret Razumov's action: if it is justified as an act of self-preservation, then why does he confess at the end? His claim to have betrayed himself "back into truth" (358) is itself ambiguous, since the designation of his life, pre-Haldin as "truth" is unsustainable. Were *Under Western Eyes* only about Razumov then it would endorse one position rather than another; instead it is about the foreignness of the Russians generally to the Western mind, necessitating the presence of the Teacher of Languages, speaking as a Westerner to Westerners, in a narrative where language itself is no longer reliable and where Western value-judgements no longer apply.

Works cited

Baines, Jocelyn. *Joseph Conrad: A Critical Biography*. London: Weidenfeld & Nicolson, 1959.
Bradbury, Malcolm. *The Modern World: Ten Great Writers*. London: Penguin, 1989.
Conrad, Jessie. *Joseph Conrad and His Circle*. London: Jarrolds, 1935.
Eagleton, Terry. *Exiles and Émigés*. London: Chatto & Windus, 1970.
Fleishman, Avrom. *Conrad's Politics: Community and Anarchy in the Fiction of Joseph Conrad*. Baltimore: Johns Hopkins Press, 1967.

Guerard, Albert J. *Conrad the Novelist*. Cambridge, Mass.: Harvard University Press, 1958.

Ignatieff, Michael. *The Needs of Strangers*. London: Hogarth Press, 1990.

Jackson, Holbrook. *The Eighteen Nineties* [1913] New York: Capricorn Books, 1966.

James, Henry. *The Princess Casamassima*. The New York Edition. Fairfield, NJ: Augustus M. Kelly, 1977.

Joyce, James. *Ulysses: The Corrected Text*. London: Bodley Head, 1986.

Kirschner, Paul. *Conrad: The Psychologist as Artist*. Edinburgh: Oliver & Boyd, 1968.

——. "Making You See Geneva: The Sense of Place in *Under Western Eyes*." *L'Epoque Conradienne* (1988): 101–27.

Mann, Thomas. *Past Masters and Other Papers*. Trans. H. T. Lowe-Porter. London: Martin Secker, 1933.

Najder, Zdzisław (ed.) *Conrad under familial eyes*. Translated by Halina Carroll-Najder. Cambridge: Cambridge University Press, 1983.

Sherry, Norman (ed.) *Conrad: The Critical Heritage*. London: Routledge & Kegan Paul, 1973.

Stape, J. H. (ed.) *The Cambridge Companion to Joseph Conrad*. Cambridge: Cambridge University Press, 1996.

Todorov, Tzvetan. *The Poetics of Prose*. Translated by Richard Howard. [1977] Ithaca, New York: Cornell University Press, 1992.

Tolstoy, Leo. *War and Peace*. Trans. Louise and Aylmer Maude. London: Macmillan, 1977.

Watts, C. T. (ed.) *Joseph Conrad's Letters to R. B. Cunninghame Graham*. Cambridge: Cambridge University Press, 1969.

——. *A Preface to Conrad*. Second Edition. London: Longman, 1993.

Woodcock, George. *Anarchism: A History of Libertarian Ideas and Movements*. Second edition. Harmondsworth: Penguin, 1986.

6

Conrad's Shorter Fiction

Conrad's novellas and short stories were collected in seven volumes. Spanning twenty years of his career as a writer, they provided a lucrative means of supplementing his income from novels. The burgeoning short-story market meant that this form was well-paid, yielding a much greater return for effort than the longer work. In 1901, when average earnings were around £100 per annum, Conrad earned £40 for "Amy Foster," a story of 12,500 words. Serialisation in a range of magazines also helped keep Conrad in the public eye while he worked on longer productions. For instance, *Youth: A Narrative, and Two Other Stories* (1902) and *Typhoon and Other Stories* (1903) appeared between the publication of *Lord Jim* (1900) and *Nostromo* (1904). Conrad turned to writing short fiction at around the time of his marriage to Jessie in 1896, probably on the advice of Edward Garnett. While honeymooning on the coast of Brittany, Conrad completed three of the five stories that would comprise his first volume, *Tales of Unrest* (1898). Recognition was swift: the volume earned him his only literary prize, a 50-guinea award from *Academy* magazine.

Hereafter, many of Conrad's novels would be initially conceived as short stories. For instance, what became *Lord Jim* was first mooted as a 20,000-word story towards a "book of short tales" (CL2: 62); *Nostromo* was originally envisioned as something "silly and saleable" (CL3: 4); while *The Secret Agent* began life as a short piece entitled "Verloc," intended as "a longish story" of "18000 or so" words (CL3: 320). Reciprocally, the short fiction provided Conrad with opportunities to explore themes and ideas that would acquire more substantial treatment in the novels. Thus,

"The Informer" and "An Anarchist," both collected in *A Set of Six* (1908), are stories whose subject matter, anarchism, is more fully developed in *The Secret Agent*, while "Because of the Dollars" in *Within the Tides* (1915), prefigures *Victory* in the trans-textual character of Davidson, the dramatic situation – a trio of villains in search of easy plunder – and the heroine's self-sacrifice.

Plaudits for these volumes were often lavish: the *Times Literary Supplement* pronounced each of the three tales in *Twixt Land and Sea Tales* (1912) "a masterpiece" while, to the *Standard*, they demonstrated that Conrad had become "the first king of a new country – that country of story-tellers who will combine the sense of form discovered here in England somewhere about 1890" (Sherry, ed., 1973: 30, 256). Despite this, Conrad recognised the discrepancy between the pragmatic need to produce saleable copy and aesthetic integrity. He described "The Lagoon," the first of his short stories to be serialised (in *Cornhill Magazine*), as containing "lots of secondhand Conradese" (*CL1*: 301). Reflecting the degree to which "Conradese" had become a recognisable trademark, the tale was parodied by Max Beerbohm in *A Christmas Garland* (1912). Similarly, "To-morrow," the final tale in *Typhoon*, was, according to its author: "'Conrad' adapted down to the needs of a magazine" (*CL2*: 373). Responding to John Galsworthy's criticism of *Within the Tides*, Conrad confessed that the tales derived from commercial rather than artistic impulses:

> The Planter est bien manqué! I had no time to wait for better inspiration. The others – well! You see my dear Jack this vol is not so much art as a financial operation. You have no idea what these second rate efforts have brought in. The Planter alone earned eight times as much as Youth, six times as much as Heart of Darkness. It makes one sick.   (*CL5*: 455)

Taken as a whole, Conrad's shorter fiction is uneven in quality. One reason might be that, as "Heart of Darkness" or "The Secret Sharer" demonstrate, the novella rather than the short story seemed better suited to the meditative inquiry that characterises his fiction. While some short stories, such as "Youth" (discussed in Chapter 4), achieve the fluency and depth one associates with Conrad at his best, he could also write "shockingly bad magazine stuff" (Leavis 1948: 209). These extend to potboilers whose grotesquerie – a bed that suffocates its occupants in "The Inn of the Two Witches" or a bloodthirsty ship in "The Brute" – seems designed to pander to popular tastes for the uncanny and the macabre. That said, the short fiction also gave Conrad the opportunity to experiment with style and subject matter. For example, "The Return," which Conrad described as a "left handed production" (*TU*: viii) and Albert J. Guerard called Conrad's "worst story" (1958: 96), reflects the stylistic influence of Henry James and, set in London, is Conrad's first fiction with an English setting.

The publication of *Typhoon and Other Stories* (1903) confirmed Conrad's status as a writer of short fiction. "We may well believe … that Mr. Conrad is now writing in the fullness of his power and rejoice in a period of fecundity," claimed *The Manchester Guardian,* while the *Morning Post* confirmed that Conrad had secured his own personal niche in the marketplace: "if we allow Mr. Kipling to be supreme on land, Mr. Conrad has no equal on the seas" (Sherry, ed., 1973: 19, 143). With its balance of sea and domestic tales – "Typhoon" and "Falk" are sea tales; "Amy Foster" and "To-morrow" engage with the English scene – *Typhoon* is a more coherent volume than most of Conrad's short story collections. Despite his view that "every volume of my short stories has a unity of artistic purpose, a mood of feeling and expression, that makes it different from every other" (*LL2*: 337), it is often difficult to see these collections as intrinsically unified. *Youth,* for instance, was originally intended as a Marlow Trilogy, until the evolution of *Lord Jim* into a novel meant that it was replaced by "The End of the Tether," costing the volume its initial unifying impulse. (Conrad would later argue that the three stories in the volume represented the three ages of man.) Even when an overt appeal to unity exists, as in *A Set of Six* (1908), where each tale is associated with a separate tonal quality – "Gaspar Ruiz" is subtitled "A Romantic Tale," "The Informer" "An Ironic Tale," and so on – the combination of eclectic tales and tones renders coherence of the volume questionable.

While Conrad's shorter fictions shadow the preoccupations of his novels – many are set in the colonial world and reflect such perennial themes as honour and identity – they also offer important new departures. For instance, the posthumously published *Tales of Hearsay* (1925), with a Preface by R. B. Cunninghame Graham, includes "Prince Roman," Conrad's only tale with a Polish setting, and "The Tale," his only piece of fiction to deal explicitly with the First World War. Written in October 1916, shortly after Conrad had undertaken tours of naval bases as part of the Admiralty's propaganda drive, "The Tale" was his last short story. The fact that Conrad wrote no short stories during the last eight years of his life can be traced to his financial success following the publication of *Chance* (1914): by 1916, not only was there no longer the same urgency to keep the wolf from the door, but Conrad's reputation now guaranteed other lucrative means of doing so, through the sale of manuscripts, for instance, or stage adaptations.

Nevertheless, the short fiction deserves a place in any study of Conrad. What follows is a brief account of five of the most frequently anthologised pieces, ending with that enigmatic but powerful story, "The Secret Sharer," perhaps one of the peaks of Conrad's art in the tight form of the novella.

"Karain: A Memory"

The opening story in *Tales of Unrest*, "Karain: A Memory," is pivotal to our sense of Conrad's early writing career. It was the first of his tales to be published in the prestigious *Blackwood's Magazine*, initiating his "Blackwood's period" that lasted from 1897 to 1902 and included the Marlow Trilogy ("Youth," "Heart of Darkness," and *Lord Jim*) and "The End of the Tether." "Karain" shares stylistic and thematic features with the Marlow Trilogy: all are frame narratives, dominated by haunting memories. Among the manuscripts that Conrad sold to the American collector, John Quinn, "Karain" never reached its destination, being carried across the Atlantic in the *Titanic*.

The tale, told by an anonymous member of a European gun-running trio, recalls how he, Hollis, and Jackson once smuggled guns to Karain, a Malay chief engaged in territorial disputes. An assured and haughty ruler, Karain is constantly attended by his old sword-bearer. During two years of illicit trading, a friendship develops between the smugglers and Karain, who generally visits them aboard their ship after dark and recounts tales of his past. On their final visit (because the trade is becoming too risky), Karain does not come to visit them, and they learn of his attendant's death. Then, on the eve of their departure, he startles them by arriving unannounced, having swum out from the shore alone, and tells them how he is haunted by the ghost of Pata Matara, his closest friend, whom he killed.

When Pata Matara's sister eloped with a Dutchman, bringing dishonour on the family, Karain joined his friend on his "obscure

Odyssey of revenge" (40). But, by the time the pair eventually track down their quarry, Karain has become so obsessed with his mental image of the girl that he envisions himself as her protector and lover, and when the moment for revenge comes, he slays his friend to save her life. In consequence, Karain is haunted by the ghost of his friend until he meets the old man whose presence exorcises Matara's ghost and who becomes his sword-bearer. When this protection is removed by the sorcerer's death, Karain is, once again, haunted by the ghost, and he begs the gun-runners either to take him with them to England where people "live in unbelief" or to give him "some of your strength – of your unbelief... A charm!" (44). Hollis provides Karain with a specifically English talisman, a Jubilee sixpenny piece, bearing the image of Queen Victoria, telling him: "She commands a spirit, too – the spirit of her nation; a masterful, conscientious, unscrupulous, unconquerable devil" (49). The coin succeeds in finally exorcising Pata Matara's ghost, and Karain returns to lead his people. The narrative concludes with a chance encounter in London, between Jackson and the narrator, outside a gun-shop in The Strand, where, Jackson confesses, the hustle and bustle of city life seems less real to him than Karain's story.

The story's obsession with memory is related to the idea of "haunting." Karain is doubly haunted: by both Pata Matara and Pata Matara's sister. But other people in the tale are haunted too. The Dutchman, whose elopement with Pata Matara's sister presents an interesting, post-colonial case of cultural inversion when he is deemed by her family to have dishonoured them, is haunted by the Malay Archipelago – to the extent that he decides to live there rather than return to Holland. Similarly, the only reason that the narrator recalls the tale is because it has haunted him in some way, demonstrating how fertile is the process of haunting: each case of haunting seems to generate a further one. Thus, Pata Matara's obsession generates Karain's obsession; and, Karain's story generates the narrator's story (which we read and, by repeating, demonstrate our own "obsession").

The narrator repeatedly describes the Malay world in theatrical terms: it is viewed as a "gorgeous spectacle" having the "suspicious immobility of a painted scene" (7). Here, "dressed splendidly for his part," Karain is "treated with a solemn respect accorded in the irreverent West only to the monarchs of the stage" (6). In combination with the tale's magical and romantic elements, such as the "old wizard … who could command ghosts and send evil spirits against enemies" (16), the narrative's theatrical frame implicitly questions the reality of exotic experience. In a tale concerned with cross-cultural relationships this raises doubts about whether cultures can truly understand and communicate with each other. In this light, Jackson's doubts about the reality of London at the end of the story – "I'll be hanged if it is yet as real to me as … as the other thing … say, Karain's story" (55) – offers a supreme reversal of colonial dominance by challenging the rhetoric of authority on which it depends.

Conrad's choice of European characters, a Dutchman and the English trio, reflects the interests of the area's two dominant colonial powers. In this context the gun-running presents an example of simple economics: the trio's supply of weapons caters for Karain's demand. From a revisionist perspective, however, the trade reflects European meddling in the affairs of another nation. This latter point gains when the narrator and Jackson meet at the end of the tale in London, far away from the Archipelago, and discuss territorial wars in the Archipelago, presumably sourced by guns they supplied to Karain. Given the importance of trade – and, from one perspective, the sixpence is the price paid by the traders for Karain's story – it is surely no accident that it is a coin that ultimately solves Karain's problem. The presence of the Jubilee sixpence as a charm or fetish to ward off evil spirits in this ghost story raises questions about its status. Viewed simply as a sixpence, the tale can be read as patronizing: Karain can be tricked into believing that a mere coin can ward off evil spirits. Alternatively, the sixpence can be seen to be invested with a magical property that Westerners believe in too: money is a kind of charm and, like magic, alters or seems to alter reality. As a Jubilee sixpence, minted to commemorate Queen Victoria's Jubilee, it carries an impression of her, representative of trade and Empire, reinforcing the cultural mythology of the British people. By demonstrating that Westerners, too, have their charms, "Karain" reduces any claims of cultural superiority to essential similarity with the Other.

"Amy Foster"

Set in England, "Amy Foster" is a tale of cultural assimilation and resistance with a twist: here the English are resistant to the invasion of the outside world, in the form of Yanko Gooral. This relocation of the colonial motif is narrated by Kennedy, the village doctor in Colebrook, Kent, and assumes the form of a tragic episode in local history when an emigrant from the Eastern Carpathians is washed ashore while trying to immigrate to America. Lured from his home by the prospect of wealth and a better life, Yanko Gooral travels to Hamburg and boards a ship. But his passage is ended when stormy seas capsize the vessel and Yanko, the only survivor, is washed up on this remote part of the English coast. The tale is given an added inflection by the fact that Conrad, from Eastern Europe, is writing about a fellow Eastern European's experience of English reception.

Yanko is treated with suspicion and abuse by the provincial community until he earns his first act of kindness from the tender-hearted but simple Amy Foster, who gives him "such bread as the rich eat in my country" (124). He gains further if wary acceptance when, while working as a farm hand, he saves the farmer's granddaughter from drowning. Yanko's status as an outsider is crucial to the story's exploration of cultural identity. His experience demonstrates how the rules of cultural inclusion are simultaneously those that ensure the exclusion of others. From the outset, the coastal landmarks, such as the "sea-wall" and Martello tower (105), suggest ramparts designed to repel intruders.

By contrast with the natives, who are described as "uncouth in body and as leaden on gait as if their very hearts were loaded with chains," Yanko is "lithe, supple and long-limbed" with a "freedom of movement" and "graceful bearing" that suggests "the nature of a woodland creature" (111). According to Conrad, "the essential difference of the races" provided the central idea for the "dismal story" (CL2: 402). Yanko eventually marries Amy Foster in whom he had found "a golden heart...soft to people's misery" (133). That it should be the "simple" Amy who responds thus passes its own cultural comment upon the English – as does the response of the villagers when they discover that Yanko has proposed to Amy: she is declared "mad," and "Every old woman in the village was up in arms" (134). Nonetheless, stepping outside her cultural limitations Amy marries the foreigner and bears him a son, Johnny – "Yanko," too, translates as "little John." Meeting Kennedy one day, Yanko declares women "funny" and relates how Amy had snatched Johnny from his arms when he crooned to it in his own language, "that to our ears sounded so disturbing, so passionate, and so bizarre" (137). While emphasizing Yanko's cultural aliena-tion, Amy's reaction here prefigures his story's bleak ending.

During a bad winter, Yanko falls ill and in his fevered state lapses into his native tongue. Confronted by Yanko's demands for water, which she cannot understand, the terrified Amy runs away with the child and returns to her father's cottage. The hapless Yanko struggles outdoors and collapses face down in a puddle, where Kennedy finds him. On his death-bed, the abandoned and uncomprehending Yanko's personal plight is accorded cosmic significance: "'Why?' he cried, in the penetrating and indignant voice of a man calling to a responsible Maker. A gust of wind and a swish of rain answered" (141). His final utterance, "Merciful!" (141), is, like Kurtz's in "Heart of Darkness," deeply ambiguous and no less powerful. The potential interpretations of the word include: a plea for mercy from an unheeding heaven, an ironic comment upon his treatment, a final tribute to Amy, or all of these. However we read this, Conrad's presentation of England as "an undiscovered country" (112) reverses the theme of his exotic fiction: now the exotic is England and Englishness as viewed from Yanko's perspective. More than a tale about competing cultures, "Amy Foster" also foregrounds the clash between instinct and cultural forces: initially, Amy's ability to respond to Yanko sentimentally differentiates her from the group, but these cultural habits and civilized associations are reasserted when she becomes frightened by Yanko's feverish ravings. In this manner Conrad develops the theme of cultural insularity that marks his fiction, together with the maturity of vision that shows not only the people but also the circumstances that entrap them and make their actions, to some degree, inevitable.

Insider and outsider in the local community, narrator and character, Kennedy occupies a liminal position in this story. A man of science and a traveller beyond English shores "in the days when there were continents with unexplored interiors" (106), he ensures that the popular perception of Yanko, as "a hairy sort of gypsy fellow" (118) or a "dangerous maniac" (121), is seen for what it is: irrational fear born of a failure of imagination. In doing so, however, Kennedy locates the story's cultural conflict within an English voice. In consequence, the cultural disagreement between the natives and Yanko suggests that this "voice" is divided against itself.

Not surprisingly, this tale of ethnic and linguistic differences has attracted biographical criticism. For instance, a potential source for Yanko's feverish ranting has been traced to Jessie Conrad's recollection of how, during their honeymoon in France, her husband lay delirious with fever: "Now he raved in grim earnest, speaking only in his native tongue and betraying no knowledge of who I might be. For hours I remained by his side watching the feverish glitter of his eyes that seemed fixed on some object outside my vision, and listening to the meaningless phrases and lengthy speeches, not a word of which I could understand" (1935: 26). However, the unsettling strength of the story lies in the way that England is depicted as a landscape of modern alienation in which Yanko "could talk to no one, and had no hope of ever understanding anybody. It was as if these had been the faces of people from the other world – dead people" (129).

"Falk: A Reminiscence"

Written in early 1901, immediately after "Typhoon," "Falk" shares the dubious distinction with "The Return" of never having been serialised. It was first published in the *Typhoon* volume in 1903. While cultural influence might be said to dominate in "Amy Foster," in "Falk" it is overcome by the elemental will to survive. Conrad summarized the idea behind this novella as: "contrast of commonplace sentimentality with the uncorrupted point-of-view of an almost primitive man (Falk himself) who regards the preservation of life as the supreme and moral law" (*CL2*: 402). Subtitled "A Reminiscence," the tale is recounted at a Thames-side inn, after an "execrable" dinner, by a sea captain, remembering "an absurd episode" during his first command in Bangkok (145, 147).

While delayed in Bangkok harbour, the young captain is robbed of his savings by his Chinese steward and, during his fruitless pursuit after him, he makes the acquaintance of Captain Hermann of the *Diana* – "Diana not of Ephesus but of Bremen" (149). Thankful for the diversion from problems that include delayed cargo and illness among his crew, the narrator becomes a regular evening visitor to the Hermanns. The *Diana* is floating home to the Hermanns, their four children, and their niece, whose name is never revealed. Instead, her appearance is emphasized: "she was built on a magnificent scale. Built is the only word. She was constructed, she was erected, as it were, with regal lavishness" (151). Barely nineteen, she has attracted the attentions of Christian Falk, another regular visitor to the Hermanns' floating home. The niece's thoughts and feelings are not revealed. Instead, she is presented as a silent presence throughout the story while complementary images of the "world proof" *Diana* provide an objective correlative. This "pat-riarchal old tub" is seemingly immune to the sea "with its horrors and its peculiar scandals": "Her venerable innocence apparently put a restraint on the roaring lusts of the sea. ... The roaring dis-closure was, in the end, left for a man to make; a man strong and elemental enough and driven to unveil some secrets of the sea by the power of a simple and elemental desire" (156).

Falk, a taciturn Scandinavian, owns the only tugboat on the river and is essential to the young captain's departure. But, wrongly believing the young captain to be a rival for the niece's hand, Falk refuses to tow his ship down river. This comedy of misunder-standing spurs Falk to thwart the captain's attempts to secure an alternative pilot and, at one point, to tow away Hermann's boat, a "simple towing operation" that suggests "the idea of abduction, of rape. Falk was simply running off with the *Diana*" (170). During a meeting with Falk at Schomberg's hotel, the narrator, discovering that "Self-preservation was his only concern" (198), assures Falk that not only is he not a rival suitor for Hermann's niece but will actively undertake to present Falk's suit to Hermann and act as go-between with the young woman. At this stage, the story seems to be about a romantic confusion, but this is all preparation for the shock discovery upon which it hinges.

During his clumsy courtship Falk feels driven to reveal a grisly incident that happened ten years previously: "'Imagine to yourselves,' he said in his ordinary voice, "that I have eaten man" (218). The episode took place aboard the *Borgmester Dahl* when, damaged and stranded among the ice floes in the southern Pacific and the ship "possessed by the pitiless spectre of starvation" (232), cannibalism had been the only means of survival. As Falk, whose surname recalls the first syllable of falcon, a bird of prey – and whose given name, Christian, adds further resonances – asks rhetorically: "But was I, too, to throw away my life?" (235). His dramatic revelation casts significant new light on apparently innoc-uous earlier references to food in the tale, and, in particular, to Falk's habit of eating alone and being vegetarian. It also powerfully underscores the place of appetite, romantic and elemental, in the tale while giving an added twist to such claims as: "He was hungry for the girl, terribly hungry, as he had been terribly hungry for food" (224). In one of the tale's many classical analogies, Falk is com-pared with Hercules, "a strong man, susceptible to female charms, and not afraid of dirt" (201). The reference to "dirt" overtly recalls the legend of Hercules cleaning out the Augean stables; more subtly it invokes the euphemism of cannibals as "dirty eaters."

Despite the revulsion felt by Hermann and his wife towards Falk, his niece, "the siren to fascinate that dark navigator" (239), proves understanding and marries him. The tale juxtaposes elemental forces, represented by Falk and Hermann's niece, with sentimental forces, represented by the Hermanns, and the elemental survival instinct emerges vindicated. As in "Amy Foster," Conrad reveals himself to be on the side of instinct – in this case the will to live prevails over cultural taboos and the over-civilized world as represented by the Hermann household. Described as "racially thrifty" and "a caricature of a shopkeeping citizen in one of his own German comic papers" (168, 181–82), Hermann consents to his niece's marriage on economic grounds. The fact of Falk's cannibalism weighs less with him than the fear of continuing to support his niece once she has outgrown her usefulness as an unpaid governess. The apparently "Arcadian" Hermann household is, in Daphna Erdinast-Vulcan's formulation: "the apotheosis of bourgeois existence, with its sense of self-righteousness, its stale proprieties, and its mercenary concerns" (1999: 95).

In his "Author's Note" to *Typhoon*, Conrad recalls that "Falk" was rejected by a popular magazine on the grounds that Hermann's niece "never says anything" (viii). Presumably its gory subject matter must also have left Edwardian editors concerned about its success with their readership. To the charge about the niece's taciturnity, Conrad points out that, in the scenes involving her, "she either has no occasion or is too profoundly moved to speak" (viii). By identifying her with actions rather than words, the story associates her with Falk, her husband-to-be, and her silence constitutes a further challenge to "civilized" behaviour in the tale: as Falk's reputation suggests, the medium of language has itself been debased, reduced to the status of mere gossip. Furthermore, by contrast with the "world proof" *Diana*, Falk is described as centaur-like, a "composite creature. Not a man-horse ... but a man-boat" (162). In and of his element, Falk's behaviour, whether manifest in his sexual desire or his monopoly of the river trade, asserts the same primeval appetites that drove him to eat human flesh to survive. The mythological fashioning of the story simultaneously confirms such elemental forces and preserves a hint of humour in its Classical referencing, as Falk the "centaur" waylays the *Diana*, whose name recalls both chastity and hunting.

"Il Conde"

"Il Conde" is the final tale in *A Set of Six* (1908), where it is subtitled: "A Pathetic Tale." According to Conrad, this short story – a mere 6,000 words – took him ten days to write, in late 1906 (*CL*4:104). It is set in Naples, which the Conrads visited in 1905 when they spent four months in Capri, and was suggested by a tale recounted to Conrad by Count Szembek, a Polish aristocrat whom he met in Capri. The Count of the story's title – Conrad later acknowledged that the title was misspelled: it should read "Il Conte" (although the "d" may register a Southern Italian pronunciation) – is a fastidious, elderly gentleman whom the narrator meets while staying in a hotel in Naples. The pair strike up a friendship before the narrator has to leave to look after a friend who has fallen ill in Taormina – extending the illness-theme: the Count has travelled to Naples for his health. Ironically, the tale bears the epigraph *"Vedi Napoli e poi mori"* – "See Naples and die."

Upon his return ten days later, the narrator finds the Count devastated after an "abominable adventure" (274). During a visit to the Villa Nazionale, a public pleasure ground, he found himself sharing a table with a moody "South Italian type of young man" (278). Later, strolling in the darkness, he is accosted by the same young man, who threatens him with a knife and robs him of a little money and a cheap watch. Contemptuous of his small haul, which the Count protests is "all I had on me" (282), the young man demands the rings on the Count's fingers. The Count refuses to part with these heirlooms and, closing his eyes, expects to be "disembowelled" (283), only to find, when he reopens his eyes, his assailant has made off. Humiliated and overwhelmed he makes his way home and discovers that, in his terror, he had forgotten to hand over a 20-franc gold piece that he carries for emergencies.

Visiting the Café Umberto to calm himself down, the Count sees the young man who, he learns from Pasquale, the waiter, is the chief of a "very powerful Camorra" (287), or secret society. When the "young *Cavaliere* from Bari" sees the Count paying with the gold piece, he insults him and, before leaving, threatens: "you are not done with me yet" (288). Knowing himself to be "a marked man," the Count makes arrangements "for leaving Southern Italy for good and all" (288). As the narrator perceives: "His delicate conception of his dignity was defiled by a degrading experience. He couldn't stand that" (288). As he bids his friend farewell at the station, the narrator muses: "*Vedi Napoli*! ... He had seen it!" (289). This justly celebrated story thus bears out its epigraph.

In "Il Conde" Conrad returns to an idea that clearly fascinated him, involving a character, placed in a situation that destroys his self-image through the collapse of his circumscribed world. Practically, the Count can no longer continue in Naples because of the presence of the young mugger; more seriously, he cannot live with himself because of his inadvertent lie: like Jim or Falk before him, the Count's conception of his honour has been compromised. Much of the impact of this story lies in precisely this recognition, which also has a bearing upon the old Count choosing his point of death. The dissolution of the European self remains a perennial feature of Conrad's fiction, whether dealing with Continental aristocracy or exotic adventurers.

Where criticism once viewed "Il Conde" in symbolic terms, an old Europe menaced by a new generation, recent interpretations have tended to refashion the tale in sexual terms, arguing that the Count's adventure is incommensurate with the devastation he subsequently experiences. Instead, drawing support from the fact that Naples and Capri had reputations as sites for homosexual encounters, and Conrad's friendship with Norman Douglas, who he first met in Capri in 1905, Il Conde's stroll in the Villa Nazionale is seen as an instance of "cruising," and the young mugger is recast as a would-be hustler. For example, to Douglas A. Hughes the Count is "actually a lonely, vulnerable pederast who becomes involved in a sordid incident" (1975: 18).

"The Secret Sharer"

Conrad's satisfaction with his achievement in "The Secret Sharer" is evident in a letter to Garnett: "between you and me, is *it*. Eh? No damned tricks with girls there. Eh? Every word fits and there's not a single uncertain note. Luck my boy. Pure luck" (*CL5*: 128). Moser regarded it as the last work of the "major Conrad" (1957: 2). It was collected in *'Twixt Land and Sea Tales* (1912), the volume that ushered in the period of Conrad's popular acclaim: *Chance* appeared a year later. He described the stories in this volume as written in his "second manner": "less forcible, more popular than the Typhoon set and in another tone than the Six" (*CL4*: 503–04).

"The Secret Sharer" is a tale of initiation. Narrated by a young sea-captain, it recounts how he achieves the self-understanding necessary to exert authority aboard his first command and thus assume the responsibility of captaincy. He does this through the agency of Leggatt, a stowaway on the run after killing a fellow sailor during a storm, and to whom the captain gives secret refuge in his cabin. At the heart of the tale is the curious dilemma of identity: while the story is narrated in the first person, and like so many such narratives has as its central theme the creation of a personality, there is a displacement of the subject as the young captain is shown to be a composite of himself and Leggatt, uniting both lawful and lawless attributes. His identity, in other words, is "shared," and the literal journey sustains a metaphorical journey towards knowing oneself.

The tale begins with a leave-taking as the captain's unnamed ship, towed to the mouth of the Meinam River, is left "at the head of the Gulf of Siam" (92) to begin her homeward journey. The attention to geographical detail that marks the opening quickly attracts attention: "On my right hand there were lines of fishing stakes ... To the left a group of barren islets ... and, far back on the inland level, a larger and loftier mass, the grove surrounding the great Paknam pagoda" (91). These navigational landmarks introduce the subject of orientation while suggesting a reluctance to leave the known world of the land for the unknown world of the sea. The first-person narration also conveys this reluctance while stylistically conveying the impression of a sensibility alienated from the rest of the crew.

The young captain is self-consciously aware of his own inexperience: "what I felt most was my being a stranger to the ship; and if all the truth must be told, I was somewhat of a stranger to myself" (93). Signs of the captain's inexperience soon call attention to themselves: the first mate reacts with "astonishment" (95) when the captain volunteers to take his watch on their first night. It is during this watch that he encounters Leggatt who has escaped incarceration and swum away from his ship, the *Sephora*, in which he served as first mate. During a storm, and acting on his own initiative since his captain "hardly dared give the order" (118), Leggatt ordered that a reefed foresail be set. The insubordination of a member of the crew led Leggatt to attack and kill him. Attending strictly to the letter of the law, the *Sephora*'s captain wants Leggatt tried in a court of law, but the young captain recognises that the setting of the reefed foresail saved the ship (118) and decides to help Leggatt to escape. Leggatt is repeatedly described by the captain as "my double" in the story. Sharing the captain's private space aboard ship, the stowaway also shares his professional experience: the men were both schooled in the *Conway* training-ship, and, hidden from the crew, they discuss the captain's plight together, "as if the ship had two captains to plan her course for her" (134). It thus makes sense to view Leggatt as the secret sharer of the captain's personality. In harbouring Leggatt the captain assumes responsibility for him and, in the process, paradoxically demonstrates his fitness to captain his ship.

As the ship is navigated through the Gulf of Siam, exotic adventure is refashioned as psychological adventure. The tale's elegant symmetries promote the idea of the double or *Doppelgänger*: not only is Leggatt presented as the captain's double – stowed away in the captain's cabin and dressed in the captain's clothes, the impression of "a double captain busy talking in whispers to his other self" (105) is created – but the ship from which he is fleeing, the *Sephora*, is unfavourably contrasted with the young captain's command. Similarly, in a tale about identity, the fact that the narrator cannot recall the name of the *Sephora*'s captain – "it was something like Archbold" (116) – speaks volumes.

The captain's already vulnerable psychological state is compounded by having to dissemble before his officers – and to add to the problem of concealing the stowaway, his command is becalmed at the head of the Gulf of Siam. The ship's inability to get underway provides an obvious metaphor for the captain's sense of impotence. Desperately needing off-shore breezes to propel his ship, the captain decides to steer her precariously close to the island of Koh-ring on the eastern side of the Gulf. This dangerous manoeuvre succeeds, allowing Leggatt to make his escape unnoticed and, with the ship at last "drawing ahead" (143), earning the captain the respect of his crew. It is significant that the ship can only make way once Leggatt has departed from her: Leggatt's agency is necessary in helping the captain realise his *own* potential.

Under the shadow of Koh-ring and needing some marker to identify his rate of progress, the captain sees his own white hat floating on the dark water – he had given it to Leggatt. This provides the necessary guide, "the saving mark" (142), that allows him to steer the ship and attempt to escape the becalming waters of the Gulf. Symbolically, this marker, an extension of himself, proves that the captain can now depend upon his own resources for his success. The description of the ship's progress at the end of the tale is rhapsodic: "Already the ship was drawing ahead. And I was alone with her. Nothing! no one in the world should stand now between us, throwing a shadow on the way of silent knowledge and mute affection, the perfect communion of a seaman with his first command" (143). For his part, Leggatt, who is, like Jim, the son of a parson, departs to be "hidden for ever from all friendly faces, to be a fugitive and a vagabond on the earth" (142). The bond with Leggatt, that forced the captain to assume personal responsibility for his actions, has facilitated and, finally, been replaced by the bond with his ship, while the sensuality in the description confirms the intimate quality of the captain's success.

The captain's cabin, an L-shaped room, also has a dual identity: it is a place of refuge, to which the captain escapes from the burden of his responsibilities, and another prison for Leggatt, whose name has connotations of legality. The captain's decision to aid Leggatt's escape rather than surrender him for trial by "an old fellow in a wig and twelve respectable tradesmen" (131) suggests that, unlike the captain of the *Sephora*, he privileges the "law of the sea" over that of the land. But this decision, a further assumption of responsibility, introduces a moral dilemma: as the figure of authority, the captain countermands the letter of the law. He is thus allied with Leggatt and the potential for lawlessness that, as the story reveals, is the "secret sharer" of personality. Conrad asked Pinker to choose from three suggested titles for this story: "The Secret Self," "The other Self," and "The Secret Sharer" – adding that he felt the latter "may be too enigmatic" (*CL4*: 300). In the event, "The Secret Sharer" deals with the enigma of self, and has inevitably attracted much psychoanalytical criticism. The captain's is a universal human quest for mirroring affirmation and individuality in the face of the perils of solitude and fragmentation. The twinning of the captain and Leggatt, together with the conflicted human psyche that this entails, places "The Secret Sharer" in the tradition of Dostoevsky's *The Double* (1846) or Stevenson's *The Strange Case of Dr. Jekyll and Mr. Hyde* (1886).

Works cited

Conrad, Jessie. *Joseph Conrad and His Circle*. London: Jarrolds, 1935.

Erdinast-Vulcan, Daphna. *The Strange Short Fiction of Joseph Conrad*. Oxford: Oxford University Press, 1999.

Guerard, Albert J. *Conrad the Novelist*. Cambridge, Mass.: Harvard University Press, 1958.

Hughes, Douglas A. "Conrad's 'Il Conde': 'A Deucedly Queer Story.' " *Conradiana* 7 (1975): 17–25.

Leavis, F. R. *The Great Tradition: George Eliot, Henry James, Joseph Conrad.* London: Chatto & Windus, 1948.

Moser, Thomas. *Joseph Conrad: Achievement and Decline.* Cambridge, Mass.: Harvard University Press, 1957.

Sherry, Norman, ed. *Conrad: The Critical Heritage.* London: Routledge & Kegan Paul, 1973.

7

Conrad at the Crossroads: *Chance, Victory,* and *The Shadow-Line*

With the publication of *Chance*, Conrad scored his first financial success in the marketplace. It secured the public acclaim that had eluded his writings thus far and initiated a final decade of popularity that culminated in his promotional visit to America in 1923, where he was feted and lionised. Ironically, this period of popular success was achieved with novels whose merits have been the subject of critical dispute. In 1957, Thomas C. Moser published his influential study, *Joseph Conrad: Achievement and Decline*, which charts the period of Conrad's "decline" from *Chance* onwards and traces this, first, to Conrad's engagement with the "uncongenial subject" of romantic relationships, and, secondly, to a sense of prevailing creative weariness that manifests itself in sentimental affirmation.

The development and bibliographical history of *Chance* is among the most vexed of Conrad's novels. It was first mentioned in a letter of 1898 (*CL2*: 62) but only completed in March 1912, while serialisation was already under way in the *New York Herald* (21 January–30 June 1912). *Chance* was published in book form in America by Doubleday, Page in October 1913 and in England by Methuen in January 1914 – the cause of the delay in publishing the first English edition being a bookbinders' strike. Conrad's comments in his letters reveal that he continued to tinker with the manuscript of *Chance* while working on *The Secret Agent* and *Under Western Eyes*. With unconscious prescience, in February

1907 he referred to "the famous *Chance* that is going to bring a real turn of luck" (*CL3*: 411). The composition of the novel seems, albeit unintentionally, designed to try the patience of his long-suffering and faithful literary agent, Pinker. For instance, his correspondence shows that Conrad had intended *Chance* to follow *The Secret Agent*, suggesting in a letter of 25 May 1907: "it is quite possible it may be finished in three months from now" (*CL3*: 442). Conrad's letter of 30 July 1907 revises this: "I reckon 4 months for Chance counting from 1st of Augst" (*CL3*: 460), and that of 3 August offers "early in December" as a conclusion date (*CL3*: 462). Instead of which, the end of the year finds Conrad occupied not with completing *Chance* but with developing "Razumov," the story that would develop into *Under Western Eyes*.

As the extreme example of *The Rescue*, begun in 1896 but only completed in 1916, demonstrates, the composition of *Chance* conforms to a pattern: an initial conception, in this case for a short story, suspended for a lengthy period, during which the initial conception gestates and mutates, to emerge finally, newly inflected. If *The Secret Agent* and *Under Western Eyes* distracted Conrad from composing *Chance*, their emphasis upon the broader subject of international politics is given a more refined focus in the novel written, or at least contemplated, in their interstices. The increasingly politicised role of women in the previous three novels now becomes Conrad's focus, not against an obvious backdrop of international politics – despite Conrad's claim on 20 December 1909 that it would be "a Malay sea tale" (*CL4*: 303) – but within a sociocultural context that has as its historical foundation the campaign for women's votes in the late nineteenth century that politicised gender in the pursuit of a revised concept of British "citizenship" and was co-ordinated through such organizations as Mrs Fawcett's National Union of Women's Suffrage Societies (founded in 1897) and the Pankhursts' Women's Social and Political Union (1903). The term "feminism" came into use in the 1890s. In this sense, in *Chance*, creative invention becomes an extension of cultural debate. As H. G. Wells's *Ann Veronica* (1909) demonstrates, Conrad was not alone in addressing the "condition of woman" issue in fiction. In a letter of 7 April 1913, Conrad suggested that *Chance* was "the sort of stuff that *may* have a chance with the public," offering as his reason: "All of it about a girl and with a steady run of references to women in general all along, some sarcastic, others sentimental, it ought to go down" (*CL5*: 208). Conrad also referred to *Chance* in correspondence as "my girl-novel" (*CL5*: 236).

Chance

To begin with an obvious point: *Chance* is the only novel by Conrad
to carry chapter titles. This concern with arrangement extends
to the novel's division into two parts, "The Damsel" and "The
Knight," that, in turn, serves as a structural debt to Dickens' *Little
Dorrit*. Not only does *Chance* echo many of the ideas and themes
of *Little Dorrit* – physical and psychological imprisonment, the
plight of women in society, and the redemptive power of love –
but the spectre of Dickens haunts the narrative, both in Conrad's
evocation of London and as a touchstone of melodramatic yet
emotive literary reference. His impressions of Flora de Barral's life
strike Marlow as "Pictures from Dickens – pregnant with pathos"
(162). Similarly, the division of *Chance* into "The Damsel" and
"The Knight" indicates Conrad's concern with romance and evokes
medieval ideas of chivalry. Captain Anthony is cast as "the rescuer
of the most forlorn damsel of modern times" (238).

   Chance begins in a riverside inn on the Thames estuary where
Marlow and an unnamed frame-narrator dine with Charles Powell.
The latter describes how he secured his first appointment as second-
mate, under Captain Roderick Anthony in the *Ferndale*. After
Powell's departure, Marlow explains to the narrator how he came
to know of Captain Anthony, through the Fynes, his neighbours
during successive holidays in the country, when Mr Fyne and Marlow would meet irregularly to play chess. On one such holiday,
Marlow chances upon a young woman walking the Fynes' dog
dangerously close to a precipice above a quarry and, awakening her
from her reverie, escorts her back to the Fynes. On a subsequent
holiday, Marlow learns that the girl, one of the "girl-friends" of the
feminist Mrs Fyne, has gone missing. Marlow's recollections of her
lead to the suspicion that she may have committed suicide, and so
he and Mr Fyne unavailingly visit the quarry to look for her. The
following day, a letter from the young woman arrives with news
that she has eloped to London with Mrs Fyne's brother, Captain
Anthony. Marlow discovers that her name is not "Miss Smith"
but Flora de Barral: she is the daughter of a discredited financier,
imprisoned for fraud.

   This news initiates a summary of Flora's past and the impact
upon her life of her father's ruin. In particular, this sequence charts
her traumatic experiences on the eve of her sixteenth birthday at
the hands of her Governess who transforms from "the wisdom,
the authority, the protection of life, security embodied and visible

and undisputed" (117) into "an emanation of evil" (116) once she learns of de Barral's demise and, hence, the collapse of her hopes of profiting from the family's wealth, towards which she is working by cultivating a relationship between Flora and her nephew, Charley. Before abandoning her, the Governess wreaks revenge, securing "an atrocious satisfaction" (121) by undermining Flora's belief in herself and the world around her. In this state she is taken up by the Fynes, who by chance are spending a week in Brighton, where Flora lives, when news of the financial scandal breaks.

Back in the narrative present, Marlow accompanies a reluctant Mr Fyne to London, where he has been sent by his wife to dissuade Captain Anthony from marrying Flora. While Fyne is engaged with Captain Anthony in the Eastern Hotel, Marlow encounters Flora on the pavement outside. While Fyne is poisoning Captain Anthony's mind against Flora – arguing that she is using him to secure a future for her soon-to-be-released father – Flora is recounting the stages of her involvement with Captain Anthony and how he came to be her "rescuer." Fyne reappears and, without seeing Flora, takes his leave of Marlow, who, receiving "a prosaic offer of employment on rather good terms" (252), embarks on a long foreign voyage.

"The Damsel" thus offers an ontological study of Flora's origins that subtly counterpoints the "chance" by which Powell enters the freedom of the man's world of the sea with the contrasting restrictedness of Flora's dependent woman's world that is blighted by ill fortune. In Part 2, "The Knight," Marlow relays the rest of Flora's story that he has learned from Powell. Powell joined the *Ferndale* seven months after Flora's marriage to Captain Anthony, and on the eve of her father's release from prison. The state of the marriage is one of paralysis: Anthony, believing Fyne, is convinced that Flora does not love him and that their union, like the *Ferndale*, provides his wife with an expedient refuge from the world; and Flora, in the wake of the Governess' deprecation and her husband's detachment, is convinced "that she was in some mysterious way odious and unlovable" (263). Compounding this strained state of affairs aboard ship, in which Anthony and Flora act out of a mistaken sense of duty towards each other, is de Barral himself. Once the *Ferndale* sets sail for southern Africa, with her cargo of dynamite, he feels that he has merely exchanged one form of incarceration for another, and, in the belief that his daughter wishes to be rid of Captain Anthony, whom he alludes to as "the jailer" (307), works to poison her mind against her husband.

Life aboard ship is fraught and disrupted. For instance, to the consternation of his officers, Captain Anthony gives up his cabin to Flora and her father, "Mr. Smith," and isolates himself. Furthermore, as Powell notes, between the Captain and his wife there was "some constraint," while her father's attitude suggested that he was always "keeping watch over her" (314). Marlow declares his interest in the "moral atmosphere": "that tension of falsehood, of desperate acting, which tainted the pure sea-atmosphere" (415). Matters come to a head when Powell, accidentally discovering that he can see into his Captain's cabin through the skylight in which a broken pane of coloured glass had been replaced by a clear pane, is shocked to discover a hand emerging from behind a curtain and doctoring the Captain's drink. He rushes downstairs and warns Anthony just in time. Overwhelmed, and to the delight of the chuckling de Barral, Anthony decides to release Flora from their union. But her response is firm: "You can't cast me off like this, Roderick. I won't go away from you. I won't –" (430), and, when the couple retire, de Barral, confronted and unmasked by Powell, drinks the poisoned cup and dies. On the pretext of awaiting his Captain's orders, Powell summons Anthony and the two men carry de Barral's corpse to his bed to be discovered by the steward in the morning. After this, the narrative rapidly concludes: the six years of happiness in the Anthony marriage, and Captain Anthony's dramatic death at sea "this four years or more" (438), are glossed in summary fashion. The last pages reveal that Powell frequently visits the widowed Flora, whom Marlow has seen only "yesterday" (447) to press the young man's suit.

The intimacy and immediacy of first-person narration in *Chance* complements this tale that "has arguably the happiest ending of all of Conrad's works" (Knowles and Moore, 2000: 58). And Marlow's reappearance gains from his previous reliability in other tales. But the Marlow of *Chance* is less reliable than the autobiographical persona of "Heart of Darkness" or *Lord Jim*. Instead he seems to offer a compendium of Edwardian male attitudes among which Flora de Barral finds herself alone and isolated. The composition of *Chance* comfortably spans the era of King Edward VII, who succeeded his mother, Queen Victoria, in 1901 and reigned until his death in 1910. An historical bridge between Victorian glories and impending horrors of the First World War, the Edwardian era also offered "a political and social revolution, accompanied and sustained by an explosion of intellectual and artistic energy" (Hattersley, 2004: 1). In the marketplace, *Chance* rode the tide of the major social issue of the day: the rise of feminism in the suffragist movement.

The cast of daughters metaphorically imprisoned by their fathers and father surrogates in Conrad's early fiction includes Nina by Almayer, Aïssa by Omar, and Jewel by Cornelius. In *Chance* this extends to the narrating voice. For instance, according to Marlow: "As to honour – you know – it's a very fine mediæval inheritance which women never got hold of. ... In addition they are devoid of decency. I mean masculine decency" (63). Unsurprisingly he later confesses: "I am not a feminist" (146). Indeed, Marlow's misogynistic attitude towards women in *Chance* echoes the attitude of the Teacher of Languages towards Russia in *Under Western Eyes*. Mrs Fyne is satirically portrayed as an exploitative, possibly lesbian, dogmatist who, together with the malicious Governess, is largely responsible for Flora's insecurities. But if Mrs Fyne's militant feminism owes something to the ideas of Sylvia Pankhurst, she herself is the victim of an overbearing father, the "poet-tyrant" (148) Carleon Anthony, who provides a satirical portrait of Coventry Patmore (1823–96), author of the verse novel *The Angel in the House* (1854–63) that sentimentalised the role of the Victorian wife and mother. The fact that Carleon Anthony, like Peter Ivanovitch in *Under Western Eyes*, idealises women in public whilst tyrannising over them in private suggests that part of Conrad's intention in *Chance* was to expose outmoded patriarchal attitudes. As such, *Chance* can usefully be thought of as a "condition-of-Edwardian England" novel. Significantly, Conrad referred to *Chance*, in a letter of 28 March 1912, as: "English in personages and locality" (*CL5*: 45).

Marlow's discovery of Flora walking along the edge of a precipice offers a symbolic representation of the vulnerability of women in a world where the people, codes, and conditions that should support them are hopelessly flawed. While this image implicitly endorses the contemporary challenge to inherited hierarchies of authority and power, Mrs Fyne's "knock-me-down doctrine" (59) of feminism is derided. Jeremy Hawthorn argues that *Chance* is disfigured by Conrad's own uncertainties about feminism: "narrative hesitations seem traceable back to ideological contradictions or confusions: it is as if Conrad's inability to decide what he believes gets in the way of ... narrative clarity" (1990: 140–41). Contradictions in Conrad's attitude are not hard to find. In the advance publicity for *Chance* he wrote: "I aimed at treating my subject in a way which would interest women. That's all. I don't believe that women have to be written for specially as if they were infants" (*CL4*: 531–32). Yet in Marlow's claim that "women ... so often resemble intelligent children" (171), purity and innocence cannot be separated from implied dependence upon men.

The novel rejects any easy distinction between male oppression and feminist salvation. Hypocritically, once Flora has espoused her "feminist doctrine" (58), Mrs Fyne then attempts to thwart her chance of happiness with Captain Anthony. Having eloped herself to escape her tyrannical father, Mrs Fyne will not countenance the same impulse in Flora. In Marlow's words, Mrs Fyne's brand of feminism "can't forgive Miss de Barral for being a woman and behaving like a woman" (189). That Flora's "salvation" comes through two men – first Captain Anthony and then Powell – only adds to the anti-feminist impression. Yet the male-constructed, "man-mismanaged" (183) world is equally damned. In *Chance*, Flora is placed in an analogous position to the hero of *Lord Jim*: Jim's masculine ideal of himself has collapsed just as her feminine ideal of herself has been destroyed. Alone, moneyless, and friendless, she cannot do what Jim did to make reparation and, instead, needs to be taken care of. Such dependency gives added force to her cry to her husband later in the novel: "But I don't want to be let off" (261). Instead, though Flora suffers a similar defeat to Jim's, *Chance* ends happily.

The contrast between Captain Anthony's concern – "He was gentleness itself" (230) – and the world in which Flora exists "under a harsh unconcerned sky" (204) is starkly represented, nowhere more so than in the depiction of her as an economic victim. Even as Fyne is engaged with Captain Anthony, poisoning her future happiness, Flora stands on the pavement outside with Marlow, depicted as vulnerable and trapped in a world in which she is "of no account":

> Every moment people were passing close by us singly, in twos and threes; the inhabitants of that end of the town where life goes on unadorned by grace or splendour; they passed us in their shabby garments, with sallow faces, haggard, anxious or weary, or simply without expression, in an unsmiling sombre stream not made up of lives but of mere unconsidered existences whose joys, struggles, thoughts, sorrows and their very hopes were miserable, glamourless, and of no account in the world. ... It was as if the whole world existed only for selling and buying and those who had nothing to do with the movement of merchandise were of no account. (208–10)

That Flora should recount to Marlow the story of her elopement in this environment, punctuated by "ugly street-noises" (216), dramatises the social point. More poignantly, that she should do so while subject to the stares of three "abominable, drink sodden loafers, sallow and dirty" (230) commodifies her within a world over which her father once held sway. As Daniel R. Schwarz argues, "*Chance* discovers a heart of darkness beneath the civilized exteriors of Edwardian London" (1980: 53).

Henry James's reaction to *Chance* stung Conrad, who professed that this was "the *only time* a criticism affected me painfully" (*CL5*: 595). James's survey of "The Younger Generation" of novelists, subsequently expanded into "The New Novel," questioned whether Flora's relatively simple story warranted such a complex narrative. The essay, that described Marlow's method as a "prolonged hovering flight of the subjective over the outstretched ground of the case exposed," also cast Conrad, "absolutely alone" among his contemporaries, as "a votary of the way to do a thing that shall make it undergo most doing" (Sherry, ed., 1973: 267, 265). This last quotation reminds the reader that Conrad was not absolutely alone in this method: it applies equally to James himself, who Conrad addressed in letters as "Cher Maître." None the less, James' was not a lone dissenting voice. The review of the novel in the *Glasgow News* of 5 February 1914 also criticised Conrad's method: "somehow *Chance* suggests a formidable scaffolding that people watch being constructed intricately for days, only to find that at the end it was designed for nothing more than the placing of a weather-cock on a steeple" (in Sherry, ed., 1973: 283). According to Martin Ray, however, it is Marlow's status as "the only disinterested observer" and his position "very much at the margins of the story" that "enables him to serve as a corrective to the egoism, vanity, or naivety of the other narrators" of Flora's story (1990: xiv, xviii).

The narrative commences with young Powell's "chance" appointment as an officer in the *Ferndale*. This anticipates a number of such "chances" that drive the plot. For instance, arriving on board his ship, Powell is told by the dock policeman that only "a most extraordinary chance" (27) has prevented him from being waylaid by night prowlers; when Marlow tries to explain why Flora should be subject to the Governess' malice he says: "Why, by chance! By the merest chance as things do happen, lucky and unlucky, terrible or tender, important or unimportant" (99–100); and Powell puts his ability to see into his captain's cabin down to "the precise workmanship of chance, fate, providence, call it what you will" (411). As Marlow suggests: "It was as if the forehead of Flora de Barral were marked. Was the girl born to be a victim; to be always disliked and crushed as if she were too fine for this world? Or too luckless – since that also is often counted as sin" (309). Coupled with this emphasis on chance is an equally persistent emphasis on characters' personal histories. Their respective pasts have an important bearing upon the behaviour of such characters as Mrs Fyne, the Governess, Roderick Anthony, and Flora herself. Within the tale's logic, chance provides the only safeguard against the damage wrought by experience, while the most contingent of all chances, gender itself, provides the novel's focus.

But the division of the world into sets of alternative options – man's world versus woman's world, or land versus sea values, for example – coexists with contradictory, confused definitions that threaten such distinctions: Carleon Anthony is a "poet-tyrant" and de Barral a "financier-convict" (148); Roderick Anthony, the son of an erotic poet, is himself paralysed emotionally and sexually; the *Ferndale* is both haven and prison; Mrs Fyne is stung by Flora's letter, which offers "an echo of her own stupid talk" (443). Structurally, Marlow's misogyny, which serves to establish the hostile social environment surrounding Flora, offers a counterpoint to Mrs Fyne's feminism, but his voice is polyphonic, blending a range of male attitudes from sentimentality, for instance when he match-makes between Powell and Flora, to scepticism: "the incapacity to achieve anything distinctly good or evil is inherent in out earthly condition. Mediocrity is our mark" (23). While declaring that "there is enough of the woman in my nature to free my judgment from glamorous reticency" (53), Marlow, who lives in the exclusively male world of the "brotherhood of the sea," also claims: "it's towards women that I feel vindictive mostly, in my small way" (150). In other words, he destabilizes the oppositions and sympathies that are set up in the narrative. As he says, "when it comes to dealing with human beings anything, anything may be expected" (59).

Victory

In the spring of 1912 Conrad began working on a short story, whose working title was "Dollars." Despite his pessimistic claim to André Gide, "I don't feel the push. I am well aware that I have written too much" (*CL5*: 100), "Dollars" evolved into two works, both including the character of Captain Davidson and a plot in which the hero is ultimately saved by a woman: the short story "Because of the Dollars" (collected in *Within the Tides* [1915]) and the novel *Victory*. By October 1912, Conrad could offer the following broad outline of the novel to his agent: "it has a tropical Malay setting – an unconventional man and a girl on an island under peculiar circumstances to whom enters a gang of three ruffians also of a rather unconventional sort – this intrusion producing certain psychological developments and effects. There is philosophy in it and also drama – lightly treated – meant for cultured people – a piece of literature before everything" (*CL5*: 113–14).

In *Victory* Conrad both returns to the site of his early fiction, the Malay Archipelago, and to some of its plotting: as in *Lord Jim*, the outside world intrudes on a supposed haven. The novel also develops further such themes as emotional isolation, paralysed sexuality, and female entrapment addressed in *Chance*. The remarketing of Conrad occasioned by *Chance* continued, as is evident in the fact that when *Victory* was published by Methuen in May 1915, the dust-jacket described it as a novel of "love and jealousy." But this is only part of the story, for this is also a novel of ideas, in which Conrad's concern is nothing less than the prevailing mood of scepticism itself.

Conrad wrote *Victory* against steadily gathering plaudits. October 1912 saw the publication of *'Twixt Land and Sea*, a collection of short stories that, according to one critic, provided "unmistakable proof of his genius." By the time he had completed a first draft of the novel in June 1914, *Chance* had appeared to such acclaim as: "Joseph Conrad is one of the marvels of our literature" (Sherry, ed., 1973: 256, 282). Essential to Conrad's financial prosperity were his American publishers, Doubleday, Page, whose aggressive marketing of *Chance* led to sales of 10,000 copies within the first week of publication. In 1914, Doubleday, Page set about acquiring the American rights to Conrad's works for a collected edition, that began to appear in 1921. Besides the obvious material improvements in the family's fortunes – for instance, in 1912 Conrad bought his first car, a second-hand Cadillac, described by Henry James as "the most dazzling element for me in the whole of your rosy legend" (Stape and Knowles, eds, 1996: 90) – his new-found wealth enabled him to pay off his considerable debts to his patient agent, Pinker.

Conrad's first reference to the novel's title occurs in a letter to Pinker of 1 July 1914, written three days after the assassination of Archduke Franz Ferdinand, heir to the Hapsburg throne, in Sarajevo, hastened the outbreak of the First World War. In his "Note to the First Edition" of *Victory* Conrad revealed that the title was to have been the "last word" (vii) of the novel: "Nothing!" (412). This "Note" also voices Conrad's misgivings about the altered title: "There was also the possibility of falling under the suspicion of commercial astuteness deceiving the public into the belief that the book had something to do with war" (vii). Conrad voiced his qualms in a letter to Iris Wedgwood of 28 January 1915: "It seems almost criminal levity to talk at this time of books, stories, publication" (*CL5*: 439). None the less, the uplifting title cannot have hurt the book's chances in the marketplace and, continuing the trend established with *Chance*, it sold well, despite the upheaval of the time. It is, furthermore, salutary to recall a comment Conrad made after the war, in a letter to Doubleday of 21 December 1918: "A piece of work of any sort is only fully justified when it is done at the right time" (*CL6*: 332). While not about the world events of its age, *Victory* is thematically relevant to them. The question posed by the novel is that raised by the general instability of life at the time of writing: is detachment the best solution to the incoherence of experience? *Victory* is a novel about faith in human relationships; in an age of moral crisis, it is about the possible victory of such faith over faithlessness. With remarkable appropriateness, the opening paragraph of *Victory* provides an image that conjures up the instability of the period in its reference to "the age in which we are camped like bewildered travellers in a garish, unrestful hotel" (3).

* * *

Victory begins with a portrait of the reticent central character, Axel Heyst. An English-educated Swede, Heyst has spent fifteen years drifting and trading among the islands of the Malay Archipelago: "a circle with a radius of eight hundred miles drawn round a point in North Borneo was in Heyst's case a magic circle" (7). The narrative relates how Heyst rescued Captain Morrison and his ship from the Portuguese port-authorities in Delli (now Dili) and, as a consequence, became Morrison's partner in the Tropical Belt Coal Company, with its headquarters on Samburan – "the 'Round

Island' of the charts" (5) – in the Java Sea. The venture is short-lived, and after Morrison's death in England and the liquidation of the company, Heyst remains on Samburan, isolated from the world and attended only by Wang, his Chinese servant, and "an indolent volcano" as his "nearest neighbour" (4). Despite the fact that Heyst has "turned hermit" (31), he is kept alive in island gossip fostered by Schomberg who spreads malicious rumours about Heyst, claiming that he has robbed and murdered Morrison. After a year-and-a-half on Samburan, Heyst unexpectedly returns to society, travelling to Sourabaya in Captain Davidson's steamship, the *Sissie*. But when Davidson returns three weeks' later to collect Heyst, he discovers to his surprise that not only has Heyst already left the hotel but that he has also returned to Samburan with Lena, a young violinist who has run away from the Zangiacomo travelling ladies orchestra and whom Schomberg was attempting to seduce.

Part II fills in the details of Heyst's stay at Schomberg's hotel during the residency of the Zangiacomo orchestra, whose performance strikes him as "not making music; it was simply murdering silence with a vulgar, ferocious energy" (68). Heyst, who is "temperamentally sympathetic" and "could not defend himself from compassion" (70, 79), instinctively responds to the mistreatment of Lena, who confesses: "I haven't come across so many pleasant people as all that, in my life" (75). In Lena, Heyst, whose father's sceptical attitudes have left with "a profound mistrust of life" (91), recognises a companion spirit, seeking refuge from the world, furthermore, her glance provides "the most real impression of his detached existence – so far" (93). Following Heyst's departure with Lena, and with Schomberg still smarting from "the pangs of wounded vanity and of thwarted passion" (97), a trio of desperadoes arrive at his hotel, led by "plain Mr. Jones ... a gentleman at large," to whom the world is "one great, wild jungle without law" (103, 113). Mr Jones, an extreme misogynist who declares that women "give me the horrors" (102), is accompanied by Martin Ricardo, his knife-carrying "secretary," and their servant, Pedro, "a nondescript, hairy creature" (99). They quickly intimidate Schomberg and establish an illegal gambling operation, using his *table d'hôte* as a cover. Increasingly desperate at having to deal with this trio – "A spectre, a cat, an ape" (148) – Schomberg eventually gets rid of them by offering Ricardo an "inducement" (154) that will spur his master to leave. The inducement also serves Schomberg's desire for revenge: he tells Ricardo that Heyst is wealthy and provides the means for the trio to get at him. Ricardo, of course, keeps Lena's presence on Samburan a secret from Jones.

The scene then changes to Samburan in Part III, where Heyst and Lena have lived for the last three months. Heyst senior had advocated detachment from the world: "Look on – make no sound" (175). While this philosophy seems validated by the plight of first Morrison and then Lena, the latter's presence on Samburan also threatens his isolation, both literally and emotionally, as he feels an increasing need for her presence near him. Lena reveals that she has heard Schomberg's version of Morrison's fate, that Heyst murdered him. This calumny, "a moral stab in the back" (259), seems further to vindicate Heyst senior's vision of the world; it also adds to the couple's already strained relationship. And when Heyst takes up one of his father's books, he reads: "Of the stratagems of life the most cruel is the consolation of love – the most subtle, too; for the desire is the bed of dreams" (219). Undermining Heyst's assurance to Lena that "Nothing can break in on us here" (223) and echoing the arrival of Gentleman Brown in Patusan, the trio arrive exhausted and thirsty, "guests whom the renounced world had sent him thus at the end of the day" (238). Heyst settles the men into the disused counting house of the Tropical Belt Coal Company. His fears are for Lena: the trio's visit, that he recognises "could bode nothing pleasant," makes him realise that "He no longer belonged to himself" (248, 245). Compounding his defencelessness, Heyst discovers that his revolver is missing.

The final part of the novel dramatises the eventful day that resolves the established tensions. Ricardo, who has been spying on Heyst, breaks into his bungalow and tries to assault Lena. When she defends herself against his "feral instincts" (285), Lena's strength stems from her newfound belief in herself as gained through her relationship with Heyst: "because she was no longer deprived of moral support; because she was a human being who counted; because she was no longer defending herself for herself alone" (292). Mistakenly believing Lena and himself to be "Born alike, bred alike" (297), Ricardo tries to enlist her in the plan to rob Heyst. Lena helps Ricardo escape when Heyst returns, but Wang, who is now armed with Heyst's revolver and has heard Ricardo in Lena's room, chooses this time to desert his master. He also refuses to provide sanctuary for Lena in the Alfuro village on the other side of the island and cut off by a barrier erected "against the march of civilization ... the product of honest fear – fear of the unknown, of the incomprehensible" (344).

When Heyst visits Jones that evening, against the backdrop of a stagily dramatic storm, "the ill-omened chaos of the sky" (355), Ricardo returns to the bungalow and prostrates himself before Lena, who secures Ricardo's weapon: "The very sting of death was in her hands; the venom of the viper in her paradise, extracted, safe in her possession" (399). Jones, with Heyst as his captive, breaks in upon the scene and fires at Ricardo. Although he only wounds his secretary, the shot fatally injures Lena. In a rapid and bloody finale, Davidson arrives, Lena dies, Wang kills Pedro, and Jones kills Ricardo before drowning. With the dying Lena in his arms Heyst curses "his fastidious soul, which even at that moment kept the true cry of love from his lips in its infernal mistrust of all life" (406). Finally, as Davidson recounts "the mystery of Samburan" (408) in the novel's final chapter, we learn that Heyst burnt the bungalow and died in the same fire that consumes Lena's body. With virtually his last words, Heyst exposes the failings of his – and his father's – philosophy: "Ah, Davidson, woe to the man whose heart has not learned while young to hope, to love – and to put its trust in life" (410).

* * *

Since its publication, reviewers of *Victory* have been exercised by the uneasy combination of psychologically developed characters, Heyst and Lena, and the trio of melodramatic figures ranged against them. But that is how the world and its agents appear to the sceptical Heyst. As he tells Ricardo: "You people ... are divorced from all reality in my eyes" (364). *Victory*, like such late Shakespeare plays as *The Tempest*, employs a mixture of genres and literary combinations whose juxtaposition calls into question the status of reality and creates a new one. As one contemporary reviewer noted: "we appear to be witnessing not a murderous contest between men, but a struggle between the spiritual powers of the universe temporarily incarnate in a little group of human beings on a lonely Pacific island" (in Sherry, 1973: 288). The narrative thus invites consideration of its allegoric patterning. For example, Heyst's self-definition as "the original Adam" (175) casts Lena in the role of Eve; her triumph over "the venom of the viper in her paradise" (399), symbolised by Ricardo's knife, rehabilitates woman by overturning the Biblical vision of her as the weak link.

Victory also provides a recognisable extension of an earlier theme in Conrad's writing: the moral ambiguity in *Lord Jim* is complicated in *Under Western Eyes*, where it is shown to be indissociable from the political situation; in *Victory* this is refocused as a philosophical ambiguity in the question of whether the world itself has existence – a question anticipated in Natalia Haldin's claim: "The whole world is inconceivable to the strict logic of ideas. And yet the world exists to our senses, and we exist in it" (106). To accommodate this development, the novel includes differing representations of reality, from the psychological realism of the relationship between Heyst and his father, or the discreet relationship between Heyst and Lena, to the very differently treated desperadoes.

Once one considers *Victory* as a novel of ideas, the full scale of Lena's "victory" becomes apparent. Both Mr Jones, in his misogyny, and Heyst himself, in his suspicion about her love, are mistaken in their interpretations of her. Furthermore, Heyst's scepticism about the world, inherited from his father, is proved wrong. The fact that the sources of these erroneous views are all male ensures that her victory is also affirmative because she has triumphed over masculine sceptical pessimism. If this suggests that the novel's concern is less with "fact" than with the "ideal" then Conrad suggests such to be his concern as an author. In an often-quoted letter of 1 March 1917, he surveyed his critical reception thus:

> Perhaps you won't find it presumptuous if after 22 years of work I may say that I have not been very well understood. I have been called a writer of the sea, of the tropics, a descriptive writer, a romantic writer – and also a realist. But as a matter of fact all of my concern has been with the "ideal" values of things, events and people. That and nothing else. The humourous [*sic*], the pathetic, the passionate, the sentimental *aspects* came in of themselves – mais en vérité c'est les valeurs idéales des faits et gestes humains qui se sont *imposé[e]s* a mon activité artistique [But the truth is that the ideal values of things and human events have imposed themselves on my artistic activities]. (*CL6*: 40)

The different psychological treatment accorded to the characters in *Victory* reinforces the novel's concern with the materiality of the universe as the reader is made to question what is "real" and what is not. Heyst remembers the "guidance" offered to him by his father: "You believe in flesh and blood, perhaps? A full and equable contempt would soon do away with that, too. But since you have not attained to it, I advise you to cultivate that form of contempt which is called pity" (174). Heyst follows Decoud and Razumov in the line of Conrad's sceptics who cannot love, and when love finds them, it destroys them because the mind gets in the way. Lena demolishes Heyst senior's pernicious philosophy with her body, protecting "paradise" by vindicating the feminine principle. The novel thus represents the victory of women over men at various levels.

In *Victory*, love is identified as the source of faith in the material world. Symbolically, when Heyst tells her: "I have lost all belief in realities," his next words are: "Lena, give me your hand" (350). As Lena lies on her deathbed, "convinced of the reality of her victory over death," and Heyst condemns himself for his lack of faith, the tropical storm abates: "Over Samburan the thunder had ceased to growl at last, and the world of material forms shuddered no more under the emerging stars" (406). The extent to which the narrative inhabits the borderline between fact and fantasy – and so justifies the presentation of the trio of desperadoes – persists in Lena's dying words, where the force of belief is set against the force of doubt:

> "Who else could have done this for you?" she whispered gloriously.
> "No one in the world," he answered her in a murmur of uncon-
> cealed despair. (406)

Lena's sacrifice finally convinces Heyst that his scepticism is hollow. Ironically, Heyst is converted to faith in flesh and blood existence at the moment when life leaves Lena's body. The destruction of the bungalow, that serves as a funeral pyre for both Lena and Heyst, now "purified" (411) in Davidson's words, also destroys Heyst-senior's portrait and books. Humorously, these books have been written to prove that nothing exists. As Conrad claimed in a letter of 4 May 1918: "irony is not altogether absent from those pages" (*CL6*: 211). Symbolically, Heyst destroys his father at this point, and, appropriately, in so doing destroys the destroyer of faith in life.

* * *

Lena threatens Heyst's defence against life in a manner comparable to the trio's invasion of Samburan. Heyst's isolation on Samburan mirrors his attempt to find refuge from the world in sceptical philo-sophy. His isolation is his protection: "that solitude which was like an armour for this man" (270). Like Brown's arrival in Patusan in *Lord Jim*, the trio's arrival in Black Diamond Bay provides the chink in this armour. (A further parallel between the novels links the two women characters: both Jewel and Lena show a greater determination to defend themselves than their men folk.) As both Jim and Heyst come to realise, to have faith in the world is to have faith in one's own actions. In the realm of heroic action, both men fail: Jim because he lacks faith in himself and Heyst because he mistakenly assumes that Lena is identified with Jones's world. Jones's misogyny provides an emanation of Heyst's own detachment. In *Lord Jim*, Jim doesn't think of a world "out there" in favour of his actions. Rather, his failure stems from the gap created between the objective world of values and his own subjectivity. As Marlow says: "of all mankind Jim had no dealings but with himself" (339). For Heyst, on the other hand, the world of values is a purely subjective creation, and he is objectively looking on. For him, the problem arises only if he believes that the world is meaningful.

A paradox begins to emerge in Conrad's representation of subjective commitment and the world of values to which one commits oneself: on the one hand, there is no meaning, but, on the other, unless we live as if life has meaning, then life is impossible. Whereas aboard the *Patna* Jim fails by not living up to the code of heroic values he has defined for himself, Heyst fails because he cannot believe in the possibility of such a code – in his case, love. (This failure to perceive the world as having value accommodates the variable degrees of realism in *Victory*.) Priest and Philosopher, the fathers of Jim and Heyst instil different creeds in their sons: in Jim's case this leads to action, in Heyst's to inaction. At the moment of choice, Jim fails in his beliefs. Heyst is the opposite: he does not mismanage or wrongly interpret the situation, yet he has still failed in some sense – even though, for him, there is neither failure nor success. By way of religious analogy, his is the contradiction of the believer who believes but does not live by: how *can* one believe but not live by? Thus, how *can* Heyst feel that he has failed in terms of a world he does not believe in or claims is meaningless? Commitment to a code of conduct may well prove illusory in Conrad's novels, but there seems to be little respect for anyone without such illusions. As the narrator of *Victory* claims: "every age is fed on illusions, lest men should renounce life early and the human race come to an end" (94).

Nostromo reveals that, for Conrad, faith is illusory. At the centre of Charles Gould's being, his faith, is the San Tomé mine. Characters who lack faith are shown to be destructive, even pointless, whilst those who do are shown to be inadequate. Like Jim, Doctor Monygham betrayed himself, when confessing under torture. Consequently he believes his life to be meaningless, because he is without meaning. Jim, however, is never cynical – and Monygham is, like Mrs Gould, an idealist, able to transcend his cynicism. In *Victory*, Heyst's rescue of Lena represents an act of commitment to the world, yet he then feels betrayed as he fails to understand her and misinterprets her feelings.

As part of its philosophical and cultural inheritance from the nineteenth century, the twentieth century was left to grapple with the problem of how to jettison God and still retain meaning in life. For Conrad, this translates into a problem of how to justify a code of being once the social dimension, so often traced back to the ship, has been abandoned. In *Victory*, Heyst's struggle to find faith in love, embodied in Lena, serves as a moral parable: Heyst would not have, finally, recognised this commitment had he not acted out of faith for Lena. To Conrad, such commitment involves commitment to the group. For instance, in *Lord Jim*, Marlow, who pronounces himself "aggrieved" because Jim has "cheated" him of "a splendid opportunity to keep up the illusion of my beginnings" (131), defines "the real significance of crime" as "its being a breach of faith with the community of mankind" (157). Yet, as Conrad's social novels demonstrate, there is no group to whom commitment makes sense. Instead, there are only individuals, amongst whom one's code of belief has to be self-explanatory. Thus commitment itself is, to some degree, illusory. Conrad may question cynicism but he also distrusts its alternatives. His essay "Autocracy and War" (1905) includes the observation: "it must be confessed that the architectural aspect of the universal city remains as yet inconceivable – that the very ground for its erection has not been cleared of the jungle" (*NLL*: 143).

* * *

Conrad described *Victory* as "a book in which I have tried to grasp at more 'life stuff' than perhaps in any other of my novels" (*LL*2: 342). Powerfully supporting this sense of inclusiveness are the literary allusions with which the narrative is littered. From the opening paragraph, where the mention of a "portable form of property" (3) recalls Wemmick in Dickens' *Great Expectations*, the novel's breadth of reference includes Shakespeare – like Pericles, Heyst hears "the music of the spheres" (66) – and Coleridge's *The Rhyme of the Ancient Mariner*, in the reference "like a painted ship on a painted sea" (178). In addition, as critics such as Paul Kirschner (1968) have noted, *Victory* contains phrases from French authors, like Maupassant and Anatole France. Together with the many biblical allusions and the obvious connection with *The Tempest* in the narrative, the intertextual echoes create a network of associations between *Victory* and other depictions of "reality." This impulse is further strengthened by the novel's use of allegory, a traditional device for conveying two meanings, the literal, surface meaning and the underlying, figural meaning, simultaneously.

For example, at the beginning of Part III, Heyst observes: "There must be a lot of the original Adam in me after all" (173). This idea then develops through a connection between action and naming:

> There was in the son a lot of that first ancestor who, as soon as he could uplift his muddy frame from the celestial mould, started inspecting and naming the animals of that paradise which he was so soon to lose.
>
> Action – the first thought, or perhaps the first impulse on earth! The barbed hook, baited with the illusion of progress. (173–74)

There follows Heyst's last memories of his father's final words to him, including the injunction to "Look on – make no sound" (175), culminating in his decision to settle on the Round Island after the liquidation of the Tropical Belt Coal Company, "as though he had never departed from the doctrine that this world, for the wise, is nothing but an amusing spectacle" (178). But, no sooner has the influence of his father's philosophy of detachment been affirmed than it is contradicted in terms of the action/naming impulse that links Heyst to Adam and exposes his "apostasy" (177) to his father. First, we learn that "Heyst and Morrison had landed in Black Diamond Bay, and named it" (180) and then that Heyst, "after several experimental essays in combining detached letters and syllables" (186) has named Lena. Such a tissue of connections with the Eden myth is too dense to admit only a surface reading of the text. Unsurprisingly, in a letter to Pinker, written on 19 February 1914, Conrad said of *Victory*: "That tale is the very devil to manage. It has too many possibilities" (*CL5*: 356).

Emblems of intertextuality, literary allusion and buried verbal fragments set off their own internal resonance in *Victory* even as they exploit the mimetic capacity of language. A "fiddle-scraping girl picked up on the very threshold of infamy" (353), Lena is associated with several myths. Introducing herself to Heyst at Schomberg's hotel, she says: "They call me Alma. I don't know why. Silly name! Magdalen too" (88). Her names recall both Edmund Spenser's *The Fairie Queene*, where Alma, meaning "soul" or "spirit" in Spanish and Italian, is the Lady of the House of Temperance, and Mary Magdalen in the Bible. She thus unites the twin extremes of the patriarchal Madonna-whore designation of woman. Since Lena is the diminutive of Helena, Watts (1984) detects a further "covert" invitation to read the plot as a parodic counterpart to the legend of Helen of Troy, where abduction results in invasion, disaster, and conflagration. The fact that Lena is identified with various myths, whose appropriateness is left to the reader to determine, suits a narrative preoccupied with the nature of reality. This is complemented in the interlocution of narrative voices and perspectives that provide the novel's organisational principle.

Heyst's scepticism about existence is communicated to the reader through a fluctuating focus of perception so that the reader, too, is sceptical about the "real" version of events. Besides the formal narrators, the omniscient narrator, the first-person narrator, and Davidson, the tale is recounted through a host of internal perspectives: those of Heyst, Lena, Schomberg, Jones, Ricardo, and Wang. Together, these shifts in focus confuse the moral issues in the novel by creating doubts about the motives of Heyst, Lena, and Wang especially. For instance, in an early chapter, Part I Chapter 3, during which Heyst is variously defined as "Heyst the Spider" "wandering Heyst," "Naïve Heyst," "enchanted Heyst," "a Swedish baron or something," and "Heyst the Enemy" (21, 23, 24), two perspectives regulate the flow of information to the reader: a first-person narrator, who has pieced together some of Heyst's story, and Schomberg. Their combination invites the reader to accept the vague focalisation of the former over the vulgar certitude of the latter.

Heyst views the trio of "envoys of the outer world" as "fantasms from the sea – apparitions, chimæras!" (329). And yet, their arrival precipitates his philosophical crisis: "the sceptical carelessness which had accompanied every one of his attempts at action, like a secret reserve of his soul, fell away from him. He no longer belonged to himself. There was a call far more imperious and august" (245). Jones' startling self-definition – "I am the world itself, come to pay you a visit" (379) – has a grim appropriateness, especially in the light of Heyst's description of the world's "envoys" as "evil intelligence, instinctive savagery, arm in arm. The brute force is at the back" (329). Jones, whose misogyny Ricardo views as "a sort of depraved morality" (266) and whose sexual nature has provoked speculation among critics, claims to be "a rebel ... coming and going up and down the earth" (317–18). Alongside this allusion to Lucifer, Jones consistently defines himself as a "gentleman." Together these claims recall Edgar's observation in *King Lear*: "The Prince of Darkness is a gentleman" (3:4:140). Jones is thus both "divorced from all reality in [Heyst's] eyes" (364) *and* instrumental in the myth in which Lena envisions herself, in which the trio arrive as a "sort of retribution from an angry Heaven" (354) and she defends Heyst from the "sting of death" – a phrase that is itself an echo of St Paul: "O death, where is thy sting? O grave, where is thy victory?" (1 *Corinthians* 15:55). The question that follows, since Heyst doesn't see Lena's actions in these terms, is: to what degree is this a "victory"?

These shifting perspectives ensure a relativistic attitude towards reality and also act as an elaborate instance of delayed decoding. Structurally, there is a convergence of knowledge at the end of the novel so that the reader shares in Heyst's realisation: the physical revelation of Lena's death to the reader coincides with the moral revelation to Heyst about the extent of Lena's sacrifice. But both pathos and ambiguity surround the ending. Lena dies clinging "to her triumph convinced of the reality of her victory over death" (406) and believing that Heyst "was ready to lift her up in his firm arms and take her into the sanctuary of his innermost heart – for ever!" (407). But how does Heyst see this moment? Heyst finally recognises the extent of Lena's sacrifice, as his words to Davidson reveal, but communication between the couple arrives too late, as if the sacrifice has to be made before it is understood. The ending of *Victory* is thus comparable to the ending of *King Lear*: both tragic, because the revelation comes too late, and optimistic, because through his madness and the loss of Cordelia, Lear learns something – indeed, it may be hope itself that kills him. *Victory* questions our ability to understand anything outside ourselves except through the ultimate experience of separation. Lena's "victory" finally destroys Heyst's scepticism but, like Decoud before him, deprived of this negative form of belief or faith, he has nothing whatsoever and thus destroys himself. Ironically, the only way to defeat scepticism and affirm the reality of life seems to be through death, its negation.

The Shadow-Line

Another product of a lengthy gestation period, Conrad's first reference to the story that would eventually became *The Shadow-Line* occurs in a letter to William Blackwood of 14 February 1899, where he mentions two stories, "First Command" and "A Seaman," which "creep about in my head" but have yet "to be caught and tortured into some kind of shape" (*CL2*: 167). It is unclear what became of "A Seaman," but "First Command" was the working-title for this novella of some 40,000 words that Conrad returned to in February 1915, writing to Pinker: "I propose to write a story for the Met[ropolitan Magazine]: It's an old subject something in [the] style of Youth. I've carried it in my head for years under the name of First Command" (*CL5*: 441). The following month he announced: "By the way the title will be: *The Shadow-line* it having a sort of spiritual meaning" (*CL5*: 458). Completed by the end of the year, the novella was published first in serial form, in the *English Review* (September 1916 to March 1917), and then in book form, by J. M. Dent in England (March 1917) and by Doubleday, Page in America (April 1917).

The Shadow-Line was Conrad's most sustained piece of writing during the First World War. His letter of 17 August 1915 to Eugene F. Saxton, an editor for Doubleday, Page, in which Conrad mentions the impending enlistment of his son, Borys, vividly recreates the prevailing mood of anxiety and uncertainty under which the novella was composed:

> Just before I began this letter we were all out in our garden listening to the hum of an airship's engines filling the still night air, and straining our eyes to catch the elusive shadow gliding against the stars. Ten minutes later came two heavy reports of guns in the distance to the north, and we heard faintly, across the dark fields, the steam-syrens of the railway-workshops in Ashford sounding the alarm. Zeppelin – or English patrol airship? We won't know till the morning. Now, midnight, a perfect quiet reigns over the countryside all calm and dark. Everybody we know has lost someone ... They all go. My boy's turn will be coming presently to start off.
>
> The shadow lies over this land. This is a time of great awe and searching of hearts and of resolute girding of loins.   (*CL5*: 500)

Written in the year that, according to D. H. Lawrence, "the old world ended" (*Kangaroo*, 220), Conrad's letter conveys the quiet apprehension and illusory calm of rural England, living under a "shadow" and steadily being denuded of her sons. Conrad pinned his faith on the nation rather than its leaders, writing to Doubleday in January 1917: "We are all feeling the strain more and more, but the national determination to see this thing through hardens as the cruel days go by. It's a pity better use is not made of it. But leaders of genius are rare" (*CL6*: 14). To Conrad, the war was primarily the nation's struggle for survival, and *The Shadow-Line* explores in miniature the nature of such a struggle. As Berthoud puts it, the protagonist "is taught that he could not have survived the ordeal to which he is exposed without a full reciprocity of dependence between himself and his crew. This lesson may seem banal enough; yet Conrad shows that it supports the entire edifice of human life" (1986: 14).

*   *   *

The Shadow-Line begins by identifying the principle that the story will proceed to dramatise: "One goes on. And the time, too, goes on – till one perceives ahead a shadow-line warning one that the region of early youth, too, must be left behind" (3). The first-person narrator, never identified, recalls the "rash moment" in "an Eastern port" (4), which turns out to be Singapore, when, suddenly disillusioned with sea-life, he resigned his post. His reasons for "Signing off for good" (7) and returning to England remain obscure to everyone, including himself. During his residence at the Officers' Sailors' Home while waiting for a homeward-bound mail-boat he comes to realise that far from wanting to give up the sea, his desire is to command a ship of his own. This desire is brought home to him by Captain Giles, "An expert – how shall I say it? – in intricate navigation" (12). Ostensibly this expertise relates to the waters of the Archipelago; more pertinently it refers to his ability to steer the narrator towards his as yet unacknowledged longing to advance his career. When an official communication from Captain Ellis, the harbour master, arrives at the Sailors' Home, the Chief Steward withholds it from the narrator until, directed by Captain Giles, he confronts the Steward and discovers that it advertises a captaincy. Following his instincts, the narrator successfully applies for the position: "I discovered how much of a seaman I was, in heart, in mind, and, as it were, physically – a man exclusively of sea and ships; the sea the only world that counted, and the ships the test of manliness, of temperament, of courage and fidelity – and of love" (40).

He sails to Bangkok to take up his new command, travelling in the *Melita* whose captain embodies "The spirit of modern hurry" (46). After a voyage of four days, he arrives in Bangkok harbour and he sees his command for the first time, pronouncing her: "one of those craft that in virtue of their design and complete finish will never look old. ... I knew that, like some rare women, she was one of those creatures whose mere existence is enough to awaken an unselfish delight. One feels that it is good to be in the world in which she has her being" (49). Like the young Captain-narrator, the ship is never named. In her saloon, the narrator identifies himself with the "dynasty" of former captains, "continuous not in blood, indeed, but in its experience, in its training, in its conception of duty, and in the blessed simplicity of its traditional point of view on life" (53). In conversation with the first mate, Mr Burns, the captain learns that his predecessor, an eccentric, violin-playing man who seemed intent upon destroying his ship, died at sea. Unsurprisingly, the narrator views the former captain's conduct as "a complete act of treason" (62). It transpires that Burns had hopes of advancement when his captain died, which explains his taciturnity. When the mate declares that, but for family responsibilities, he would have asked to be discharged, the young Captain counters by saying: "I shall expect you to attend to your duty and give me the benefit of your experience to the best of your ability" (64).

The ship's departure is delayed due to ill health among the crew. First, the steward dies, and then Mr Burns is transferred to the hospital suffering from fever. From his sickbed, the mate pleads with the Captain not to be left behind when the ship sails. Despite the doctor's caution, the Captain respects Mr Burns' wish, framed in a discourse of mutual values: "You and I are sailors" (70), and, trusting to the healing potential of the sea as "the only remedy for all my troubles" (71), the Captain makes his delayed departure with an unfit crew. Not only is the ship's progress across the Gulf of Siam tortuously slow, but it quickly becomes clear that the ship has not left sickness behind her in Bangkok as the crew succumb to tropical fever. Only the Captain and Ransome, the cook, who has a weak heart, "a deadly enemy in his breast" (68), and must be spared heavy duties, remain unaffected. Mr Burns blames the ship's distress upon the malevolent influence of the former Captain, buried at sea "right in the ship's way ... out of the Gulf" (83).

While rejecting his mate's interpretation, the Captain's own use of phrases such as "the evil spell held us always motionless" (83) sustains the possibility of a malign supernatural influence at work on board.

No sooner does the Captain put his faith in the ship's supply of quinine to combat the fever than, weighing out doses of this "unfailing panacea" (88) one morning, he discovers that the remaining bottles are filled not with quinine, which the previous Captain is suspected of selling, but with a replacement powder. Haunted by guilt at not having personally checked these supplies, the Captain sets his course for Singapore in order to replenish his medical supplies. Still the ship moves at a snail's pace, and extracts from the Captain's diary detail his despair on this "death-haunted command" where his every order, obeyed by an increasingly diminished "tottering little group," is issued with "a pang of remorse and pity" (98). Despite their enfeebled state, the crew's endurance and lack of reproach render them, in the Captain's phrase that also provides the novella's epigraph, "worthy of my undying regard" (100). This is simultaneously a tale about the Captain's capacity to command in the face of seemingly overwhelming odds, and makes of his previous experience "a fading memory of light-hearted youth, something on the other side of a shadow" (106). Just as he has convinced himself of his unfitness to command – "I am no good" (107) – than a storm threatens, and when alerted by Ransome he responds "briskly" (108).

As the rain begins to fall, and with the ship still becalmed, Mr Burns who has spent the voyage incapacitated in his cabin and obsessed with the idea that the former captain is responsible for the ship's state, crawls onto the deck in order "to scare the old bullying rascal" (116). Just as Mr Burns had defied the Captain when alive, by laughing at him, so he now issues a "provoking, mocking peal" of laughter (119) that, while it causes him to faint, is immediately answered by winds that fill the sails. The spell broken, the ship makes good progress for Singapore – although the sailors' exertions have overwhelmed them, leaving her "a ship without a crew" (123). It is left to the Captain, Ransome, and Mr Burns to bring the ship into harbour, after a three-week journey from Bangkok. As the crew are removed to hospital, the Captain regards each one as "an embodied reproach" (129). Ashore, he tells Captain Giles: "I feel old" (131), to which the old sailor advises: "one must not make too much of anything in life, good or bad" and "a man should stand up to his bad luck" (131, 132). The Captain's announcement that he intends to ship a new crew immediately and continue his voyage at daybreak earns Captain Giles' simple commendation: "You'll do" (132). Having exerted himself unwisely during the ship's ordeal, Ransome requests to be discharged, and the narrative ends with the Captain reluctantly letting him go: "I listened to him going up the companion stairs cautiously, step by step, in mortal fear of starting into sudden anger our common enemy it was his hard fate to carry consciously within his faithful breast" (133).

The Shadow-Line is subtitled "A Confession," and Conrad repeatedly described it as autobiographical. For instance, in a letter to John Quinn, to whom Conrad sold the manuscript, he described it as "a sort of autobiography – a personal experience – dramatised in the telling" (*CL5*: 543). As Norman Sherry's research in *Conrad's Eastern World* has shown, the novel draws on Conrad's experiences of his own first command. Conrad signed off the *Vidar* in Singapore in January 1888. While staying at the Sailors' Home, he was offered and accepted his only command, the *Otago* (whose captain had died), on 19 January, and then travelled to Bangkok in the *Melita* to join his command. The early part of the *Otago*'s voyage, to Australia, was beset with the troubles fictionalised in *The Shadow-Line*: after a delayed departure from Bangkok and calms in the Gulf of Siam, illness aboard forced the ship to call at Singapore in order to replenish her medical supplies and take in fresh crew members before continuing her voyage in early March. In *The Shadow-Line*, although the paper he reads at the Officers' Sailors' Home is "old and uninteresting," the narrator records that they were "filled up mostly with dreary stereotyped descriptions of Queen Victoria's first jubilee celebrations" (16). As these Golden Jubilee celebrations took place in June 1887, the fictional action occurs at approximately the same time as its autobiographical counterpart. But while the tale told in *The Shadow-Line* draws upon Conrad's own experiences of "first command," the autobiographical element has larger implications.

The novella is dedicated to the Conrads' eldest son, Borys, who enlisted in September 1915 and was attached to the Mechanical Transport Corps. He attained the rank of second lieutenant and suffered shell shock during the closing months of the war. The dedication reads: "To Borys and all others who like himself have crossed in early youth the shadow-line of their generation / with love." In his "Author's Note" to *The Shadow-Line*, Conrad likens the two experiences, his own and those of Borys and his contemporaries, while emphasising their incomparability:

> Primarily the aim of this piece of writing was the presentation of certain facts which certainly were associated with the change from youth, care-free and fervent, to the more self-conscious and more poignant period of maturer life. Nobody can doubt that before the supreme trial of a whole generation I had an acute consciousness of the minute and insignificant character of my own obscure experience. There could be no question here of any parallelism.   (x)

The point is not that the narrator's and the soldiers' experiences are equivalent but, rather, that each involved crossing a "shadow-line." Conrad's letters of January 1917, after Borys had come home on a 10-day leave, during which he celebrated his nineteenth birthday, repeatedly refer to how "mature" his son has become. (A shadow-line is also that cast by an upright pole on a sundial, demarcating time.) His letter to Cunninghame Graham of 17 January expresses proudly that Borys has "the respect of his seniors" and "a deep democratic feeling as to values in mankind" (*CL6*: 10). The personal, first-person narrative in *The Shadow-Line* is, thus, emblematic of the mass transition from innocence to experience forced on an entire generation, caught up in a war and, in Conrad's words, "falling like cornstalks under the scythe" (*CL6*: 27). To this end, the narrative resounds with apocalyptic phrases that, while emotively conjuring up the young Captain's impressions, simultaneously evoke the destruction and horrors of war against which it was composed: he envies Mr Burns for being "So near extinction – while I had to bear within me a tumult of suffering vitality, doubt, confusion, self-reproach, and an indefinite reluctance to meet the horrid logic of the situation" (92–93); he describes the trial in universal terms as "the formidable Work of the Seven Days, into which mankind seems to have blundered unbidden. Or else decoyed. Even as I have been decoyed into this awful, this death-haunted command. ... " (97–98); and, when it finally arrives, the storm affords only "the closing in of a menace from all sides" (108) upon a ship "poised on the edge of some violent issue, lurking in the dark" (115). One of the pleasures of the novella lies precisely in recognising its richness as both a fictionalised autobiography and an oblique commentary on an historical moment, both the work of an individual and the product of a culture.

Returning to Eastern waters in *The Shadow-Line*, Conrad revisited earlier maritime-themes with social implications. Prominently, *The Shadow-Line* engages with the rights and responsibilities of authority. Conrad's earlier essays on this idea, in *The Nigger of the "Narcissus"* and "Typhoon," had been extended in "The Secret Sharer" (1910), written during the composition of *Under Western Eyes*. In its vision of captaincy, "The Secret Sharer" offers a corrective to Alistoun's – and a wry contrast to his "secret ambition" "to make her accomplish some day a brilliantly quick passage which would be mentioned in nautical papers" (31). The stratified ship's community found in the *Narcissus* remains, but the mutual dependence of commander and commanded strikes a new note. As the ordeal demonstrates, authority is as much imposed as allowed in this ship. With autobiographical immediacy, this Captain recounts – and, metaphorically, commands – his own narrative, where professional responsibility goes hand-in-hand with moral responsibility: the Captain's right to command is sanctioned by the marine community, extending from Captain Ellis to the crew. This broader vision, the benefit of reflection and maturity, is evident when Ransome, in a symmetrical complement to the narrator, demands his "right" to leave the ship: the Captain sees "under the worth and the comeliness of the man the humble reality of things" (129).

* * *

In *The Shadow-Line* Conrad returns to writing "sea stuff." Charting the young Captain's confrontation with his own potential, his fitness to command, the novella simultaneously confirms faith in the values of collective action. To readers familiar with Conrad's fiction the tale offers persistent and identifiable themes: the solidarity and interdependence of the crew, man's solitary struggle with the sea that reveals his own worth, and a voyage that provides an initiation into seamanship. Noticeably few of the crew are identified, and the Captain-narrator is never named. Instead the sailors are presented, often as a shadowy and emblematic group, as a testament to the self-effacing image of common duty performed for the good of the ship. When Gambril, one of the few named sailors, is at the wheel, he preserves "finely that air of unconsciousness as to anything but his business a helmsman should never lose" (111). As such, *The Shadow-Line* affords a dual tribute to the enduring claims of tradition: the tradition of British seamanship – owned by an Arab, "and a Syed at that" (4), the ship flies the Red Ensign, the flag of the British Merchant Service – and an extension of the fictional tradition established in Conrad's earlier works, such as "Youth" and *The Nigger of the "Narcissus."* In *The Shadow Line* Conrad reconfigures the dangers posed by the sea: while the *Judea*, the *Narcissus*, and the *Nan-Shan* all endure the violence of storms the sea, here the drama stems from its contrary: a death-inducing placidity. Together, Conrad's sea tales thus reveal his enduring faith in a code of seamanship that, while idealised, is ubiquitous. In a letter of 1917 he wrote: "my ideas were settled and my character formed long before I began to write" (*CL6*: 27).

The voyage itself occupies less than half of the narrative, with the first three chapters (of six) devoted to the narrator's period in the Officers' Sailors' Home, taking up his command, and the preliminaries for setting sail from Bangkok. Structurally this emphasises the weight of the past upon the story, by setting the narrator's impulsiveness and uncertainty against the claims of tradition embodied in the seafaring community and established through the characters of Captain Ellis, the Harbour Master, and, above all, Captain Giles. Despite his own initial ennui, the narrator is distinguished from the loafers who, according to Captain Giles, "go soft mighty quick" out East where things are "made easy for white men" (14). His rejection of this easy option speaks volumes about the young mate's professionalism. If a degree of arrogant, wilful blindness renders him impervious to Captain Giles' promptings about his future, the narrator's dependence upon such assistance confirms a central truth in the tale: this account of a first command is simultaneously a recognition that such command depends upon the service of those one commands, a recognition elevated to the status of personal tribute in both the novella's sub-title, "A Confession," and its epigraph, "worthy of my undying regard." Quoted from the text itself (100), this epigraph is a testament to the sailors whose supreme efforts have resulted in his twin authority, as both Captain and narrator.

When instructed to hoist the mainsail, "The shadows swayed away from me without a word. Those men were the ghosts of themselves" (109). The proximity of "shadows" to "ghosts" here confirms the Classical associations of the term: where "shades" or "shadows" refer to the dead. Not only is their presentation as "shadows" literally apt – the crew are decimated by illness and in need of medical attention – but it also forms part of a persistent impulse in *The Shadow-Line* to align itself with Classical and maritime mythology. For instance, Captain Ellis strikes the narrator as "Our deputy-Neptune" (31), while Mr Burns condemns his previous skipper for "Acting the Flying Dutchman in the China Sea" (94). The first English edition of the novella carried an advertisement describing it as "a prose counterpart of *The Ancient Mariner*" and, as Hawthorn (2003) has shown, *The Shadow-Line* contains a number of textual echoes of Coleridge's poem with its "ghastly crew." While the ship's predicament certainly recalls her literary prototypes – "She's running away with us now. All we can do is to steer her. She's a ship without a crew" (123) – the Captain's dependence upon his crew suggests an engagement designed to rehabilitate these.

The presence of the supernatural in *The Shadow-Line* also forms part of the network of associations that link it to earlier literature. Dismissed as "silly fancies" and being "like a case of possession" (102, 103), Mr Burns' obsession with the idea that the former captain is somehow haunting the ship none the less influences the Captain's thinking: he refers to "the fever-devil who has got on board this ship" (103) and describes the ship's predicament as "like being bewitched" (84). As with Singleton's belief that it is Wait who is impeding the ship's progress in *The Nigger of the "Narcissus,"* while it is tempting to dismiss Burns' ideas as nothing more than sailor-superstition, the "facts" of the story bear out his ideas: once he has challenged the "old dodging Devil" with "a hair-raising, screeching over-note of defiance" (116) the ship finally makes headway. According to the Captain: "By the exercising virtue of Mr. Burns' awful laugh, the malicious spectre had been laid, the evil spell broken, the curse removed" (125). Two interpretations, meteorological facts and Mr Burns' "silly fancies," are thus juxtaposed. Insisting upon their mutual validity within the story, Conrad reminds us that superstition also has its place in the mythology of seafaring, the irrational being one means of confronting a reality as vast as the sea.

As Frenchy's insistence that "he had a jump or two left in him" (112) or Gambril's description of his enfeebled state with "no complaint in his tone" (111) demonstrate, those who can continue in their duties unswervingly, even willingly. In particular, the Captain depends upon "the unfailing Ransome" (105). When Ransome, "a priceless man altogether" (112), leaves to go about his duties the

Captain feels "as if some support had been withdrawn" (112). Nor does such dependence upon the crew offset the affirmatory quality of *The Shadow-Line*; rather, this tale of a young captain's initiation demonstrates and reinvigorates the concept of mariners as a fraternity. Ransome's unwise but dutiful exertions while hoisting the mainsail leave him "sobbing for breath" (109), causing the Captain to wonder: "putting out his strength – for what? Indeed for some distinct ideal" (126). It is this "ideal" of marine service, above and beyond the call of duty and in direct contradiction to the old captain's dereliction, that is rehabilitated and celebrated in the novella.

Works cited

Berthoud, Jacques. *Joseph Conrad: The Major Phase*. Cambridge: Cambridge University Press, 1978.

——. "Introduction: Autobiography and War." *The Shadow-Line*. Edited by Jacques Berthoud. 7–24. Harmondsworth: Penguin, 1986.

Curle, Richard. *Joseph Conrad: A Study*. London: Kegan Paul, Trench, Trübner & Co., 1914.

Hattersley, Roy. *The Edwardians*. London: Little, Brown, 2004.

Hawthorn, Jeremy. *Joseph Conrad: Narrative Technique and Ideological Commitment*. London: Edward Arnold, 1990.

——. "Explanatory Notes." *The Shadow-Line*. Edited by Jeremy Hawthorn. "Oxford World's Classics." 113–29. Oxford: Oxford University Press, 2003.

Kirschner, Paul. *Conrad: The Psychologist as Artist*. Edinburgh: Oliver and Boyd, 1968.

Knowles, Owen, and Gene Moore. *Oxford Reader's Companion to Conrad*. Oxford: Oxford University Press, 2000.

Lawrence, D. H. *Kangaroo*. [1923] London: William Heinemann, 1970.

Moser, Thomas. *Joseph Conrad: Achievement and Decline*. Cambridge, Mass.: Harvard University Press, 1957.

Ray, Martin. "Introduction" to *Chance*. Edited by Martin Ray. "Oxford World's Classics." vii–xix. Oxford: Oxford University Press, 1990.

Schwarz, Daniel R. *Conrad: The Later Fiction*. London: Macmillan, 1982.

Sherry, Norman, ed. *Conrad: The Critical Heritage*. London: Routledge & Kegan Paul, 1973.

Stape, John, and Owen Knowles, eds. *A Portrait in Letters: Correspondence to and about Conrad*. Amsterdam: Rodopi, 1996.

Watts, Cedric. *The Deceptive Text: An Invitation to Covert Plots*. Brighton: Harvester Press, 1984.

8

Late Novels and the Growth of a Reputation

The final phase of Conrad's writing career yielded four novels: *The Arrow of Gold* (1919), *The Rescue* (1920), *The Rover* (1923), and the unfinished *Suspense*, published posthumously in 1925. These were years of prosperity for the author. Besides royalties from the late novels, Conrad benefited financially from the sale of his manuscripts, film rights to his novels, and collected editions of his works that sold well in England and the United States. A measure of Conrad's prosperity is reflected in his domestic circumstances: in 1919, the Conrads moved to the last and largest of their residences, Oswalds, in Bishopsbourne, near Canterbury. The annual rent for this Georgian house was £250 and the household staff, or "crew" as Conrad called them, included a butler/valet, chauffeur, cook, housemaids, gardeners, and a nurse-companion for Jessie. Oswalds became the site of pilgrimage for numerous friends and admirers of the ageing novelist and hosted musical evenings and lavish weekend gatherings. The sums of money that Conrad commanded in the closing stage of his career were phenomenal. For example, selling the film rights to his work netted Conrad £3,080, after Pinker's commission had been paid. Similarly, the "Note Book of Joseph Conrad," now housed at the Bodleian Library, Oxford, and composed of copies of and extracts from Conrad's contracts with his publishers, records that the serial rights alone of *The Arrow of Gold* and *The Rescue* brought in £1,000 and £2,500 respectively. Although such comparisons are notoriously difficult to verify, according to <concertina.com> (accessed January 2006), the contemporary equivalent for £3,500 in 1920 is a staggering £348,000.

But, although Conrad's late novels were financially successful and the critical acclaim that greeted their publication often excessive, it is as if contemporary reviewers and the book-buying public were making up for their neglect of his earlier writings. Reading the novels now one gets the sense of a career drawing to a close and, with it, that his gift for prose had deserted him. A possible factor here may be that Conrad's working method had altered: chronic gout affected his wrists and left him unable to write, so all of these works were dictated, a situation made more acute by Conrad's documented unease about his spoken English. Appropriately, the epigraph to *The Rover*, the best of these works, is inscribed upon his tombstone: "Sleep after toyle, port after stormie seas, / Ease after warre, death after life, does greatly please." Taken from Edmund Spenser's The Faerie Queene (Book I Canto 9:40), the words are those spoken by Despayre to the Red Crosse Knight, urging him to commit suicide.

Taken together, the late novels offer a settling of accounts with the world. Most obviously, in late May 1919, twenty-three years after starting it, Conrad eventually completed *The Rescue*, begun in March 1896 and returned to intermittently and perfunctorily across his writing career. His sense of relief upon reaching the end is palpable: "I am settling my affairs in this world and I should not have liked to leave behind me this evidence of having bitten off more than I could chew" (*CL6*: 444). With *The Rescue* Conrad finally completed the Lingard trilogy of novels with which his writing career had commenced. The novel is Conrad's farewell to the Eastern waters that, as an early reviewer predicted, he had "annexed" in his writings. Together, *The Arrow of Gold, The Rover*, and *Suspense* provide another belated settling of accounts – this time, with nineteenth-century European history. In a letter of 1923 Conrad wrote: "I think that I am not taking too much upon myself in saying that I am a good European, not exactly in the superficial, cosmopolitan sense, but in the blood and bones as it were, and as the result of a long heredity" (*LL2*: 296). Set in Marseilles, *The Arrow of Gold* returns to the site of his interregnum years, between 1874 and 1878, as Conrad made the transition from Polish aristocrat to British sailor. Like Conrad, M. George travels to the Caribbean, while his gun-running exploits recall the author's own, impossible to verify, reminiscences.

The novel might have succeeded in the marketplace, but it failed to convince his peers. Galsworthy noted how Conrad's return to youthful experiences had, on this occasion, let him down, writing to Garnett: "read *Youth* alongside of it. Both are reproductions of Conrad's own youth. Both are glamorous subjects. But Youth has glamour; this hasn't a speck of it" (Garnett, 1934: 235). Both *The Rover* and *Suspense* are set against the backdrop of the Napoleonic era, a subject that increasingly preoccupied the novelist during his last years. Of *The Rover*, a novel spanning the years from 1796 to 1804, shortly before the Battle of Trafalgar, and concerned with old age and death, he confessed: "I have wanted for a long time to do a seaman's 'return' (before my own departure) and this seemed a possible peg to hang it on" (*LL2*: 339). On the evidence, *Suspense* – not Conrad's title but conferred posthumously – is half-finished. Conrad added little to the work after December 1922, when he informed Gide: "la moitié a peu près est faite" [about half is done] (*CL7*: 630). The author's provisional titles, presumably referring to Elba, include *The Isle of Rest* and *The Island of Rest*, and he claimed, to Ford, that the novel would conclude with Napoleon's departure from Elba (*CL7*: 107, 127, 394), but the surviving work neither reaches Elba nor introduces Napoleon.

While European history provides a context for the late novels, it has, more often than not, only a tangential bearing upon their central action and the weight of historical circumstance is somehow absent. While M. George's gun-running exploits in the Carlist cause in *The Arrow of Gold* establish political sympathies with Doña Rita de Lastaola, who was once the mistress of Don Carlos, history itself reduces to a framing device. In *The Rover*, the eponymous hero, Peyrol, returns to France after a life spent at sea among the piratical "Brotherhood of the Coast," arriving when Revolutionary fervour is on the wane and Napoleon's political power increasing. After three chapters, the historical setting is reconfigured as the action moves forward eight years to 1804, shortly before Napoleon's coronation. Facilitating the love between Arlette and Lieutenant Réal, Peyrol sacrifices his own life to outwit Captain Vincent of the English fleet, ensuring that faked documents about French naval strategy in Egypt pass into English hands. But while this ensures that Peyrol's bravery is thrown into relief by a Napoleonic backdrop, rather than that of the Revolution, an historical irony remains: Peyrol's "victory" over Captain Vincent anticipates by a few months the Battle of Trafalgar. Peyrol's patriotic sacrifice is emphasised when Nelson, who has a cameo role in the novel, compares himself to the rover: "I am like that white-headed man you admire so much, Vincent. ... I will stick to my task till perhaps some shot from the enemy puts an end to everything" (275–76). Despite this, however, the historical frame cannot but rob Peyrol's suicide of some of its glory.

While the late fiction explores the elusiveness of self-knowledge, a perennial Conradian concern, these works are also dominated by the obscurity of relations between women and men, and the losses that thwart human desire for union and communion. Dubbed Conrad's "uncongenial subject," by Moser (1957), love provides a recurrent and connecting theme of these novels. Yet Conrad's treatment of the subject is often stilted and static. It is para-lysed desire that characterises the relationship between Lingard and Mrs Travers in *The Rescue*, while *The Rover* charts Arlette's gradual emergence from emotional trauma stemming from her youthful encounter with the sanguinary fanaticism of the French Revolution. Reflecting this sense of paralysis, the symbolically stranded yachts in *The Rescue* or the eight-year elision in *The Rover*, during which "time seemed to have stood still" (40), sustain a sense of ennui and emphasise procrastination.

It is not simply the subject matter, but rather its treatment that attracts attention. Conrad has a reputation for being a "man's writer": at the outset of his career, H. G. Wells had chided him for not making "the slightest concessions to the reading young woman who makes or mars the fortunes of authors" (Stape and Knowles, eds, 1996: 21). But while it is true that the world of Conrad's novels is, predominantly, masculine – the colonial world, the world of the sea – the action he presents is, by and large, meditated action, that quickly set him apart from many of his contemporaries. In the late novels, this often amounts to a lack of clarity. For example, the triangular relationships of M. George, Doña Rita, and her childhood persecutor, Ortega, in *The Arrow of Gold*, or between Lingard, Mrs Travers, and her husband, in *The Rescue*, evade the dramatic intensity they promise. In the case of *The Arrow of Gold* this stems, in part, from the presentation of Ortega, Rita's wealthy cousin, as a stock, underdeveloped villain, crippled by stilted speeches that veer between abuse and devotion: "you are in all your limbs hateful ... your body is cold and vicious like a snake ... I cannot live without you" (318). When M. George and Doña Rita eventually withdraw from Marseilles and enjoy a six-month love idyll, their relationship is glossed over in summary. In *The Rescue*, the triangular relationship is reformulated, both because of Mr Travers' apparent diffidence towards his wife and, more importantly, because his place is eclipsed by the presence of Hassim and Immada. It is Lingard who provides the contested site here, as he is torn between illicit desire for Edith Travers and his duty to his Malay friends: he has promised to restore Hassim to power in Wajo in the Celebes (present-day Sulawesi). In the event, he fails on both counts.

More fruitful in this respect is the relationship in *The Rover* between Arlette, Peyrol, and Scevola, a fanatical Jacobin who poses an insistent sexual threat to Arlette. Within the emotionally fraught dynamic of the Escampobar farm on the Giens Peninsula, Peyrol finds himself cast in various male roles in his relationship with Arlette, from potential lover to father-figure: she refers to him as "Papa Peyrol." Returning to his native soil to retire after "forty years or more of sea-life" (5), Peyrol is psychologically exempt from the corrosive force of the historical context that has rendered Arlette mentally unstable and Scevola tormented and marginalized. No less damaged is the functionary, Lieutenant Réal, torn between his love for Arlette and his commitment to duty. (The coda to the novel reports that he is wounded at the Battle of Trafalgar.) Adopting the lieutenant's suicidal mission, Peyrol removes at a stroke the threat posed by Scevola, who is killed alongside Peyrol, and ensures the love between Arlette and Réal.

The Arrow of Gold

Published in 1919, *The Arrow of Gold* has the reputation of being Conrad's worst novel. One contemporary reviewer claimed that, in this novel, Conrad had become "Conrad's shadow and imitator" (Sherry, ed., 1973: 327). E. M. Forster's mother spoke for many readers when she waggishly renamed it "The Arrow of Lead." Subsequent critics have been equally scathing about its inert plotting and laboured writing: to John Batchelor it is "the worst of the late works" (1994: 265). Acknowledging the "note of disappointment in almost every review," Conrad claimed in his own defence: "This is the penalty for having produced something unexpected" (CL6: 464–65).

Conrad's claim that the novel offers a tale of "initiation ... into the life of passion" (ix), sustained by the obvious background metaphor of military and political upheaval, suggests M. George, the young narrator, as the central subject. This impression gains from the claim that his recent "adventures" in the West Indies "had not matured" him (8). However, in a letter of 18 February 1918, Conrad identified Rita as the novel's true subject: "the novel may be best described as the Study of Woman" that "deals with is her private life: her sense of her own position, her sentiments and her fears" (*CL6*: 185–86). This "double focus" yields two plots. In the first, M. George is introduced to Rita through the discourse of his male friends, Mills and Blunt; then he meets Rita and comes to share her allegiance to the Carlist cause; and finally, their relationship having become increasingly more intimate, it is consummated. This reading of the novel is undermined by the summary account of the six months the couple spend in the Maritime Alps. Significantly, the climactic scene in the locked room, which recalls the shelter in which, as a young goatherd, she used to hide from Ortega, involves laying the ghost of not M. George's but Rita's past. Described as "slowly awakening from a trance" (329), Rita frees herself from the trauma of her past to love on her own terms. M. George's "initiation" thus becomes a function of Rita's. Her history is one of social mobility: a Basque peasant girl, Rita left Lastaola for Paris, to stay with her uncle, an orange merchant. In Paris she meets the artist Henry Allègre, becoming his model and then his companion, and finally inherits his fortune. Her wealth gives her access to influential political circles, where she becomes the mistress of Don Carlos and hence is associated with Carlist politics.

The emphasis upon art and aesthetics in *The Arrow of Gold* draws attention to Rita's construction as an object of male fascination, constituted by the so-called "male gaze." For instance, Allègre first encounters Rita "sitting on a broken fragment of stone-work buried in the grass of his wild garden, full of thrushes, starlings, and other innocent creatures of the air" (41). From this innocence spring his paintings of Rita, such as "Girl in the Hat" and "Byzantine Empress" (36), successive artistic transformations that parallel her social transformation from peasant goatherd into Doña Rita, Allègre's "most admirable find ... amongst all the priceless items he had accumulated" (23). In short, the presentation of Rita is indistinguishable from the claims of male proprietorship: she is both an art-object and, as Blunt and Mills demonstrate, constituted by male discourse. In this light, the claim that Rita reflects "something of the women of all time" (28) assumes an added poignancy.

The narrative self-consciously advertises its concern with both the world of art and itself as a work of art. Its structural "framing" between two notes is only part of the emphasis upon perspective, whereby M. George's relationship with Rita is played out in the foreground against a background of gun-running and the Carlist enterprise. Sustaining this connection with art, characters are repeatedly described as figures in paintings. M. George's first sight of Rita leaves him with the sense that "the visual impression was more of colour in a picture than of the forms of actual life" (66); Rita's sister, Therese, looks to have stepped from "an old, cracked, smoky painting" (139); while Mrs Blunt appears as "a perfect picture in silver and grey, with touches of black here and there" (180). M. George, whose memories provide the source of this narrative and who provides the focus of perception in the tale, is described by a friend in comparable terms: "he may be an artist in a sense. He has broken away from his conventions. He is trying to put a special vibration and his own notion of colour into his life" (166).

More pragmatic concerns are also responsible for Rita's fascination. For example, Mrs Blunt pursues Rita on behalf of her son, attracted by her wealth. For his part, and reflecting his mother's "perfect pride of Republican aristocracy" (185), Blunt cannot conquer his feelings of social superiority towards the heiress to Allègre's fortune. Conrad's "Study of Woman" in *The Arrow of Gold* repeatedly envisions Rita as subject to the definition of others, chiefly men: from Allègre's abbreviation of her name to a monogram on fabric to her status as mistress to the Pretender. Her disappearance at the end of the novel may well constitute the final, damning comment upon the male-centred world she inhabits.

The Rescue

Set in 1860, *The Rescue* completes Conrad's Malay trilogy-in-reverse and in its presentation of a younger Lingard helps to explain his character in *Almayer's Folly* and *An Outcast of the Islands*. For example, Lingard's "adoption" of the young girl who becomes Mrs Almayer, in the former, and of Willems, in the latter, can now be traced to his failure in *The Rescue* to protect Immada and Hassim, who are "like his children" (330). Read chronologically, the Malay Trilogy charts a pattern of imperial demise centred on Lingard: from his failure to keep his word and save Hassim and Immada in *The Rescue*, through the loss of his trading monopoly in *An Outcast of the Islands*, to his disappearance in *Almayer's Folly*, where he is but a memory.

The Rescue recounts the thwarted plans of Captain Lingard to restore their country of Wajo to the exiled prince and princess, Hassim and Immada. His encounter with the Europeans aboard the *Hermit* – Mr and Mrs Travers and their guest Mr d'Alcacer – frustrates his intentions, especially when Travers and d'Alcacer are kidnapped and Lingard undertakes their rescue. In its juxtaposition of European and Malay worlds, the novel dramatises their respective claims on Lingard: his feelings for Edith Travers and his debt of honour to Hassim and Immada. As such, *The Rescue* is a tale about various kinds of desire: his commitment to the Wajo cause locates him within "the circle of another existence, governed by his impulse, nearer his desire" (99); while his "desire" for Mrs Travers will, ironically, destroy the Rajah Laut's power on the Shore of Refuge. Lingard's divided cultural loyalties are traced to his divided nature. Caught between competing claims on his assistance, Lingard muses: "Conflict of some sort was the very essence of his life. But this was something he had never known before. This was a conflict with himself. He had to face unsuspected powers, foes that he could not go out to meet at the gate. They were within" (329).

Stranded on the shallows off the Shore of Refuge, and viewed as a source of potential plunder by the Illanun pirates, the *Hermit* provides an image of paralysed Western force. The intermediary between two cultures, Lingard is powerless to honour his word to the Malay because frustrated by the Europeans, who view him as "our only refuge" (308). But, if the arrival of the European yacht frustrates Lingard's political plans to restore Hassim to power in Wajo, his encounter with Mrs Travers extends this failure to his emotional life in a frustrated European romance. Read chronologically, the trilogy of Malay novels that virtually frame Conrad's writing career contain a romance narrative that is steadily re-formed: the thwarted European romance in *The Rescue* precedes the tragic cross-cultural romance between Willems and Aïssa, in *An Outcast of the Islands*, which, in turn, is revised in the fruitful Malay romance in *Almayer's Folly*, between Nina and Dain. Viewed thus, the trilogy is characterised both by a developing sense of the exotic as eroticised and, inversely proportional to this, a chronicle of Lingard's demise. While the backdrop of revolutionary instability in *The Rescue* provides a fitting context for the encounter between Lingard and Edith Travers, the sheer difference in scale between background and foreground renders the latter myopically self-serving.

Edith Travers claims Immada as her "humble and obscure sister" (153). But, consistent with its presentation elsewhere in the Malay Trilogy, the exotic remains beyond the comprehension of the Europeans, preserving its "otherness" – just as the "exotics" are unable to comprehend the Europeans. The pageant and politics of the Malay world appear unreal to Mr Travers, himself an English politician, and, pointedly, his illness includes symptoms of delirium. To his wife, the names of native politicians, "Belarab, Daman, Ningrat," are "barbarous sounds" possessing "an exceptional energy, a fatal aspect, the savour of madness" (163). Lingard's indictment of European judgement is unambiguous: "They take a rajah for a fisherman" (136), he tells Hassim. Instead, the narrative is concerned with margins and liminal spaces – topographical, cultural, and moral.

As in *Almayer's Folly* and *An Outcast of the Islands*, *The Rescue* invites comparison of the parallels between Occidental and Oriental culture to reveal their shared impulses and debunk any Western claims to superiority. In d'Alcacer's wry distinction, the superiority of European civilization reduces to its "methods": to not being "speared through the back in the beastliest possible fashion" (408). For his part, Lingard has "wandered beyond that circle which race, memories, early associations, all the essential ambitions of one's origin, trace round every man's life" (121–22), and, in a life divested of cultural origins, found a paradoxical stability in rootlessness, claiming: "if I lost her [the *Lightning*] I would have no standing room on the earth" (229). The mercurial nature of his cultural reference is conveyed in a narrative whose story is itself, in Conrad's claim, "in a fluid – in an evading shape" (*CL2*: 50).

When Mrs Travers, attempting to rescue her husband, sails to the Shore of Refuge with Lingard, she enters an annihilatory void: "The darkness enfolded her like the enervating caress of a sombre universe. It was gentle and destructive. Its languor seduced her soul into surrender. Neither existed and even all her memories vanished into space. She was content that nothing should exist" (245). Her gradual acceptance of the reality of the Malay world in which she finds herself, and which she had initially viewed as "a mere pageant marshalled for her vision with barbarous splendour and savage emphasis" (367), corresponds with the awakening of her desire for Lingard. Geddes suggests that: "she must discard her education, or *feel* her way back into life" (1980: 152). Cultural displacement both mimics and facilitates Edith Travers' encounter with repressed elements in her sexual psyche, with comparably disorienting consequences. Immada blames her for the emotional hold she exerts over Lingard: "You are a cruel woman! You are driving him away from where his strength is. You put madness into his heart, O! Blind – without pity – without shame! ... " (234). Their relationship loosens ties of fidelity, as Mrs Travers responds to her feelings for Lingard, and honour, as Lingard is distracted from Hassim and Immada.

For both Mrs Travers and Lingard, private impulses conflict with social responsibility, and a state of emotional stalemate ensues. The manifest indicators of stasis and entrapment in the narrative, such as the stranded *Hermit* or Belarab's stockade, extend naturally to the couple's frustrated desires – just as the novel's title directs us beyond the literal rescue of Mr Travers and Mr d'Alcacer (not to mention the failure to "rescue" Hassim and Immada) to the rescue from neglect of emotional and sexual potential. This theme of thwarted emotion, implicit in such characters as Dr Monygham and developed more prominently from *Chance* onwards, finds its extreme expression in the character of Arlette in Conrad's next novel, *The Rover*.

The Rover

The critical reception of *The Rover* sounded a "note of disappoint-ment" (*LL2*: 337). Indeed, where the novel was praised, it was in terms that must have jarred with the author. The *Spectator* review, for instance, claimed that Conrad "writes in a familiar convention and is true to type, the type being the adventure novel beloved of boys, which G. A. Henty turned out regularly every year and Stevenson raised to a classic in *Treasure Island*" (Sherry, ed., 1973: 35). However, focused upon the emotional trauma brought about by revolutionary excess, *The Rover* also touches upon the themes of political authority, civic responsibility, and cultural loyalties. In Peyrol, returned to his native France with a captured English ship and encountering witnesses of the revolutionary terror, Conrad describes a character who strains against historical circumstance and, in the process, presents history not as a chronicle of great events (these have all happened before the action or take place "off stage") but as a way of analysing a nation's soul.

214JOSEPH CONRAD

The Rover is a novel of ageing and maturity in which personal
and national narratives are entwined. The stunted and traumatised emotional lives at Escampobar bear the imprint of revolutionary fervour as the consequences of doctrinaire violence and
religious repression are reflected in the portraits of Arlette, her aunt
Catherine, Réal – and even Scevola. But it is through Peyrol that
the relationship between the individual and the state is examined
and revivified. When he presents himself to the Port authorities
in Toulon at the beginning of the narrative, Peyrol is wearing an
emblematic tricolour outfit of red, white, and blue; he is finally
remembered by Réal as "not a bad Frenchman" (286). Having lived
for much of his life as a freebooter beyond the influence of society,
"Citizen" Peyrol returns to a society transformed since "the time
of kings and aristocrats" (4) and yet paralysed by the excesses of
revolution, whose legacy remains in the emotional and temporal
stasis that Peyrol discovers and from which he will rescue Arlette
and Réal. Returning to his native soil, Peyrol steps into national
history. During his eight years at Escampobar, a political transformation occurs in France, "The years of political changes ending
with the proclamation of Napoleon as Consul for life," and yet
these years "had not changed Peyrol except as to his strong thick
head of hair, which was nearly all white now" (38).

Instead, Peyrol's physical isolation on the Giens Peninsula, whose
neck is "impregnated with salt and containing a blue lagoon" (15),
dramatises the psychological isolation of the other residents of
Escampobar, whose lives are stunted by history: Old Catherine,
who fell in love with a priest when she was eighteen; Arlette who,
"touched by the red hand of the Revolution" ran "ankle-deep
through the terrors of death" (260); and Scevola, a retired *sans-
culotte* and enthusiastic "blood-drinker" in the time of the Terror.
To these can be added Michel, who has "no place in the life of the
village" (82), and the cripple of La Madrague, who tells Peyrol:
"since those Republicans had deposed God and flung Him out of
all the churches I have forgiven Him all my troubles" (96). By
contrast, Peyrol, who "did not want to own any part of the solid
earth for which he had no love" (12), has his own ideas about the
principles of the Revolution, fashioned by his experiences among
the Brotherhood of the Coast:

> Liberty – to hold your own in the world if you could. Equality –
> yes! But no body of men ever accomplished anything without a

chief.... He regarded fraternity somewhat differently. Of course brothers would quarrel amongst themselves... In his view the claim of Brotherhood was a claim for help against the outside world". (132)

The structural symmetry of Peyrol handing over a captured English ship at the beginning of the novel and outsmarting Captain Vincent of the *Amelia*, a captured French ship, at the end provokes other parallels with historical and national implications. Ultimately, Peyrol breaks the temporal and emotional deadlock at Escampobar, ensuring a future for Arlette and Réal, through action. Whether his self-sacrifice is motivated by patriotism, altruism, or egoism, his battle of wits with Captain Vincent symbolically redirects the forces of the Revolution. The tartane that Peyrol has restored and in which he dies has a ghoulish history as a charnel house that includes the massacre of "a lot of fugitive traitors, men and women, and children too" (86), whose bloodstains he cleans from her woodwork. In this guise, the tartane, cleansed of her past, is restored to patriotic service, and Peyrol exchanges identification with the Brotherhood of the Coast for identity with the nation. Following Peyrol's example, Réal retires from the navy to lead "a quiet and retired life," eventually becoming the Mayor of the Commune in a little village near Escampobar, "that very same little village which had looked on Escampobar as the abode of iniquity, the sojourn of blood-drinkers and of wicked women" (283). Like the marriage itself, Réal's position is testimony to the resurgent communal impulse inspired by the actions of Old Peyrol.

In the light of the eight-year ellipsis in the narrative (between Chapters III and IV), it is tempting to speculate why Conrad did not simply commence the novel in the Napoleonic era. The answer would seem to be that this period provides a backdrop of war and honour against which Peyrol's self-sacrifice can be measured that is altogether different from that provided by the revolutionaries. In other words, the erstwhile pirate's return to the France of the Revolution not only dramatises his aloofness from such events but also offers his own brand of lawlessness as a preferable alternative to revolutionary lawlessness. As Andrew Busza has claimed:

> In a world warped and still trembling from the aftershocks of a major social upheaval, the homecoming outlaw Peyrol offers, through his inner independence and hard serenity, not only a firm psychological

purchase, but also in his attitude to life what is in effect a perfect antidote to the violent artifice of revolutionary thought and praxis".

(1992: xvii)

In its presentation of Peyrol, *The Rover* signals a development in Conrad's portrayal of the outlaw. Conrad's unequivocal defence of the law-abiding in his early fiction, where the portrayal of Kurtz or Gentleman Brown is underwritten by tacit approval of the enforcement of the law, gradually gives way to such characters as Leggatt (in "The Secret Sharer") who, though outlaws, exist in large part to assist the law-abiding. In *The Rover* society and not the outlaw is perceived as the transgressor, and it is the victims of society that Peyrol saves.

The question that Jim's character poses in *Lord Jim* – whether the world holds a place for the romantic – is implicit in the pattern of Peyrol's life: having put his sea-life behind him, he comes out of retirement both because of the call to action to which his nature cannot but respond and because of his new-found desire to protect Arlette. But whereas in *Lord Jim* the interest lies in Jim's redemption in his own eyes, in *The Rover* Peyrol has no such doubts about himself, lacking Jim's self-reflection and psychological unconsciousness. Instead, unusually, Conrad presents a central character whose past experiences fail to trouble him. At the novel's end, Peyrol is recalled as "the man of dark deeds, but of large heart" (286). While his large-heartedness inspires his self-sacrifice, his "dark deeds" are strangely muted. Having "seen decks swimming with blood and ... helped to throw dead bodies overboard after a fight" (86), the inconsequentiality of his memory seems strangely out of place, especially in a narrative where past experience hangs so heavily over the lives of the other characters. By comparison with such sceptics as Razumov or Heyst, who are forced to become involved in life, Peyrol is at once the apogee of unreflective consciousness and sentimental enough to sacrifice his life for France and for Arlette.

Although his past is as turbulent as that of Arlette, Catherine, or Réal, Peyrol stands conspicuously apart as being untroubled by its memories. Rather, he is contrasted with Scevola: "The necessities of a lawless life had taught Peyrol to be ruthless, but he had never been cruel" (35). The emphasis falls upon the fact that although Peyrol has killed, he has done so unselfconsciously, un-idealistically, while Scevola and the *sans-culottes* kill in the name of an ideal – as does Haldin in *Under Western Eyes*, or, had they energy, the anarchists in *The Secret Agent*. To Réal, "The sincere lawlessness of the ex-Brother of the Coast was refreshing. That one was neither a hypocrite nor a fool. When he robbed or killed it was not in the name of the sacred revolutionary principles or for the love of humanity" (209). Thus, what one might term "clean" killing is redeemable. This extends to killing as a military performance – like Vincent's shooting of the tartane crew – as a patriotic act, performed out of a sense of duty.

In a letter of 4 December 1923, Conrad confessed to his "secret desire to achieve a feat of brevity": "This is perhaps my only work in which brevity was a conscious aim. I don't mean compression. I mean brevity *ab initio*, in the very conception, in the very manner of thinking about the people and the events" (*LL2*: 327, 326). The pared-down style of *The Rover* – described by Geddes as "a kind of descriptive short-hand" (1980: 182) – serves a double purpose: whilst it helps to convey the sense of emptiness and alienation in the lives of those left emotionally repressed by the Terror, it also mimics the "undemonstrative" (1) and unemotional nature of Peyrol. From the priest's garden "choked with weeds" (147) to the tartane that acts as a symbolic substitution of Arlette's mental state, the narrative turns instead to poetic imagery to provide objective correlatives that both explain and preserve the stunted emotional lives of the characters.

The Growth of a Reputation

Modernism in the arts is characterised by a prevailing mood of scepticism. Thus Ezra Pound's definitive injunction to artists to "Make It New" is consistent with Nietzsche's claim in *The Will to Power* (1901): "What is needed above all is an absolute skepticism towards all inherited concepts" (Kaufmann, ed., 1968: 221). When offering advice to John Galsworthy in 1901, Conrad wrote: "you want more scepticism at the very foundation of your work. Scepticism the tonic of minds, the tonic of life, the agent of truth – the way of art and salvation" (*CL2*: 359).

* * *

Ideologically, the Modern age responds to the combined challenges of Darwin, Marx, and Freud, while Nietzsche's famous dictum "God is dead" (Introduction, *Thus Spake Zarathustra*) provides its watchword. It is also a schizophrenic age, in which the *avant-garde* coexists with a Romantic and nostalgic impulse: James Joyce's *Ulysses*, for instance, derives its structural cohesiveness from Homer's *Odyssey*, while Picasso's cubist portraits draw recognisably upon "primitive" African art. In May 1902, When William Blackwood declined to purchase the copyrights of *Lord Jim* and *Youth*, declaring that Conrad was a loss to the firm, the author famously responded in a letter: "I am *modern*, and I would rather recall Wagner the musician and Rodin the Sculptor who both had to starve a little in their day ... They too have arrived. They had to suffer for being 'new'" (*CL2*: 418). Indeed, according to Conrad, suffering was a necessary condition of artistic integrity and creativity, as he suggests in this intimidating advice to an aspirant novelist in 1913: "Suffering is an attribute almost a condition of greatness, of devotion, of an altogether self-forgetful sacrifice to that remorseless fidelity to the truth of his own sensations, at whetever [*sic*] cost of pain and contumely which for me is the whole credo of the artist" (*CL5*: 239).

Although Conrad claimed to have had to work "like a coalminer in his pit quarrying all my English sentences out of a black night," and despaired as late as 1907 that "English is still for me a foreign language whose handling demands a fearful effort" (*CL4*: 112; *CL3*: 401), he is one of the great stylists in the language. His linguistic maturity is even more impressive for being in his third tongue. Always vexed by the difficulties of pronunciation, his ear for language is evident in the cadence and elegance of his sentences, in his presentation of the poetry of everyday life in epiphanies of the mundane, and in his alertness to the ironic potential of English that provides his fictions with their definitive tone. In his early artistic credo, the "Preface" to *The Nigger of the "Narcissus,"* he claimed: "My task which I am trying to achieve is, by the power of the written word to make you hear, to make you feel – it is, before all, to make you *see*. That – and no more, and it is everything" (x). Reflecting on his decision to write in English, in his "Author's Note" to *A Personal Record*, he states: "English was for me neither a matter of choice or adoption. The merest idea of choice had never entered my head. And as to adoption – well, yes, there was adoption; but it was I who was adopted by the genius of the language" (vii). Responding to a review of *An Outcast of the Islands*, he says, with obvious delight: "the 'Aberdeen F[ree] P[ress]' extols my English – and that is a real, a great pleasure; for I *did* try to earn that kind of notice" (*CL1*: 277).

Conrad's technical experiments with disrupted chronology or multiple narrating voices are as definitively Modernist as the Jamesian sentence or Woolf's use of interior monologue. He eschewed what he saw as the transitory "formulas of art" because of their dependence upon "things variable, unstable and untrustworthy; on human sympathies, on prejudices, on likes and dislikes, on the sense of virtue and the sense of propriety, on beliefs and theories that, indestructible in themselves, always change their form – often in the lifetime of one fleeting generation" (*NLL*: 5–6). Yet he admitted himself to be "haunted, mercilessly haunted by the *necessity* of style" (*CL2*: 50). In Conrad's books, truth resides as much in the words on the page as in the mind of the reader. As he wrote in a letter: "the reader collaborates with the author" (*CL2*: 394). This approach is echoed in Marlow's qualities as a narrator in "Heart of Darkness": "to him the meaning of an episode was not inside like a kernel but outside, enveloping the tale which brought it out" (*Y*: 48). Even Marlow's first-person narration, simultaneously assertive and speculative, reveals a technical concern with revelation and identity. His narrative is typified by locutions such as "seemed," "like," and "as though," and his delayed decoding of incident designed to replicate the hesitancies and vulnerabilities of the first-person narrator caught in the act of deciphering experience. In a literary analogue to the Symbolist notion of art as sensory counterpart to experience, interpretive responsibility is shared with the reader who responds to meaning generated through narrative rhythm. The narrative complexity of Conradian fiction is characteristically Modernist in its concern with aesthetic form. He shares the age with Stravinsky and Picasso.

In "A Familiar Preface" to *A Personal Record*, Conrad observes: "Those who read me know my conviction that the world, the temporal world, rests on a few very simple ideas; so simple that they must be as old as the hills. It rests notably, among others, on the idea of Fidelity" (xxi). He expanded upon this credo in a letter of 1913, saying: "For me the artists [*sic*] salvation is in fidelity, in remorseless fidelity to the *truth of his own sensations*. Hors de là, point de salut. [Beyond there, no salvation.] ... For what I believe in most is responsibilities of *conduct*" (*CL5*: 238). In response, his fictions chart the universal quest for mirroring affirmation and individuality, while also acknowledging the perils of solitude and fragmentation. Tinged with a deep, melancholic fatalism, part of his paternal inheritance, his chosen forms are

220 JOSEPH CONRAD

frame narration, palimpsest, and doubles. As he claimed in a letter to
the *New York Times "Saturday Review"*: "The only legitimate basis
of creative work lies in the courageous recognition of all the irreconcilable antagonisms that make our life so enigmatic, so burdensome,
so fascinating, so dangerous – so full of hope!" (*CL2*: 348–49).

* * *

Despite poor early sales of his works, Conrad's originality and genius
were readily recognised, and important strands in his subsequent critical reception were, broadly, delineated by early reviewers. So, too,
was the difficulty of his fiction that would prevent him becoming popular in the first half of his career. Thus, while his first novels were
heralded as the work of "a writer of genius" (Sherry, ed., 1973: 6),
H. G. Wells' caution that Conrad made no concessions "to the reading young woman who makes or mars the fortunes of authors" (Stape
and Knowles, eds, 1996: 21) proved insightful. Later, *The Nigger of
the "Narcissus"* earned such plaudits as "Mr. Conrad ... gives us the
sea as no other story-teller of our generation has been able to render
it," the novella was criticised for having "no plot and no petticoats"
(Sherry, ed., 1973: 99, 95). The problem of "petticoats" dogged Conrad's subsequent reception although, ironically, it was his treatment
of Flora de Barral in *Chance* (1914) that secured his popularity with
the reading public.

  With the publication of *Lord Jim* in 1900, however, his originality was recognised and his critical reputation established. It brought
Conrad "into the front rank of living novelists" (Sherry, ed., 1973:
120), and he was able to proclaim himself "the spoiled child of the
critics" (*CL1*: 313). Criticism of the novel centred on the question
of narrative style that, according to one reviewer, left the reader
"wandering in a morass of wonderful language and incomprehensible events" (Sherry, ed., 1973: 124). Even reviews of *The Nigger of
the "Narcissus"* had pointed up "the uncompromising nature of his
methods" as debarring Conrad from a wide popularity (Sherry, ed.,
1973: 93). Wells had already raised this issue in his review of *An
Outcast of the Islands* – in which he said: "his story is not so much
told as seen intermittently through a haze of sentences. His style
is like river-mist" (Sherry, ed., 1973: 74) – and it would persist:
in his essay "The New Novel" (1914), Henry James, in a famous
instance of the pot calling the kettle black, described Conrad as

"absolutely alone as a votary of the way to do a thing that shall make it undergo most doing" (1984: 147).

Critics of the *Youth* volume, although widely praising the title-story, largely overlooked "Heart of Darkness" until Edward Garnett's influential review in *Academy and Literature*, identifying the tale as "the high-water mark of the author's talent" (Sherry, ed., 1973: 132), realigned the focus of the book's reception. As Conrad wrote to Garnett, "Heart of Darkness" would have been dismissed as "dreary bosh – an incoherent bogie tale" but for the fact of his timely intervention (*CL2*: 468). Curiously the tale's treatment of colonialism had to wait for another generation before its subversive potential would be recognised. In his "Author's Note" to that volume, Conrad recalled the reviews of *Typhoon*, published in 1903, as marked by "a warmth of appreciation and understanding, a sympathetic insight and a friendliness of expression for which I cannot be sufficiently grateful" (ix). Along with reviews of *The Nigger of the "Narcissus"* and "Youth," however, they did help to cast Conrad as a "sea writer," a tag that, like a writer of Malay romances, he tried to shake off, fearful of being stereotyped.

Public reaction to Conrad's three political novels, written in the first decade of the twentieth century disappointed the author. He described the response to *Nostromo* as "the blackest possible frost" (*CL5*: 139), pronounced *The Secret Agent* "an honourable failure" (*CL4*: 9), and remembered *Under Western Eyes* as "a failure with the public" ("Author's Note", viii). Whilst praised for their psychological insights, these novels wrong-footed the critics. "Mr. Conrad generally sails in Eastern Seas," lamented the *Scotsman* on the publication of *Nostromo*, while the *Times Literary Supplement* called it "an artistic mistake" (Sherry, ed., 1973: 20, 164) Furthermore, the critics, again following Garnett's lead, began to approach Conrad in terms of his "foreignness," as if this somehow explained the complexity and "strangeness" of the narratives. The *Times Literary Supplement* declared him "an alien of genius," the *Glasgow News* "alien to our national genius," and, to Robert Lynd, writing in the *Daily News*, he was "without either country or language" (Sherry, ed., 1973: 185, 195, 211). To John Galsworthy, however, Conrad's foreignness was a virtue: "Prisoners in the cells of our own nationality, we never see ourselves; it is reserved for one outside looking through the tell-tale peep-hole to get a proper view of us" (Sherry, ed., 1973: 208). Conrad generally over-reacted to negative criticism. Nevertheless, in 1919, admittedly with his fame and popular reputation secure, he would write: "I must confess that, in truth, I never did care what anybody said. It may appear a most brutal and ungrateful thing to come from a man who has been so well understood" (CL6: 530).

Following the publication of *Chance* in 1914 Conrad was fêted as "one of the marvels of our literature" (Sherry, ed., 1973: 282), receiving critical plaudits and, as importantly, the financial rewards of popularity that had eluded him thus far. A review of *Victory*, for example, claimed Conrad as "not only one of the favourite novelists of the elect but one of the favourite novelists of the many" (Sherry, ed., 1973: 33). With the benefit of hindsight, it is easy to see in the appreciation for Conrad's late fiction a belated recognition of the earlier works whose genius had been obscured by complexity. The applause in which Conrad revelled drowned out his fears about "being a writer of any 'coterie' of some small self-appointed aristocracy of the vast domain of art and letters" (CL6: 333). The period is also marked by Conrad's return to techniques and settings with which he had already made his name: Marlow returns as the narrator of *Chance*, for instance, while *Victory*, *The Shadow-Line*, and *The Rescue* all return to Eastern waters for their settings.

But if Conrad had now become the grand old man of English letters, as Sherry calls him (ed., 1973: 33), the works of his last years received mixed reviews. *The Arrow of Gold* occasioned reviews that detected "a just perceptible falling away from the abilities of the artist" and found its "'story' elements ... popularly conceived and contrived," while the claim that *The Rescue* was Conrad's "finest work" went hand-in-hand with the suspicion that his "best work was already done" (Sherry, ed., 1973: 33, 314, 343). The subject of love in the late novels also attracted adverse criticism, and some critics felt that, by the time *The Rover* was published in the year before his death, Conrad's audience could enjoy reading him "unmitigated by any necessity for intellectual strivings." Indeed, with this novel Conrad seemed to have come full circle, as comparisons were made with the exotic romances of Henty (Sherry, ed., 1973: 35). By the time of Conrad's death his body of work was already being reappraised, to the detriment of the late novels. In her obituary of Conrad, Virginia Woolf claimed, with remarkable percipience, that "It is the earlier books ... that we shall read in their entirety" (1925: 291) while John Galsworthy confessed, in a letter to Edward Garnett: "I can't put up, like the younger generation, with these later books" (Garnett, ed., 1934: 236).

* * *

Serious critical consideration of Conrad's works came, initially, from friends and fellow writers, such as Edward Garnett, Hugh Clifford, and John Galsworthy, who claimed in a review-article in 1908 that the volumes Conrad had published by that date were "the only writing of the last twelve years that will enrich the English language to any great extent" (Sherry, ed., 1973: 206). The studies of Conrad published during his lifetime – initiated by Richard Curle's *Joseph Conrad: A Study* (1914) – tend to combine discussion of the author's "exotic" life and examination of the work, but Conrad's place within the Modernist pantheon was also being staked by chapters in John Freeman's *The Moderns* and William Lyon Phelps' *The Advance of the English Novel*, both published in 1916. Led by Ford Madox Ford's *Joseph Conrad: A Personal Remembrance* (1924), reminiscences of Conrad began to appear soon after his death, including Jessie Conrad's *Joseph Conrad as I Knew Him* (1926) and *Joseph Conrad and His Circle* (1935), and Conrad's friend and first biographer, G. Jean-Aubry, brought out *Joseph Conrad: Life and Letters* in 1927. Alongside these, other voices were being sounded that would generate lines of future critical inquiry. In 1930 appeared Gustav Morf's *The Polish Heritage of Joseph Conrad*, a psychoanalytic study that read the works as coded confessions in which Conrad sought to expiate his "desertion" of Poland. Thus, for example, Jim's jump from the *Patna* in *Lord Jim* symbolises, in Morf's reading, Conrad's desertion of Poland or *Polska*. Despite this line of inquiry, the decade was generally belletristic in approach, the highpoint of which is Edward Crankshaw's *Joseph Conrad: Some Aspects of the Art of the Novel* (1936). As often happens after a writer's death, there was some stock-taking. Elizabeth Bowen noted: "Conrad is in abeyance. We are not clear yet how to rank him; there is an uncertain pause" (Sherry, ed., 1973: 39). The 1940s, however, would both cement Conrad's critical reputation and ground it in "fidelity" to scholarship, beginning with John Dozier Gordan's path-breaking analysis of the biographical and textual sources of Conrad's art in *Joseph Conrad: The Making of a Novelist* (1940).

In the following year F. R. Leavis' "Revaluations: Joseph Conrad" was published, in two instalments, in *Scrutiny* and subsequently reprinted in *The Great Tradition* (1948). The influential Cambridge critic identified Conrad as "among the very greatest novelists in the language – or any language" (226) and the natural inheritor of the tradition of the English novel that included Jane Austen, George Eliot, and Henry James. Leavis identified a Conrad canon, stretching from *Nostromo* to *The Shadow-Line*, and recognised in the sea fiction the author's commitment to British national traditions. Leavis and the "practical criticism" he espoused – based upon a detailed analysis of the text – exerted considerable influence on Conrad studies, and English studies in general, over the three decades that followed. By then, however, two new, equally influential, critical studies from across the Atlantic had appeared.

As its title indicates, Thomas C. Moser's *Joseph Conrad: Achievement and Decline* (1957) argued that the Conrad canon is composed of a period of greatness – 1898–1911 – followed by sharp decline, a thesis already proposed by some early reviewers. According to Moser, the works of Conrad's greatness are those concerned with the "anatomy of moral failure." Two reasons are proposed for Conrad's decline after 1911: first, his preoccupation with the "uncongenial subject" of love in his novels; and, second, his "affirmative" themes in the later fiction, which Moser reads as a sign of Conrad's creative exhaustion. Following this, Albert J. Guerard's *Conrad the Novelist* (1958) used psychoanalysis to reveal latent, archetypal patterns in the fictions, including the presence of a Jungian "night journey." This study, also notable for its critical reading of Conrad's "impressionist" literary style, concurs with Moser's achievement-and-decline theory, calling *Victory* "one of the worst novels for which high claims have been made by critics of standing" (273). Bernard C. Meyer's *Joseph Conrad: A Psychoanalytic Biography* (1967) provides a logical extension of these two works written in the wake of Freudian-influenced literary criticism.

Challenging both the reduced critical status of *Victory* and the increasingly popular achievement-and-decline thesis, John A. Palmer's *Joseph Conrad's Fiction: A Study in Literary Growth* (1968) reformulated Conrad's work into three phases, each with its own "achievement" and unified by an underlying set of moral imperatives: dilemmas of private honour and individual fidelity; psycho-moral social challenges; and the metaphysical basis of moral commitment. Palmer, who saw *Victory* as the high point of the third phase, downgraded *Nostromo*, which is often viewed as Conrad's masterpiece, to the status of a transitional work. Perhaps unsurprisingly, Conrad criticism of the 1960s was dominated by political readings by two American critics: Eloise Knapp Hay's *The Political Novels of Joseph Conrad* (1963) and Avrom Fleishman's *Conrad's Politics: Community and Anarchy in the Fiction of Joseph Conrad* (1967). Hay traced in Conrad's work the persistent presence of politics and the entrapment of the individual in overwhelming political forces, while Fleishman's study examined the complicated nature of the individual's commitment to the nation and the implications of this for the fate of the community. The 1960s were also marked by Paul Kirschner's *Conrad: The Psychologist as Artist* (1968) which, while expounding Conrad's treatment of the psycho-moral dimensions of the self, as importantly pioneered the study of Conrad's borrowings from Continental authors, tracing the influence of Turgenev, Maupassant, and Anatole France on his fiction. Of the wealth of criticism that followed, special mention must go to Ian Watt's *Conrad in the Nineteenth Century* (1980) which generously blended textual exegesis with the contextual influences – biographical, philosophical, scientific, and literary – that shaped Conrad's thought and art; and Jacques Berthoud's *Joseph Conrad: The Major Phase* (1978), which provided an advanced introduction to the moral bearings of Conrad's characters during the period spanned by *The Nigger of the "Narcissus"* and *Under Western Eyes*. Once again, the shape of the Conrad canon was being settled.

* * *

By this time, Conrad, along with other major authors, was generating an academic industry, with dissertations, monographs, edited collections of essays, journal articles, and scholarly editions of the fiction appearing regularly. This trend continues today as Conrad studies reflect the changing nature and fashions of literary criticism. Nor was the "fidelity" to scholarship that underpins Conrad studies idle during these years. In 1959, Jocelyn Baines' *Joseph Conrad: A Critical Biography* appeared. The first properly researched biography, this set standards that would inspire Conrad's subsequent biographers: Frederick R. Karl's *Joseph Conrad: The Three Lives* appeared in 1979 and Zdzisław Najder's magisterial *Joseph Conrad: A Chronicle* in 1983. Norman Sherry's tireless research into Conrad's life culminated in *Conrad's Eastern*

World, in 1966, and *Conrad's Western World*, in 1971. This professional attitude to Conrad scholarship continues in the Cambridge University Press nine-volume edition of *The Collected Letters of Joseph Conrad* (1983–2007).

In the wake of the "structuralist revolution" in universities in the 1960s and 1970s, literary studies became increasingly theory-driven during the closing decades of the twentieth century, and Conrad studies inevitably reflected this. Among the varied approaches, feminism, post-colonialism, deconstruction, and new historicism were all applied to Conrad, often with revealing results, to expose inherent power relations in the texts. In the light of the male narrator's claim in "Because of the Dollars" that "Ours ... was a bachelor crowd ... There might have been a few wives in existence, but if so they were invisible, distant, never alluded to" (*Within the Tides* 175), a feminist approach to the fiction was both fitting and timely. Similarly, the representation of the racial "Other" in Conrad's work has received considerable attention from post-colonial critics, particularly in the light of the charge made by the Nigerian novelist, Chinua Achebe, in a lecture given in 1975, that, in "Heart of Darkness," Conrad reveals himself to be "a bloody racist" (1977: 788). In the ensuing debate, which situated "Heart of Darkness" at the centre of post-colonial studies, Conrad has been both attacked and defended, a testament to the health and wealth of critical discourse surrounding his writings.

Of Conrad's works, "Heart of Darkness" continues to receive the lion's share of critical attention. The history of its critical reception reflects the interpretive trends of the twentieth century. To early reviewers, such as Garnett, who stressed the novella's presentation of psychology, politics, and style, Kurtz was the tale's focus. In the 1950s, the emphasis shifted from Kurtz to Marlow as Guerard and Moser viewed Marlow's as a journey of self-discovery. This shifted the focus from the tale to the telling, with the consequence that its ambiguity now came to be seen as a virtue rather than a weakness. The following two decades offered a reassessment of the presentation of colonialism, as critics such as Bruce Johnson and Fleishman highlighted such issues as alienation and disruption. Alongside this, the critical focus was increasingly directed towards language and narrative techniques in the work of Cedric Watts (1977) and Jeremy Hawthorn (1979). Despite the famous proclamation of the "death of the author," the closing decades of the century saw a return of interest in the author behind the work (Schwarz, 1980). Revisionist studies were and continue to be in the ascendant: Conrad's debunking of Victorian progress was addressed by Ian Watt, while J. Hillis Miller (1989) addressed the deconstruction of European identity, and Peter Firchow's (2000) study usefully contrasted such terms as "racism" as employed in the 1890s with their current, narrowly ideological definitions. In addition to the full scale studies mentioned, Conrad's work has been subject to critical scrutiny by a singularly active and international scholarly community. Not only do their studies fill three journals (published in England, France, and the United States) each year, but there is a lively series of conferences held on a regular basis.

While "Heart of Darkness" is the most studied of his fictions and integral to any university course on modern literature, Conrad's legacy continues outside the academy. There have been a wealth of adaptations, operatic, theatrical, and, above all, cinematic – to date there have been almost a hundred film versions of his fiction including, most famously, Francis Ford Coppola's *Apocalypse Now* (1979), a controversial Vietnam War film based loosely upon "Heart of Darkness." His influence upon generations of writers, from André Gide and F. Scott Fitzgerald to Graham Greene and V. S. Naipaul, continues unabated, particularly in the so-called "Third World", where his influence looms large. His popular influence is variously reflected, in "classic" comic books, in popular music – Bob Dylan, for instance, used *Victory* as the basis for the song "Black Diamond Bay" on his *Desire* album in 1976 – and, perhaps above all, in the fact that he has "entered the language," becoming part of the idioms of everyday speech: thus, the expression "heart of darkness" has become a byword and lazy cliché for human atrocity. In every sense of the phrase, Conrad remains, as Marlow claimed of Lord Jim, "one of us."

Works cited

Achebe, Chinua. "An Image of Africa." *Massachusetts Review* 17 (1977) 782–94.
Baines, Jocelyn. *Joseph Conrad: A Critical Biography*. London: Weidenfeld & Nicolson, 1959.
Batchelor, John. *The Life of Joseph Conrad*. Oxford: Blackwell, 1994.
Berthoud, Jacques. *Joseph Conrad: The Major Phase*. Cambridge: Cambridge University Press, 1978.
Busza, Andrew. "Introduction." *The Rover*. Edited by J. H. Stape and Andrew Busza. ix–xxx. Oxford: Oxford University Press, 1992.
Conrad, Jessie. *Joseph Conrad as I Knew Him*. London: Heinemann, 1926.
———. *Joseph Conrad and His Circle*. London: Jarrods, 1935.

Crankshaw, Edward. *Joseph Conrad: Some Aspects of the Art of the Novel.* London: Lane, 1936.

Curle, Richard. *Joseph Conrad: A Study.* London: Kegan Paul, 1914.

Fleishman, Avrom. *Conrad's Politics: Community and Anarchy in the Fiction of Joseph Conrad.* Baltimore: Johns Hopkins University Press, 1967.

Ford, Ford Madox. *Joseph Conrad: A Personal Remembrance.* London: Duckworth, 1924.

Firchow, Peter Edgerly. *Envisioning Africa: Racism and Imperialism in Conrad's Heart of Darkness.* Lexington: University Press of Kentucky, 2000.

Freeman, John. *The Moderns.* London: Robert Scott, 1916.

Garnett, Edward, ed. *Letters from John Galsworthy: 1900–1932.* London: Jonathan Cape, 1934.

Geddes, Gary. *Conrad's Later Novels.* Montreal: McGill-Queen's University Press, 1980.

Gordan, John Dozier. *Joseph Conrad: The Making of a Novelist.* Cambridge, Mass.: Harvard University Press, 1940.

Guerard, Albert J. *Conrad the Novelist.* Cambridge, Mass.: Harvard University Press, 1958.

Hawthorn, Jeremy. *Joseph Conrad: Language and Fictional Self-Consciousness.* London: Edward Arnold, 1979.

Hay, Eloise Knapp. *The Political Novels of Joseph Conrad: A Critical Study.* Chicago: University of Chicago Press, 1963.

James, Henry. *Literary Criticism: Volume One.* New York: Library of America, 1984.

Jean-Aubry, G. *Joseph Conrad: Life & Letters.* 2 vols. London: William Heinemann, 1927.

Johnson, Bruce. *Conrad's Models of Mind.* Minneapolis: University of Minnesota Press, 1971.

Karl, Frederick R. *Joseph Conrad: The Three Lives.* London: Faber and Faber, 1979.

Kirschner, Paul. *Conrad: The Psychologist as Artist.* Edinburgh: Oliver & Boyd, 1968.

Leavis, F. R. *The Great Tradition: George Eliot, Henry James, Joseph Conrad.* London: Chatto & Windus, 1948.

Meyer, Bernard C. *Joseph Conrad: A Psychoanalytic Biography.* Princeton: Princeton University Press, 1967.

Miller, J. Hillis. "'Heart of Darkness' Revisited." In *Heart of Darkness: A Case Study in Contemporary Criticism.* Edited by Ross C. Murfin, 209–24. New York: St Martin's Press, 1989.

Morf, Gustav. *The Polish Heritage of Joseph Conrad.* London: Samson Low, Marston, 1930.

Moser, Thomas. *Joseph Conrad: Achievement and Decline.* Cambridge, Mass.: Harvard University Press, 1957.

Najder, Zdzisław. *Joseph Conrad: A Chronicle.* Cambridge: Cambridge University Press, 1983.

Nietzsche, Friedrich. *The Will to Power.* Edited by Walter Kaufmann; translated by Walter Kaufmann and R. J. Hollingdale. New York: Vintage Books, 1968.

Palmer, John A. *Joseph Conrad's Fiction: A Study in Literary Growth.* Ithaca, NY: Cornell University Press, 1968.

Phelps, William Lyon. "Conrad, Galsworthy and Others." *Bookman* XLIII (May 1916): 297–304. Reprinted in *The Advance of the English Novel.* New York: Dodd, Mead: 1919.

Schwarz, Daniel R. *Conrad: Almayer's Folly to Under Western Eyes*. London: Macmillan, 1980.

Sherry, Norman. *Conrad's Eastern World*. Cambridge: Cambridge University Press, 1966.

———. *Conrad's Western World*. Cambridge: Cambridge University Press, 1971.

———, ed. *Conrad: The Critical Heritage*. London: Routledge & Kegan Paul, 1973.

Spenser, Edmund. *Faerie Queene*. Edited by J. C. Smith. 2 vols. Oxford: Clarendon Press, 1978.

Stape, J. H., and Owen Knowles, eds. *A Portrait in Letters: Correspondence to and About Conrad*. Amsterdam: Rodopi, 1996.

Watt, Ian. *Conrad in the Nineteenth Century*. London: Chatto & Windus, 1980.

Watts, Cedric. *Conrad's "Heart of Darkness": A Critical and Contextual Discussion*. Milan: Mursia International, 1977.

Woolf, Virginia. *The Common Reader*. London: Hogarth Press, 1925.

Note

Chapter 4: "Youth," "Heart of Darkness," and *Lord Jim*

1. A good counter argument is provided by Firchow, 2000: 55.

Index

238 INDEX